"What can I make that's different?"

If that's your daily complaint, it's time to take a test.

Have you tried poaching eggs in wine? Do you know how to make a chicken and banana casserole? Can you cook broccoli with bacon and parsley? Ever try a Japanese omelette . . . steak à la Denmark . . . or Hungarian ham puffs?

If your answer is "No" to the above, then you need a copy of this book.

Here are the answers to all your problems—and they come from the four corners of the earth. You'll find taste-tempting recipes from Guatemala, England, the South Seas—from Alaska to Yugoslavia—and all points between. These dishes are as easy to make as any of the American favorites you've cooked over and over—and twice as exciting! Compliments from your dazzled guests will be proof of that.

These wonderful recipes are fun to read, too. Just dip in and see. Chances are you'll stop reading to start cooking. They're all that irresistible!

🌿 🌿 🌿 🌿 🌿 🌿

" . . . very interesting reading as well as a real adventure in cooking."

Statesville (N.C.) *Record & Landmark*

A World of Good Cooking

or

**How to Fit Five Continents
into an American Kitchen**

ETHEL HULBERT RENWICK

Drawings by Paul Davis

MB

A MACFADDEN-BARTELL BOOK

THIS BOOK IS THE COMPLETE TEXT
OF THE HARDCOVER EDITION

A MACFADDEN BOOK . . . 1964

MACFADDEN BOOKS are published by
Macfadden-Bartell Corporation
205 East 42nd Street, New York, New York, 10017

Library of Congress Catalog Card Number: 62-19079

꒰꒰꒰꒰꒰꒰

CONTENTS

alphabetized in cpl.

	Foreword	9
1 •	HORS D'OEUVRES	11
2 •	SOUPS	17
3 •	EGGS	31
4 •	VEGETABLES	39
5 •	SALADS AND SALAD DRESSINGS	70
6 •	MEAT	80
7 •	POULTRY	133
8 •	FISH AND SHELLFISH	153
9 •	RICE: PILAFS AND RISOTTOS	174
10 •	SAUCES	179
11 •	GARNISHES AND RELISHES	187
12 •	PANCAKES	194
13 •	BREADS AND BISCUITS	198
14 •	DESSERTS	205
	Index	214

꒰꒰꒰꒰꒰꒰

• FOREWORD •

These recipes were originally assembled in this form for my own convenience. Having traveled around the world for several years with parents who lived abroad extensively, I found myself possessing both hundreds of recipes and a keen interest in all kinds of cooking. I quite naturally learned about foods and methods from on-the-spot observation and personal experience, such as dropping in on a charming little old lady on a country lane in Scotland and being invited into her kitchen for a cup of tea and freshly baked scones. Out of this background came my desire for a book that would be usable and fun for everyday cooking for me, Mrs. American Housewife.

My chief concerns were to include only ingredients readily available, to put all recipes in our measures for our methods, and to classify the recipes according to food (rather than according to country), so that I could see and compare, at a glance, numerous ways to prepare whatever particular food I had in mind.

I have also tried to transmit the inspiration captured in this search—the inspiration of unprofessional creativity. Hence I have incorporated suggestions and ideas from both housewives and cooks of small restaurants in various countries. I recall so vividly driving along the country roads of Hungary one bleak and stormy night and stopping at an inconspicuous, modest family eating place, there to be greeted by a burning hearth, open hearts, smiling faces, bowing gentlemen, and the moving music of gypsy violinists. What a setting for strange, chilled, and weary travelers to enjoy a steaming dish of *sült marha* (baked beef) drenched in sour cream and tomatoes!

It was interesting to observe that although various countries do have very definite characteristics in their own cooking, to which they adhere in most cases, many of them have a certain flexibility in home cooking and, therefore, some of the foods and seasonings of other countries show up just as they do in our country. I found this freedom and flexibility opening new horizons for menu planning in my own home, and I present this book in just that spirit.

Another phase of creative cookery that shows up in this book is the foreign service cooking developed by the military, by those in the diplomatic service, and by representatives of international businesses. These recipes call for a combination of foods and seasonings not completely typical of the country in which they are served but having some of its characteristics. As a matter of fact, these dishes have themselves become traditional throughout the years. To label them as coming from the country of the originator—such as England or the U.S.A. —would be incorrect, for they do not so derive; as a result, I have shown these dishes as coming from the country in which they were inspired and used. Examples are the hors d'oeuvres that are called Indian.

Another concern of mine was to incorporate the tips I found helpful in my own kitchen and way of life. This has been accomplished by adding these tips to the recipes to which they pertain and, in addition, by grouping certain foods (vegetables, sauces, salad dressings, and garnishes) that do not specify the countries from which they come. In the latter case I might add that many of these recipes and methods are used in several (even many) countries, so that their significance lies not in a defined nationality but in the special twist or accent or addition they make to the meal.

In conclusion, may I say that the recipes in this book, rather than being necessarily the criteria of the professional, are somewhat organic, being straight from people's kitchens and recipe boxes. These recipes are the discoveries made, in an adventure covering many years, by myself and my family and then put into practice in my own kitchen. My hope is that this completely new arrangement of foreign recipes will bring a variety of menus to the experienced gourmet and fun to those who heretofore have not included foreign cooking in their day-by-day living.

ETHEL HULBERT RENWICK

HORS D'OEUVRES

The world over, meals begin with appetite-stimulating delicacies—whether they are known as hors d'oeuvres, antipasto or zakouski. These tidbits can be offered as a simple first course or as an elaborate spread. In Russia they were served in a room separate from the dining room, the idea being to keep the early guests from famishment until the later guests arrived—Russian sense of time being what it was. Now, in whatever manner they are served, their appearance has become routine in homes, hotels, on ships and planes. In the great lounge of the Taj Mahal Hotel in Bombay (a gathering place for Europeans) French-fried potato strips were served to be dipped in a sharp sauce like ketchup. (Our ketchup originates in the East; its name comes from the Malay.) On a small freighter moving languidly along the east coast of Africa we were served hot sardines on toast fingers, spread with mustard and broiled. Obviously, inspiration for delicious tidbits can and does come from all parts of the world.

1 • CHINA

Wrap split water chestnuts and pieces of chicken liver with

11

pieces of bacon; secure with toothpicks. Dip in soy sauce and broil.

2 • NEW ZEALAND

Mix 3 cups minced boiled ham with 1 cup chutney and 1 cup chili sauce. Place on toast rounds. Sprinkle with grated cheese (try cheddar). Broil.

3 • FRANCE

Mince and sauté mushroom stems in butter; season with salt and pepper. Mix ½ cup stems with ½ cup flaked leftover white fish, minced garlic, 1 tablespoon chopped parsley, and 1 egg. Fill the mushroom caps with this mixture, top with crumbs, and dot with butter. Bake in a buttered pan at 350° for 15 minutes.

4 • ENGLAND

In the top of a double boiler mix 2 tablespoons butter, 2 egg yolks, 2 teaspoons minced onion, 1 tablespoon Worcestershire sauce, 1 teaspoon chopped parsley, and ¼ cup cooked chopped ham or bacon. Stir over hot water till thick. Spread on toast strips. Serve hot.

5 • SYRIA *eggplant caviar*

Peel an eggplant, slice thin, and sauté in butter. Cool. Mix together ¼ cup sesame or olive oil, ¼ cup lemon juice, 2 tablespoons chopped parsley, clove minced garlic, chopped green pepper, and ½ cup sour milk or yogurt. Saturate the eggplant with this. Chill. Serve on thinly sliced dark bread.

6 • ENGLAND

Mix together 8 ounces crab meat, 1 teaspoon curry powder, ¼ cup thick white sauce or mayonnaise, 1 tablespoon each minced pimiento and green pepper, ½ teaspoon salt, and a dash pepper. Horseradish and chopped onion may be added if desired. Spread on toast rounds, sprinkle with grated cheddar cheese, dot with butter, and brown under the broiler.

7 • FRANCE

Mix lobster, crab, salmon, or tuna with half mayonnaise, half whipped cream. Serve on artichoke hearts.

8 • ENGLAND

Cream together ¼ cup butter, 2 teaspoons dry mustard, and

12

¼ teaspoon Worcestershire sauce. Spread sardines with this mixture; dip them in crumbs and broil them. Serve on toast strips.

9 • FRANCE

Heat in a double boiler 2 cups flaked cooked lobster, 2 cups heavy cream sauce, 2 egg yolks, and ¼ cup chopped blanched almonds. Serve hot on toast, sprinkled with paprika.

10 • ENGLAND

Season oysters with cayenne pepper and lemon juice. Wrap each one in bacon, secure with a toothpick, and broil. Serve on toast.

11 • SWEDEN

Marinate 1 pound cooked shrimp in 1 cup of tarragon vinegar mixed with 2 bay leaves, 6 peppercorns, 1 teaspoon dill seed, and 1 teaspoon thyme. To serve, hang the shrimp on the edge of a bowl filled with the shrimp marinade.

12 • CHINA

Dip shelled, cleaned shrimp in soy sauce and broil.

13 • FRANCE

Thread scallops, mushroom caps, and bacon squares on skewers. Broil.

14 • SWEDEN

Roll thin slices of smoked salmon into cone shapes. Fill these cornets with cream cheese softened with cream or milk and mixed with chopped chives.

15 • ITALY

Wrap thin slices of ham (Italian prosciutto or Virginia ham) around cubes of honeydew melon. Chill.

16 • ENGLAND

Blend together equal parts of butter and chopped chutney. Spread on toast or crackers and broil.

17 • RUSSIA

Cut ½ pound butter into 2 cups of flour; add 1 tablespoon

sour cream. Form into a ball, wrap in wax paper, and chill until firm. Roll out ⅛ inch thick on a floured board. Cut into 1½-inch circles; pinch sides to form a cup. Fill each with 2 teaspoons of a mixture of chopped chicken livers and chopped mushrooms moistened with sour cream. Sprinkle with salt. Bake at 375° for 20 minutes or until lightly browned. You may add curry powder to your meat filling if you wish and use chicken or beef or lamb (as the Syrians do). Deviled ham may also be used.

18 • FRANCE

Make small pancakes (recipe #5, page 195) and fill with meat (see meatball and hash recipes, pages 127–132) or with Pancake Filling #2, page 196. Filled pancakes may be frozen and then heated for serving.

19 • RUSSIA

See Cheese Pastry, recipe #10, page 201.

20 • FRANCE

Cut rounds of bread; toast one side. Spread the untoasted side with a mixture of equal parts of butter and prepared mustard; press a chilled oyster on top, dab with mayonnaise, and sprinkle with chopped chives.

21 • RUSSIA

Mix caviar with lemon juice and chopped onions. Spread the mixture on bread rounds, top with an oyster, and sprinkle with chopped parsley.

The following cocktail balls may be made in big batches, frozen, and reheated for serving.

22 • INDIA

Form balls of 2 cups cooked rice and 1 cup grated cheese (cheddar is good for this). Spread with prepared mustard. Fry in deep fat.

23 • FRANCE

Mix equal parts of cream cheese and Roquefort or bleu cheese with chopped chives and parsley. Form into balls. Roll in sweet paprika and ground toasted almonds.

24 • ENGLAND

Add 1 cup grated cheddar cheese to ½ cup thick white sauce;

salt to taste. Spread on a flat pan and chill. Shape into balls. Roll the balls in fine crumbs, in beaten egg, and again in crumbs. Fry quickly in deep fat.

25 • FRANCE

Mix 1 cup grated cheddar cheese with 1 egg yolk, ¼ teaspoon prepared mustard, ¼ cup soft bread crumbs, salt, and pepper. Fold in 1 stiffly beaten egg white. Shape into balls; roll in fine crumbs. Fry quickly in deep fat.

26 • INDIA

Mix ½ cup minced cooked chicken with 1 tablespoon chopped parsley, 2 tablespoons chopped chives, 1 tablespoon grated onion, and 2 tablespoons fresh bread crumbs. Season with salt, cayenne pepper, and 1 tablespoon curry powder; moisten with prepared mustard. Shape into balls and chill. Dip in crumbs, in beaten egg, and again in crumbs. Fry quickly in deep fat.

The following cocktail dips may be served with any of the attractive crackers and chips available now, as well as with fried tortillas, party rye bread (sliced paper thin by your butcher, buttered, and put in the oven until browned and curled), and Italian breadsticks. For those who take their dipping seriously, there are cooked chilled jumbo shrimp (with #29 or #35), chilled oysters, sautéed chicken livers, whole small sausages or cubes of ham (with #34), and chunks of cooked turkey, chicken, or lobster. Chilled vegetables are also excellent: try cauliflower buds, asparagus tips, baby beets—all very good with salad dressing #2 (Vinaigrette), page 76—celery, raw zucchini, sweet onion chunks, and small whole onions. And, of course, you can use cubes or balls of chilled melon.

27 • LATVIA

Cream together 1 pound cream cheese, ¼ pound butter, 1 teaspoon paprika, 1 teaspoon prepared mustard, 1 teaspoon caraway seed, and chopped chives.

28 • INDIA

Blend together ¼ cup butter, 1 teaspoon Worcestershire sauce, 2 tablespoons tomato catsup, 2 tablespoons sherry, 1 teaspoon curry powder, 2 teaspoons lemon juice, salt, and pepper.

29 • HUNGARY

Combine 1 cup sour cream, 1 tablespoon lemon juice, and 2 teaspoons chopped fennel.

30 • SOUTH AMERICA

Mash 2 avocados. Mix them with 6 chopped hard-boiled eggs, 1 onion chopped fine, 3 tablespoons chopped parsley, ¼ teaspoon chili powder, and 2 tablespoons vinegar.

31 • MEXICO

Mash 2 avocados. Mix them with 1 peeled and chopped tomato, small amount minced onion, 2 teaspoons chili powder, 1 teaspoon salt, and 2 tablespoons vinegar.

32 • ENGLAND

Blend ½ pound crumbled Stilton or Roquefort cheese with ¼ pound butter, 1 teaspoon Worcestershire sauce, 1 teaspoon paprika, and ¼ cup sherry.

33 • HUNGARY

Combine ½ pound cream cheese, ½ pound butter, ½ teaspoon prepared mustard, ½ teaspoon paprika, 1 teaspoon caraway seed, generous amount chopped chives, and chopped capers (optional), with enough cream to soften.

34 • ENGLAND

Mix equal parts of butter, currant jelly, and prepared mustard. Heat together until melted.

35 • FRANCE

Mix 1 cooked mashed eggplant with 2 finely chopped onions, 4 peeled finely chopped tomatoes, 1 clove garlic minced, ¾ cup olive oil, salt, and pepper.

36 • ENGLAND

Combine ¾ cup chili sauce, ¼ cup grated horseradish, 1 tablespoon Worcestershire sauce, 10 drops tabasco sauce, 2 tablespoons lemon juice, and ¼ teaspoon salt.

37 • SCANDINAVIA

See chicken recipe #19, page 139. Prepare the mixture as described, but do not bake. Serve as an hors d'oeuvre spread.

• 2 •

SOUPS

The soup kettle has been the true melting pot for the fruits of the earth. Every nation has contributed its particular fruits, its ingenuity and love to the art of soup making. Soups can be the most satisfying of foods—in flavor, fragrance and nutrition. They may also be distinctive in their nationality and unique in their personality. Here in America, with our wide geographic and climatic range, we have the means to make most of the soups of the world. We can go from the heartiest German lentil soup to Russian fish soup, French carrot soup, delicate Chinese broth, and Scandinavian fruit soups. All subtleties are open to us.

I • BEEF

The following recipes are all made with 3 cups of beef stock. If you don't have your own beef stock on hand, the recipes may be made with (1) 1 can of consommé with 1½ cans of water or (2) 3 beef bouillon cubes dissolved in 3 cups of boiling water.

1 • GUATEMALA

3 cups beef stock
fresh or dried mint

lemon juice
avocado, cubed

Heat the consommé with the mint. Just before serving, add a few drops of lemon juice and the cubes of avocado.

2 • MEXICO

3 cups beef stock
1 cup sour cream
1 avocado, mashed
¼ teaspoon chili powder

onion juice
salt
pepper

To the cold consommé add the sour cream, mashed avocado, chili powder, a few drops of onion juice, and salt and pepper to taste. Serve chilled.

3 • ENGLAND

3 cups beef stock
1 tablespoon minced onion
2 tablespoons butter

2 tablespoons flour
1 cup scalded milk
1 cup grated cheddar cheese

Sauté the onions in butter, add the flour, and blend well. Add the consommé slowly. Simmer a few minutes. Add the milk and cheese and season to taste. Heat till the cheese is melted.

4 • FRANCE

3 cups beef stock
thin slices French bread
grated cheddar or Swiss

cheese
1 onion, chopped
butter

Fill a buttered casserole two-thirds full with layers of French bread sprinkled with cheese. Sauté the onions in butter and add them to the consommé. Pour over the bread. Bake 1 hour in a 350° oven. This is quite thick, almost solid.

5 • FRANCE

3 cups beef stock

eggs

Into each cup of hot consommé drop 1 egg; stir quickly and serve immediately.

6 • ITALY

thin slices French bread
poached eggs

grated Parmesan cheese
3 cups beef stock

Fry bread slices in butter. In each soup plate place 2 slices; top them with a poached egg and sprinkle with 1 teaspoon cheese. Pour the hot consommé carefully into the plate.

7 • AUSTRIA

3 cups beef stock
2 onions, sliced thin
2 tablespoons butter
2 tablespoons flour
½ cup red wine

1 egg, beaten
2 tablespoons cream
2 tablespoons chopped
    parsley
1 teaspoon chopped chives

Sauté the onions in butter, add the flour, and slowly add the consommé; simmer a few minutes. Add the wine and simmer 30 minutes. Combine the egg, cream, parsley, and chives. Stir about ½ cup of the hot consommé into the egg slowly; combine this with the rest of the consommé. Heat for a minute, stirring constantly, but do not boil.

8 • ITALY

3 cups beef stock
1 cup shredded cabbage
1 tablespoon butter
¼ cup cooked rice

¼ cup grated Parmesan
    cheese
sliced frankfurters (optional)

Cook cabbage in 1 cup water with the butter for 15 minutes. Drain. Mix the cabbage with the rice and cheese. Add the cabbage mixture to hot consommé. Frankfurters may be added if you wish.

9 • AUSTRIA

3 cups beef stock
¼ cup oats

1 tablespoon butter

Bring the consommé to a boil. Add the oats; cook till done. Add the butter and serve.

10 • SPAIN

3 cups beef stock
2 onions, chopped
oil
¼ pound chopped cooked
    ham
¼ cup chopped celery
1 bay leaf

¼ teaspoon thyme
⅛ teaspoon nutmeg
½ cup red wine
1 tablespoon vinegar
2 egg yolks, beaten
garlic toast

Brown onions in 1 tablespoon oil; add ham, celery, bay leaf, thyme, and nutmeg. Cook together a few minutes. Add the wine and consommé and simmer 10 minutes. Mix vinegar with the egg yolks in the soup tureen; pour soup over them and stir well. Garnish with toast that has been spread with garlic butter.

Tips: For extra richness you can add 2 tablespoons of sherry or Bordeaux to any of the above recipes. For garnish you might add slightly salted whipped cream either browned lightly under the broiler or topped with a dab of caviar.

11 • PHILIPPINES

3 cups beef stock	1 pound ground lean beef
2 onions, chopped	2 potatoes, cubed
clove garlic, minced	2 tomatoes, chopped

Sauté onions and garlic; add the beef and brown it. Add the potatoes and tomatoes and simmer a few minutes. Add the consommé, season to taste, and simmer 20 minutes.

12 • SOUTH AFRICA

3 cups beef stock	1 bay leaf
½ pound beef in small cubes	1 potato, sliced
1 onion, chopped	1 tablespoon vinegar
1 tablespoon curry powder	1 teaspoon salt

Brown the beef and onions in butter. Add consommé, curry powder, and bay leaf and simmer 30 minutes. Add potato and vinegar, season, and simmer until all ingredients are tender.

13 • SPAIN

3 cups beef stock	1 egg
¼ pound ground lamb	1 tablespoon prepared to-
¼ pound ground pork	mato sauce
½ clove garlic, minced	¼ cup browned bread
salt	crumbs (or Melba toast
pepper	or zwieback crumbs)
red pepper	1 tablespoon chopped
nutmeg	parsley

Mix all ingredients except the stock and last three. Form into small balls, roll in flour, and brown in butter. Heat the consommé. Add the bread crumbs, tomato sauce, parsley, and meatballs. Simmer 15 minutes.

14 • CHINA

3 cups beef stock
1 pound ground pork
2 eggs, beaten
3 green onions, chopped
    fine

1 teaspoon soy sauce
1 teaspoon salt
pepper
chopped parsley or mustard
    greens

Combine all ingredients except the stock and parsley and shape into balls. Cook the pork balls, covered, in consommé in the top of a double boiler over hot water for 1 hour. Garnish the soup before serving with chopped parsley or mustard greens.

15 • AUSTRIA

3 cups beef stock
¼ teaspoon salt
⅛ teaspoon pepper
½ teaspoon cumin seed

1 tablespoon flour
½ cup sour cream
½ cup sweet cream
2 potatoes, cubed

Simmer the consommé a few minutes with salt, pepper, and cumin seed. Mix the flour and sour cream; add a little of the hot consommé to this slowly, beating all the while. Stir mixture into the rest of the consommé. Add the sweet cream and potatoes and simmer 10 minutes. Don't boil.

II • CHICKEN

1 • WEST AFRICA

1 stewing chicken
3 tablespoons peanut butter
2 teaspoons tomato paste
1 potato, cubed

2 tablespoons chopped
    parsley
salt

Cut up the chicken; simmer it in 2 quarts of water for 20 minutes. Mix the peanut butter with ½ cup of the broth. Add it to the chicken with all the remaining ingredients. Simmer 1 hour.

2 • CHILE

stewing chicken, cut up
1 onion, sliced
3 potatoes, diced
½ pound squash, cubed
¾ cup green beans

1 tablespoon rice
salt
red pepper
1 egg yolk
chopped parsley

Stew chicken in enough water to cover till tender. Brown

chicken pieces in butter with the onions and potatoes. Add the broth that the chicken was cooked in, the vegetables, rice, salt, and a dash of red pepper. Simmer until the vegetables are tender. Stir in the egg yolk; garnish with chopped parsley and serve.

3 • HAWAII

chicken stock
pinch garlic powder or
   crushed garlic
salt

pinch powdered ginger or
   a little grated fresh
   ginger
papaya, avocado, or melon

Add the seasonings to the hot stock; float cubes of the fruit on top.

4 • BELGIUM

2 leeks
3 stalks celery
1 carrot
few sprigs parsley
¼ teaspoon thyme
frying chicken, quartered

lemon
1 bay leaf
1 quart chicken or veal
   stock or water, or 1
   pint water and 1
   pint white wine

Shred the leeks (onion may be used if you can't get leeks), celery and carrot; sauté them in butter, along with the chopped parsley and thyme. Butter a casserole and spread the vegetables in a layer on the bottom. Rub the chicken with lemon. Place the chicken on top of the vegetables. Pour in the chicken stock or the water and white wine. Season and add the bay leaf. Simmer 1 hour.

5 • CHINA

1 cup diced chicken meat
soy sauce
salt
½ cup celery, chopped fine
4 water chestnuts, chopped
   fine

4 cups chicken stock
1 teaspoon cornstarch dissolved in ¼ cup water
4 eggs
mustard greens

Dip chicken in soy sauce and fry in fat till done. Add celery, water chestnuts, 2 tablespoons soy sauce, salt, and chicken stock and simmer a few minutes. Stir in the cornstarch. Add the eggs: either stir them into the soup or poach them on top. Garnish with mustard greens and serve at once. (You might try any one of these touches: 1 teaspoon powdered ginger, a few drops of peanut or sesame oil, or a dash of

Mei Yen, MSG, or Accent seasoning added to the stock; extra bouillon cubes for stronger flavor; or the eggs beaten, cooked in a skillet without stirring, and cut into long strips and used as a garnish.)

6 • FRANCE

½ dozen chicken feet	and parsley
3 chicken carcasses	4 egg yolks
1 celery stalk	1 cup cream
1 carrot	salt
1 onion	pepper
bouquet of herbs: chervil	chives

Scald and peel the chicken feet. Combine carcasses, feet, and 6 cups water and bring to a boil; skim. Add cut-up vegetables and bouquet of herbs. Simmer till reduced to 1½ cups of liquid; strain. Add the egg yolks, half the cream, salt, and pepper. Cook in top of double boiler till thickened; add the remaining cream. Chill in the refrigerator in individual serving bowls until it is jelled. Serve garnished with chopped chives.

7 • WEST INDIES

2 stewing chickens	3 yams or sweet potatoes,
ham bone	cubed
¼ teaspoon chili powder	2 carrots, diced
1 stalk celery, diced	2 tablespoons tomato sauce
2 onions, chopped	1 tablespoon flour
3 potatoes, quartered	

Cut the chicken into pieces, rub with salt and pepper, and brown in butter. Add the ham bone, 3 quarts water, chili powder, celery, and onions. Bring to a boil and skim. Simmer 1 hour. Add potatoes, yams, carrots, and cook 1 hour more. Mix the tomato sauce with the flour and a little of the liquid; add to the rest of the soup. Simmer a minute or two more.

8 • INDIA

1 onion, minced	dash chili powder
2 apples, sliced	dash cayenne pepper
2 tablespoons curry powder	4 cups strong chicken stock
4 tablespoons flour	1½ cups cream
salt	¼ cup diced chicken meat

Cook the onion and 1 sliced apple in butter till tender. Add the curry powder and cook for a few minutes. Stir in the flour, salt, chili powder, and cayenne pepper. Add the stock slowly and bring to a boil. Rub through a sieve and chill. Before serving, add the cream and chicken meat. Garnish with slices of raw apple. (This may be served hot if you prefer, but do not boil after the cream is added.)

9 • AFRICA

3 cups milk
2 tablespoons cornstarch
3 cups chicken stock

¾ cup peanut butter
1 tablespoon minced onion

Slowly add milk to cornstarch. Add the remaining ingredients; simmer 5 minutes. Beat with a rotary beater 1 minute; strain and season. Serve hot.

10 • GREECE

Lemon soup

½ cup rice
3 pints chicken stock
salt
pepper

2 egg yolks
2 tablespoons lemon juice
lemon slices or croutons

Simmer rice in stock till done; season. Mix a little of the stock with the egg yolks, add it to the rest of the soup, and add the lemon juice. Serve garnished with slices of lemon or croutons.

11 • EAST INDIES

1 teaspoon powdered ginger
2 teaspoons salt
2½ quarts chicken broth
3 onions, sliced
1 cup drained bean sprouts

3 hard cooked eggs, sliced
2 cups cooked slivered
    chicken
lemon slices

Add ginger and salt to the stock and bring to a boil. Sauté onions in oil, add bean sprouts, and cook 5 minutes; add to the stock with the sliced eggs and chicken. Garnish with lemon slices.

12 • FRANCE

1 quart chicken stock
salt
pepper

½ cup sour cream
1 cup shelled walnuts,
    broken or halved

Heat the stock and season. Add the sour cream and walnuts. Serve hot.

24

III • VEGETABLE

There are innumerable vegetable soups. For variety and strength, use meat stock, consommé, or bouillon cubes dissolved in water for the liquid. You might add bean sprouts and bamboo shoots, a bit of soy sauce or a pinch of ginger, and any minced leftover meat, fried in oil, chinese style. For an Italian touch, add vermicelli (fine spaghetti), garlic or garlic powder, tomato paste, and a sprinkling of Parmesan cheese. A combination of herbs and a good dash of wine add French flavor. Indian variety is added with coconut milk and/or curry powder. The Hungarians like dill seeds, sour cream, caraway seeds, and, of course, sweet paprika. In Spain people use chili—either the whole peppers or the powdered variety—and a dash of saffron. Both cinnamon and nutmeg are used in soup in many parts of Europe. Garnishes add flavor and appeal to soup: try fresh or dried mint, fresh spinach leaves, sliced hard-boiled eggs, slices of green pepper, grated cheese, parsley, or chives. To add even more interest to soup, see pages 188-190.

1 • INDIA

½ cup lentils	¼ teaspoon chili powder
6 cups water	2 teaspoons curry powder
¼ cup chopped onion	1 teaspoon lemon juice
clove garlic, minced	salt

Cook lentils in water 1 hour. Sauté the onions and garlic in butter with the chili and curry powder. Add the mixture to the lentil soup with lemon juice and salt. Simmer 10 minutes more. Serve this way or puréed through a sieve or in the blender. (For another kind of flavor, substitute ½ teaspoon turmeric for the curry powder and garnish with sliced hard-boiled egg.)

2 • GERMANY

½ cup lentils	1 whole onion
6 cups water	6 frankfurters, sliced
1 teaspoon salt	mashed potatoes
ham bone	

Simmer the lentils in the water with salt, ham bone, and onion for 1 hour. Remove the bone. Add the frankfurters and simmer till they are heated through. Serve with a large dollop of mashed potato in each plate.

3 • CZECHOSLOVAKIA

1 pound dried split peas
1 quart meat stock or
    consommé
2 quarts water
1 stalk celery, diced
1 tablespoon chopped
    parsley

ham bone
2 onions, chopped
1 tablespoon flour
1 cup milk
6 frankfurters, sliced
salt

Simmer the peas, stock, water, celery, parsley, and ham bone together for 1 hour. Remove the bone. Mix the onions and flour and brown in butter. Add this to the soup with the milk, frankfurters, and salt. Simmer 30 minutes more. You can also purée this through a sieve or in the blender just before adding the slices of frankfurter. (The French season pea soup with a bay leaf, a pinch of thyme, a handful of spinach or lettuce leaves, or a few pea pods. Remove the pea pods before serving. If you have fresh or cooked peas, add a few and leave long enough to cook or heat through.)

4 • POLAND

1 pound dried split peas
2 quarts meat stock
1 small onion, chopped
¼ cup potato flour or
    regular flour
2 tablespoons butter

¼ teaspoon marjoram
6 frankfurters, sliced
¼ pound cubed cooked ham
salt
pepper
1 cup sour cream

Simmer the peas, stock, and onion together for 1 hour. Blend the flour and butter together and stir into the soup. Add the marjoram, frankfurters, ham, and seasoning. Simmer 5 minutes. Stir in the sour cream and serve.

5 • ITALY

1½ pounds chopped fresh
    spinach or 3 packages
    frozen spinach, cooked
    and drained
½ cup meat stock
5 cups water

¼ cup butter
¼ cup grated Parmesan
    cheese
¼ teaspoon nutmeg
salt
2 eggs, beaten

Combine all ingredients and simmer gently until the soup thickens slightly. Serve immediately with croutons. Sprinkle extra cheese on top if you wish.

6 • CHINA

½ cup lean pork, cut in
   strips
clove garlic, minced
1 tablespoon soy sauce
5 cups boiling water

1½ teaspoons salt
1½ pounds chopped fresh
   spinach or 3 packages
   frozen spinach

Fry the pork in a little oil, with the garlic and soy sauce, in the kettle. Add the water and salt and simmer 10 minutes. Add the spinach and simmer 5 minutes longer.

7 • CHINA

1 pound diced cooked pork
¾ cup soy sauce
6 cups boiling water

2 bunches watercress
2 eggs

Put the pork in the kettle; pour first the soy sauce and then the boiling water over it. Bring to a boil. Add the watercress and simmer 5 minutes more. Add the eggs, stir briskly, and serve immediately.

8 • PORTUGAL

3 medium potatoes, diced
2 cups meat stock
1 bunch watercress,
   chopped

4 egg yolks
1 cup warm milk
¼ cup grated cheese

Cook the potatoes in stock until done. Force through a sieve or put in the blender. Reheat the purée and add the chopped watercress. Mix the egg yolks with the warm milk. Combine with the soup. Season to taste and sprinkle with cheese.

IV • MISCELLANEOUS

1 • NORWAY

12 prunes
1 cup raisins
6 cups water
3 tablespoons "minute"
   tapioca
1-inch stick cinnamon

1 cup diced apple
¼ cup sugar
1½ cups grape or
   raspberry juice
1 tablespoon lemon juice

Soak the prunes and raisins in the water overnight; cook with tapioca, cinnamon, and apple until clear. Add the sugar and juices. Serve hot or cold. Fruit soup is sweetish, so it is better not to serve it before a heavy meal. (In Sweden people use 2 tablespoons cornstarch mixed with 2 tablespoons water for thickening instead of the tapioca and then force the soup through a sieve.)

2 • HUNGARY

3 cups tomato juice
salt
¼ cup sugar

2 cups white wine
sliced hard-boiled egg

Combine the tomato juice, salt, sugar, and wine; heat for a few minutes, stirring well. Chill and serve cold, garnished with slices of egg.

3 • TURKEY

3 pounds lamb with bones
1 onion
1 carrot
2 teaspoons salt
cayenne pepper

4 tablespoons butter
4 tablespoons flour
3 egg yolks
3 tablespoons lemon juice

Combine the lamb, cut up onion and carrot, water, salt, and pepper and simmer 2 hours. Pour off and strain the liquid and cool it enough to skim off the fat. Mince the meat and combine it again with the soup. Melt the butter and add the flour, making a smooth paste. Pour a little hot liquid over this and blend well. Add to the rest of the soup. Simmer 10 minutes more. Beat the egg yolks, add the lemon juice, and carefully add a little hot soup, stirring continuously. Stir into the rest of the soup. Garnish each serving with a pat of butter and a dash of paprika.

4 • NORWAY

1 cup stock or consommé
1 cup water
2 tablespoons "minute"
    tapioca
½ cup medium cream
salt
2 tablespoons white wine

1 tablespoon sugar
optional:
    ¼ cup chopped almonds
    2 tablespoons raisins
    2 teaspoons grated
        lemon rind

Simmer tapioca in stock and water for 10 minutes. Add

cream, salt, wine, and sugar. Add the optional ingredients if desired. Heat through. You can top with unsweetened whipped cream and chives.

5 • ITALY

1 onion, chopped	2 pounds shrimp, cleaned
1 carrot, chopped	¾ cup red wine
1 teaspoon chopped parsley	¼ cup rice
salt	cayenne pepper
1 bay leaf	2 cups stock or water
½ teaspoon thyme	2 tablespoons butter

Sauté the onion, carrot, parsley, salt, bay leaf, and thyme in butter; add the shrimp and ¼ cup water and cook 10 minutes. Add the wine; simmer, covered, for 15 minutes. Cook the rice and force through a sieve or put in the blender with a little liquid from the shrimp. Combine rice and shrimp mixture; add the pepper, stock, and butter. Heat through.

6 • CZECHOSLOVAKIA *Beer soups ?*

2 cans beer	salt
1 quart water	3 egg yolks
1 tablespoon butter	1 cup cream or milk
2 tablespoons sugar	

Combine beer and water; bring to a boil. Add the butter and sugar and salt to taste; simmer 30 minutes. It will reduce slightly. Beat the egg yolks and add the cream or milk. Strain the beer to remove scum and slowly beat into the egg mixture; heat but do not boil.

7 • LATVIA *Borsche ?*

2 cups diced cooked or canned beets	½ cup vinegar
	¼ cup sour cream
1 quart stock or consommé	salt
1 grated raw beet (optional)	parsley or fresh dill

Combine the beets with the heated stock; force through a sieve or put in the blender with the raw beet and vinegar. Reheat, add the sour cream, salt to taste, and serve garnished with parsley or dill.

small honéydew or casaba   *ripe*
   melons, slightly under-   *ham stock or chicken broth*

Cut off the stem end of each melon and remove the seeds. If a melon doesn't balance well on the round end, cut off a little piece of the bottom; but be careful not to cut too much or the melon will leak. Fill the melons with the stock; place them in hot water two-thirds the depth of the melons and heat thoroughly. Serve the soup in the hot melons.

9 • Poland

4 dill pickles, sliced   *1 cup stock*
flour   *1 cup sour cream*
butter

Lightly flour the pickle slices and sauté in butter till wilted. Add the stock and simmer 30 minutes. Strain, removing the pickles; add sour cream and serve.

10 • Spain

2 potatoes, diced   *1 stalk celery, diced*
2 medium white turnips,   *1 quart veal stock*
   diced   *¼ cup rice*
½ cup cooked kidney   *¼ cup vermicelli*
   beans   *salt*
½ cup chopped cabbage   *pinch saffron*

Cook the vegetables in the stock until tender. Add the rice, vermicelli, salt, and saffron and cook 20 minutes longer.

EGGS

The ubiquitous egg has been prepared and served in every form from the very simplest to the so-called "hundred-year" eggs of China. They have been cooked *in* their shells and *out* of them. They have been served *under* almost everything imaginable, and *over* it. We may not try to age our eggs as the Chinese do, but we can make "Foo Yung Tan," a kind of omelet made of chicken and duck eggs. But sometimes the simplest preparation can be the most satisfying. One morning in an English country house in the Lake district I was greeted by the maid, who came to light the fire, carrying a tray of tea with cold, hard toast. (It was my first visit to England.) Certainly an inauspicious opening. But what a delight it was to come down to the breakfast room and find cheerful coddled eggs with a dash of Worcestershire sauce. All was "right with the world."

I • SCRAMBLED EGGS

METHOD: Mix all ingredients together, beating lightly with a fork. Melt butter in skillet (peanut or sesame oil may be used in Oriental recipes), pour in egg mixture, and cook over low heat, stirring from the bottom as the egg sets. Cook until firm but still moist. Serve immediately.

1 • JAPAN

8 eggs, 2 tablespoons soy sauce, 2 tablespoons sugar, 1 tablespoon butter

2 • CHINA

8 eggs, ¼ cup sliced and sautéed mushrooms, ½ cup diced cooked pork, ½ cup drained and sliced bamboo shoots, 1 teaspoon soy sauce

3 • SPAIN

8 eggs, 1 cup chopped fresh or drained canned tomatoes, salt, pepper

4 • AUSTRIA

8 eggs, ½ cup grated Parmesan cheese, salt, 2 tablespoons butter

5 • RUSSIA

8 eggs, ½ cup chopped onions, ½ cup milk, ½ pound chopped smoked salmon, salt, pepper

6 • POLAND

8 eggs, 1 pound sliced and sautéed mushrooms, 2 tablespoons chopped chives, ¼ cup cream, salt, pepper, ¼ cup butter

7 • MEXICO
8 eggs, ½ cup orange juice, paprika, salt, pepper

II • FRIED EGGS

1 • ITALY

Slice and fry ½ pound calf's liver and 1 pair sweetbreads. Place on toast or fried bread. Top with egg fried in butter.

2 • POLAND

Make hollows in the center of 8 slices of French or Vienna

bread. Brown slices lightly in butter. Drop an egg in each; sprinkle with salt, pepper, and 1 tablespoon cream (optional). Cover skillet and cook until eggs are set.

3 • GERMANY

Cut 4 small boiled potatoes into cubes and brown in butter. Add either 4 sliced frankfurters or pieces of cooked ham to pan. Drop 8 eggs on top and cook, basting with butter, till done.

4 • AUSTRIA

Sauté 1 pound sliced mushrooms, 1 tablespoon chopped onion, and 1 tablespoon chopped parsley in butter. Remove from pan and keep warm. Fry 8 eggs, basting with butter till done. Serve with the mushroom mixture.

TIPS: Numbers 1, 3, and 4 are ideal for brunch or supper. Everything up to the final frying of the eggs can be prepared ahead of time.

III • POACHED EGGS

METHOD: Add either a little salt or vinegar to water in a saucepan and bring to a boil. Break the egg into a small dish. Stir the water briskly with a spoon and carefully slip the egg into the center of the whirlpool. Lower the heat so the water doesn't boil. Poach the egg about 3 minutes or until the white is set. Remove with a slotted spoon. Besides water and the sauces in the recipes, you can poach eggs in milk, wine, tomato juice, or consommé or other clear soups. They may also be made in an egg poacher.

1 • FRANCE

Poach eggs in the usual way. Split and toast French rolls, brioches, or English muffins. Place a slice of cooked ham or Canadian bacon on each half; set a poached egg on top. Cover with Vegetable Sauce #1 (page 180).

2 • ITALY

Poach eggs in the usual way. Serve on a bed of hot cooked spinach, flavored with a dab of anchovy paste if you wish. Sprinkle with grated Parmesan cheese. Brown under broiler or bake at 350° for 10 minutes. Cheese sauce is also delicious poured over the eggs.

3 • MEXICO

Lightly brown in oil 1 chopped onion, 1 clove garlic minced, and 1 chopped canned green chili pepper; add 2 cups canned tomatoes and salt; heat. Poach eggs in this sauce and then serve them in it.

4 • FRANCE

Simmer together for 10 minutes 1 cup red wine, 1 cup consommé, 1 clove crushed garlic, 1 chopped onion, salt, pepper, and a dash each of nutmeg and cinnamon. Poach the eggs in this liquid; then remove them and keep them warm. Reduce the liquid to 1 cup. Work together 1 tablespoon flour and 1 tablespoon butter; add to the sauce and simmer a few minutes. Place the eggs on toast or bread fried in butter. Cover with the sauce.

IV • BAKED EGGS

1 • AUSTRIA

Pour 1 cup sour cream and ¼ cup milk into a baking dish. Carefully slip in 8 eggs. Dot with butter; sprinkle with chopped chives and parsley. Bake at 350° about 15 minutes or until eggs are set.

2 • ENGLAND

Butter muffin tins. In each either (1) press ground ham mixed with a little mustard or (2) wrap a partially cooked strip of bacon. Drop an egg into each cup; sprinkle with salt, paprika, and grated cheese. Bake at 350° about 15 minutes or until eggs are set. Also good with deviled ham with a dash of Worcestershire sauce.

3 • ITALY

Scoop the seeds and juice out of 8 tomatoes. Stand the tomatoes in a buttered baking dish; sprinkle them with oil. Drop an egg into each tomato; sprinkle with more oil, salt, pepper, and oregano or basil. Bake at 350° about 15 minutes or until eggs are set and tomato skins are shriveled.

4 • FRANCE

Brown 2 large thinly sliced potatoes in butter. Place them in a baking dish and sprinkle with salt, pepper, nutmeg, and grated cheese. Carefully drop 8 eggs on top and pour in a

little cream. Bake at 350° about 15 minutes or until eggs
are set.

V • OMELETS

1 • GERMANY

1 potato, diced and cooked   ½ teaspoon chopped parsley
1 tablespoon minced onion   salt
6 eggs

Fry potatoes and onions lightly in butter. Mix beaten eggs,
parsley, and salt and pour over potatoes. Cook until set. Fold
in half and serve.

2 • CHINA

4 eggs
1 cup cooked diced fresh veg-
     etables or ½ cup cooked
     diced meat or fish
½ cup bean sprouts
     (drained)

½ cup chopped onion
½ teaspoon Mei Yen pow-
     der, MSG, or Accent
1 clove garlic, minced
1 teaspoon salt
¼ teaspoon pepper
oil

Beat eggs and add all other ingredients except oil. Heat oil
in skillet. Cook one-third of the mixture at a time, turning
to brown both sides. Drain on paper. Cut into long strips to
serve. This is served with rice and Chicken Sauce # 2 (page
185) and is called "Egg Foo Yung."

3 • SWEDEN

bread crumbs
anchovy fillets, salted salm-
     on, or ¼ pound bacon,
     cooked

6 eggs, separated
1½ cups milk
salt

Butter a baking dish and sprinkle it with crumbs. Line with
pieces of fish or bacon. Mix beaten egg yolks with milk and
salt. Fold in beaten egg whites. Pour into dish and bake at
350° for 20 minutes or until set.

4 • FRANCE

4 eggs
2 cups mashed potatoes

salt
½ cup milk

Beat eggs until light. Add potatoes, salt, and milk. Pour into a buttered skillet and cook until lightly browned. Fold over and serve. (This may also be served sprinkled with minced ham, cheese, green pepper, or tomatoes before folding.)

5 • PORTUGAL

4 eggs
½ cup minced onion
¼ cup chopped parsley

1 teaspoon salt
pepper
butter

Melt butter in skillet. Beat eggs until light. Add other ingredients and pour into skillet. Cook until bottom is brown. Place in 350° oven until dry on top.

6 • AUSTRIA

5 eggs, separated
1 teaspoon salt
pepper
3 tablespoons flour

½ cup grated Parmesan
cheese
1 cup creamed spinach

Beat egg yolks with milk; add salt, pepper, flour, and cheese. Fold into beaten egg whites. Divide into four portions and cook each portion in a buttered skillet turning to brown both sides. Place hot spinach on each omelet, fold over, and serve.

7 • PHILIPPINES

1 pound fish fillets
1 onion, sliced
1 clove garlic, minced
1 tomato, chopped
1 cup cooked peas

½ teaspoon salt
pepper
butter
4 eggs

Fry fish in butter till brown; remove from pan and cube. Add all other ingredients except eggs to pan and cook for a few minutes. Beat eggs lightly and add to pan. As eggs begin to set on bottom, lightly stir in fish on top. Cook until omelet is browned.

VI • FILLED OMELETS

Basic Omelet Recipe

6 eggs
6 tablespoons milk or
   cream or 3 tablespoons

cold water
salt
pepper

Beat eggs lightly with liquid, salt, and pepper. Pour into hot, buttered skillet. Shake pan, stirring briskly, until eggs begin to set; then lightly stir top to spread eggs quickly and let set a minute or two. Fold over and serve plain or fold in any of the following fillings. The fillings are spread across the egg mixture when it has set, and the omelet is then folded over the filling. Omelets may also be baked in a buttered dish at 350° for 20 minutes or until set.

OMELET FILLINGS

1 • POLAND

Sauté ¼ pound sliced mushrooms in butter; stir in 1 tablespoon chopped chives and a dash of paprika.

2 • JAPAN

Sauté ½ cup chopped onions and ¼ cup chopped celery lightly. Add ½ cup stock, ¼ cup soy sauce, 1 teaspoon sugar, 1 teaspoon salt, pepper, and 2 cups diced cooked fish or lobster. Keep warm until omelet is ready.

3 • FRANCE

Sprinkle omelet with two or more of the following: tarragon, marjoram, thyme, basil, chervil, rosemary, chives, parsley, garlic, onion.

4 • GERMANY

Chicken livers chopped and cooked in butter.

5 • ENGLAND

Diced cooked bacon or slivers of ham and shredded Swiss cheese.

6 • HUNGARY

Mix together 1 cup cottage cheese, ½ cup sour cream, and 2 tablespoons sugar.

7 • RUSSIA

Pieces of smoked salmon, anchovy fillets, or caviar.

8 • SPAIN

Chopped tomatoes, either alone or with chopped green pepper.

9 • ITALY

Anchovy paste and grated Parmesan cheese. The cheese may be blended into the egg mixture if desired.

10 • SWITZERLAND

Chopped fresh mint and basil.

TIPS: Other fillings used throughout the world are creamed chicken, tuna fish, crab meat, lobster, mushrooms or chipped beef, and asparagus—and any of these can be moistened with tomato paste instead of cream sauce.

Eggs combined with cheese make perfect light dishes for luncheons, late suppers, and buffets.

1 • FRANCE

12 eggs	*1 cup grated cheddar cheese*
¼ cup butter	*Salt*
¼ cup flour	*Pepper*
1 cup milk	*pinch dry mustard*

Take 6 of the eggs and separate the yolks from the whites. Melt the butter; stir in first the flour and then gradually the milk. When this mixture has thickened, add the cheese and seasonings and stir in the 6 egg yolks. Beat the egg whites stiff and fold into the cheese mixture. Butter a soufflé dish and pour in half the mixture. Make 6 impressions in it and carefully drop 1 egg into each hollow. Gently pour the remaining mixture on top. Bake in a 450° oven for 15 minutes or until puffy and golden.

2 • SWITZERLAND

3 eggs	*slivered*
3 tablespoons butter	*¼ teaspoon salt*
3 tablespoons flour	*8 slices bread*
½ pound Swiss cheese,	*fat for deep frying*

Separate the yolks from the whites of the 3 eggs. Melt the butter, stir in the flour, and carefully add the cheese, stirring until smooth. (This can be done in the top of a double boiler. If cheese is melted over direct heat, stir briskly to avoid burning.) Cool partially. Stir in the egg yolks. Spread the cheese mixture on both sides of the toast slices. Beat egg whites with salt until stiff. Dip toast in egg whites. Fry in deep fat until golden.

VEGETABLES

Most of the essentials of a well-balanced diet can be found in the vegetable kingdom. It is quite possible for man to live on a completely vegetable diet without suffering ill effects. Universal experimentation with the cooking of vegetables has resulted in some fairly universal rules. Root vegetables are best started in cold water. Dropping them into boiling water toughens some of them. Covered and brought to a gentle simmer, the center cooks to tenderness, but the outside is not over-cooked. Fresh green vegetables may, in many instances, be eaten raw; or they may be cooked gently in a small amount of water until they are tender. Seaweed, a staple of Japanese diet and frequent in Pacific areas, is cooked in this manner. Hardier vegetables, such as those in the cabbage family, are cooked in larger quantities of water and are covered. There is no excuse for lack of variety in vegetable cookery.

TIPS FOR COOKING VEGETABLES:

Boiling: Use as little water as possible so that you don't have to pour it off and lose the vitamins. Don't overcook.

39

Pressure cooking: This is a convenient method when you want to add herbs and seasonings. You can use stock instead of water as the liquid.

Steaming: This is one of the simplest and most desirable methods, especially with the new steaming racks that fit any pan.

Baking: Frozen vegetables may be done in the oven, covered, with a little butter and seasonings.

I • ARTICHOKE HEARTS

1 • ITALY

Artichoke hearts   *salt*
flour   *pepper*
1 egg, beaten   *fat for deep frying*

Dip the artichoke hearts in flour and then in the egg (which has been beaten lightly with salt and pepper). Fry in deep fat until golden.

2 • ITALY

artichoke hearts   *onion, chopped*
grated Parmesan cheese   *tomato paste*
bacon

Cook the bacon and crumble it. Chop the onion and sauté it in butter. Butter a casserole. Lay the artichoke hearts in it. Sprinkle them with grated cheese, crumbled bacon, and chopped onion. Pour over them a mixture of equal parts of tomato paste and water, enough to keep them moist. Bake at 350° for 20 minutes.

II • ASPARAGUS

1 • POLAND

1 pound fresh or 2 packages   *bread crumbs*
*   frozen asparagus spears*   *butter*

Cook the asparagus and drain. Meanwhile, brown the bread crumbs in butter. Sprinkle over the asparagus.

2 • BELGIUM

1 pound fresh or 2 packages   *egg yolks, hard-boiled*
*   frozen asparagus spears*   *chopped parsley*

Cook the asparagus and drain. Sprinkle with sieved egg yolks and chopped parsley.

3 • FRANCE

1 pound fresh or 2 packages   *Hollandaise sauce*
    frozen asparagus spears

Cook the asparagus and drain. Meanwhile, prepare Hollandaise sauce (Vegetable Sauce #1, page 180). Serve over the asparagus.

4 • POLAND

1 pound fresh or 2 packages   *grated Parmesan cheese*
    frozen asparagus spears   *butter*

Cook the asparagus and drain. Meanwhile, brown the butter by simmering it gently until it changes color. Pour the butter over the asparagus and sprinkle with cheese.

5 • FRANCE

1 pound fresh or 2 packages   *Vinaigrette dressing*
    frozen asparagus spears

Cook the asparagus and drain. Serve hot or cold with Salad Dressing #2 (Vinaigrette), page 76.

6 • FRANCE

1 pound fresh or 2 packages   *whipped cream*
    frozen asparagus spears   *lemon juice*
mayonnaise

Cook the asparagus; drain and chill. Serve with a dressing made of equal parts of mayonnaise and whipped cream, with a little lemon juice added.

7 • FRANCE

1 pound fresh or 2 packages   *mayonnaise*
    frozen asparagus spears   *prepared mustard*
toast rounds or croutons   *poached eggs*
egg yolks, hard-boiled

Cook the asparagus and drain. Sieve the egg yolks and mix with mayonnaise and a bit of mustard. Spread the rounds of toast or fried bread with this mixture. Arrange a few spears of asparagus on each toast round and top with a poached egg.

41

8 • SWITZERLAND

1 pound fresh or 2 packages
    frozen asparagus spears
4 tablespoons butter
3 tablespoons flour
2 cups milk
pinch thyme
pepper
little chopped parsley

little onion powder or
    minced onion
½ cup diced Gruyère cheese
¼ cup chopped ham or 2¼-
    ounce can deviled ham
baked pastry shell
bread crumbs

Cook the asparagus. Melt the butter, stir in the flour, and gradually add the milk, stirring till thickened. Add the thyme, pepper, parsley, and onion. Fold in cheese and ham. Line the bottom of the baked pie shell with half the asparagus; pour over half the sauce. Make another layer with the remaining asparagus and pour over the rest of the sauce. Sprinkle with bread crumbs, dot with butter, and broil until the top is browned.

III • GREEN BEANS

1 • HUNGARY

2 packages frozen green
    beans or 1 pound fresh
    beans
6 strips bacon
4 tablespoons butter

4 tablespoons flour
2 cups sour cream
1 teaspoon minced onion
bread crumbs (optional)

Cook the beans. Cook and crumble the bacon. Combine the two. Melt the butter, stir in the flour, and gradually stir in the sour cream. Add the onion and salt and mix into the beans. Simmer together 2 minutes. (Or put the mixture in a buttered casserole, sprinkle with bread crumbs, and bake at 450° until the top is browned.)

2 • ITALY

2 packages frozen French-
    cut green beans or 1
    pound fresh green beans
4 tablespoons butter
3 tablespoons flour
2 cups milk

½ teaspoon salt
2 tablespoons grated
    Parmesan cheese
2 eggs, lightly beaten
bread crumbs

Cook the green beans. Melt the butter, stir in the flour, and gradually add the milk. Add the salt, cheese, and beaten eggs and blend smoothly. Combine the sauce with the beans and pour into a buttered baking dish. Sprinkle with bread crumbs and dot with butter. Set in a pan of hot water and bake at 400° for 45 minutes or until firm.

3 • FRANCE

2 packages frozen French-cut green beans or 1 pound fresh beans	*butter* *salt* *pepper*

Sauté the green beans in butter until they are slightly browned. Season to taste with salt and pepper and add a little more butter.

4 • CHINA

2 packages frozen green beans or 1 pound fresh green beans *½ cup soy sauce*	*1 tablespoon sherry* *1 tablespoon cornstarch* *pinch powdered sugar (optional)*

Cook the beans in a small amount of water with the soy sauce, sherry, and a little salt. When they are tender, stir in the cornstarch, which has been dissolved in 2 tablespoons water. You may add a pinch of powdered sugar if you wish.

5 • ITALY

2 pounds whole green beans *2 eggs, separated*	*fat for deep frying* *salt*

Cook the beans in a small amount of water and drain them. Separate them into 8 bunches and tie with string. Beat the egg whites and gently fold in the beaten yolks. Dip the bunches of beans in the egg mixture and fry them in deep fat until golden. Drain and sprinkle with salt. Remove the string before serving.

6 • AUSTRIA

2 pounds cut green beans *2 tablespoons butter* *1 onion, chopped* *2 tablespoons flour* *½ teaspoon chopped parsley*	*2 teaspoons chopped dill (optional)* *salt* *pepper* *1 cup sour cream*

Cook the beans in a little water, drain them, and save the water. Sauté the onion in the butter until it is golden. Stir in the flour and add 6 tablespoons of the water from the beans. Add the parsley, dill, salt, and pepper. Cook 5 minutes, add the beans and sour cream, and bring just to a boil.

7 • ITALY

2 pounds green beans	oil
4 onions, chopped	1 cup tomato juice

Sauté the beans and onions together in oil for about 15 minutes or until they are tender. Add the tomato juice and season to taste. Bring to a boil.

8 • RUSSIA

2 pounds green beans	1 tablespoon sugar
chopped chervil	chopped parsley or mint

Cook the beans in a small amount of water with a dash of chervil and the sugar. Serve sprinkled with chopped parsley or mint.

TIP: Green beans can be cooked in a small amount of water, drained, and tossed with salt and butter. They can then be garnished with crisp, crumbled bacon or grated Parmesan cheese. Or, when tossing with the butter, you might add a dash of nutmeg or a little catsup.

IV • LIMA BEANS

1 • ITALY

1 package frozen lima beans	oil
2 lettuce leaves	½ cup mushrooms
coriander seeds (optional)	sugar
1 onion, sliced	poached eggs (optional)

Cook the lima beans in a little water with the lettuce leaves and a small amount of coriander; drain. Sauté the onions in oil with the mushrooms; add the beans and a little sugar. Serve plain or with poached eggs on top.

2 • FRANCE

1 package frozen lima beans	½ teaspoon salt
1 package frozen corn	pepper
1 green pepper, chopped	2 cups tomatoes
1 onion, chopped	pinch thyme (optional)
butter	

44

Cook the lima beans and the corn. Sauté the green pepper and onion in butter for 5 minutes. Combine the beans, corn, and green pepper and onion with the salt, pepper, tomatoes, and thyme. Heat through.

3 • GERMANY

1 package frozen lima beans
2 slices bacon
1 cup heavy cream

2 tablespoons lemon juice
salt
2 teaspoons chopped parsley

Cook the lima beans in a little water and drain. Cook the bacon and crumble it. Combine the lima beans with the cream, lemon juice, salt, parsley, and crumbled bacon. Heat but do not allow to boil.

V • BEETS

1 • POLAND

2 pounds beets, cooked or
    canned
2 tablespoons butter
1 tablespoon flour
2 tablespoons sugar

3 tablespoons vinegar
salt
pepper
½ cup sour cream

Grind, shred, or chop the beets. Melt the butter, stir in the flour, and add the sugar, vinegar, salt, and pepper. Add this to the beets; heat through and add the sour cream.

2 • RUSSIA

2 pounds beets
sugar
½ teaspoon tarragon

2 tablespoons butter
tarragon vinegar

Cook the beets (unless you use canned beets) and cut them into cubes. Sprinkle the hot beets with a little sugar and the tarragon. Add the butter and stir through. Serve with the vinegar on the side.

3 • AUSTRIA

4 pounds beets
½ cup butter
½ cup red wine
½ cup water
¼ teaspoon caraway seeds

1 cup consommé
4 tablespoons flour
salt
2 teaspoons sugar

Cook the beets and dice them. Combine with the butter, wine, water, caraway seeds, consommé, salt, sugar, and flour (which has been blended with a little of the liquid). Simmer together 10 minutes.

VI • BROCCOLI

1 • GERMANY

fresh or frozen broccoli *chopped parsley*
bacon *butter*

Cook the broccoli. Cook the bacon and crumble it. Garnish the broccoli with the crumbled bacon, parsley, and melted butter.

2 • ENGLAND

fresh or frozen broccoli *chopped chives*
butter

Cook the broccoli. Serve it hot, garnished with melted butter and chopped chives.

3 • ITALY

1 small bunch fresh or 1 *chopped*
* package frozen broccoli* *grated Parmesan cheese*
1 tablespoon oil *salt*
sliced onions *pepper*
few anchovy fillets, chopped *1 cup red wine*
few pitted ripe olives,

Cut the broccoli lengthwise. Pour the oil in the bottom of a saucepan and lay the broccoli in layers with the onions, anchovies, and olives. Sprinkle with salt, pepper, and grated cheese. Pour over the wine and simmer very slowly for 30 minutes.

4 • FRANCE

fresh or frozen broccoli *Hollandaise sauce*

Cook the broccoli and drain. Meanwhile, prepare Hollandaise sauce (Vegetable Sauce #1, page 180). Serve over the broccoli.

5 • FRANCE

fresh or frozen broccoli *lemon juice*
melted butter *slivered, toasted almonds*

Cook the broccoli and drain. Pour over the melted butter and sprinkle with lemon juice. Garnish with toasted almonds.

6 • ITALY

fresh or frozen broccoli   *minced garlic*
butter or olive oil

Parboil the broccoli and cut it up. Cook in a skillet with the butter or olive oil and garlic until it is tender.

VII • CABBAGE

METHOD FOR COOKING STUFFED LEAVES:
Parboil 12 large cabbage leaves 3 or 4 minutes, until they are limp enough to handle. Drain and lay flat. Place a heaping tablespoonful of the filling on the leaf and roll it up, tucking in the ends. Tie with thin string or secure with toothpicks. Bake, covered, at 350° for 2 hours or simmer, covered, for 2 hours in any of the following: (1) 1 can tomato paste and 1 can water, plus minced garlic if you wish; (2) 1 one-pound can tomatoes; (3) 1 can tomato juice; (4) 1 cup consommé; (5) 1 cup consommé with 1 tablespoon tomato paste; (6) 1 cup white wine.

METHOD FOR COOKING WHOLE STUFFED CABBAGE:
Cut off the top of the cabbage and scoop out the inside, leaving a shell about 1 inch thick. Fill with the meat mixture and replace the top. Wrap in aluminum foil, tie, and cook in boiling water for 2 hours.

ALTERNATE METHOD:
Pour hot water over the cabbage, while spreading the leaves apart. Allow the cabbage to drain; then carefully press the filling in between the leaves. Tie the whole thing with string to keep the shape and hold the filling. Place the cabbage either on a bed of sauerkraut or on a layer of chopped onion with sliced carrots or tomatoes. Using any of the liquids listed under "Method for cooking stuffed cabbage leaves," cover the pot and simmer 2 to 3 hours or until the meat is done. To serve, cut into wedge-shaped pieces.

1 • AUSTRIA

1 large head cabbage   *pepper*
1½ pounds sausage meat   *1 can tomato paste with 1*
1 onion, chopped   *can water or 1 can*
salt   *tomatoes*

Prepare the cabbage as directed on page 59. Combine all the other ingredients, stuff the leaves or the whole cabbage, and cook as directed under "Method."

2 • MIDDLE EAST

1 large head cabbage
1½ pounds ground lamb
salt
pepper

1 can tomato paste with 1
   can water or 1 can
   tomatoes

Prepare the cabbage as directed on page 47. Combine all the other ingredients, stuff the leaves or the whole cabbage, and cook as directed under "Method."

3 • FRANCE

1 large head cabbage
1 pound ground beef
1 onion, chopped
¼ cup chopped mushrooms
clove garlic, minced
2 hard-boiled eggs, chopped

1 peeled tomato, chopped
½ cup cooked rice
¼ teaspoon thyme
¼ teaspoon marjoram
salt
pepper

Prepare the cabbage as directed on page 47. Cook the onion, mushrooms, and garlic in butter. Add the meat and cook a few minutes more. Combine with all the other ingredients. Stuff the whole cabbage or leaves and proceed as directed under "Method."

4 • POLAND

1 large head cabbage
1½ pounds ground beef
1 onion chopped
¼ cup uncooked rice
2 tablespoons Worcestershire
   sauce

salt
pepper
1 can tomato paste with 1
   can water or 1 can
   tomatoes

Prepare the cabbage as directed on page 47. Combine all the other ingredients, stuff the leaves or the whole cabbage, and cook as directed under "Method."

5 • AUSTRIA

1 large head cabbage
1½ pounds cooked meat
1 onion, chopped
¼ teaspoon thyme
¼ teaspoon marjoram

½ teaspoon chopped parsley
½ teaspoon caraway seeds
salt
pepper
1 egg yolk

Prepare the cabbage as directed on page 47. Chop the meat fine; combine with all the other ingredients and brown in butter. Proceed as directed under "Method."

6 • HOLLAND

1 large head cabbage	1 teaspoon salt
1½ pounds ground beef or	½ teaspoon pepper
pork or a combination	good dash nutmeg
1 slice bread	butter
milk	

Prepare the cabbage as directed on page 47. Soak the bread in milk and squeeze it out. Combine the meat, bread, salt, pepper, and nutmeg and stuff the cabbage leaves. Lay a pat of butter on top of each cabbage roll and proceed as directed under "Method."

7 • RUSSIA

1 large head cabbage	1 can tomato paste with 1
1½ pounds ground beef	can water or 1 can
1 onion, chopped	tomatoes
½ cup cooked rice	flour
salt	butter
pepper	1 cup sour cream

Prepare the cabbage as directed on page 47. Combine the meat, onion, rice, seasoning, and tomato paste and water. Stuff individual cabbage leaves. Roll each in flour and brown in butter. Simmer 20 minutes in any one of the tomato sauces suggested under "Method." Stir the sour cream into the sauce and heat through just before serving.

8 • RUMANIA

1 large head cabbage	1 teaspoon salt
1½ pounds ground beef or	½ teaspoon pepper
pork or a combination	6 slices bacon
1 onion, chopped	sauerkraut (optional)
1 slice bread	tomato juice (optional)
milk	1 cup sour cream (optional)

Prepare the cabbage as directed on page 47. Soak the bread in milk and squeeze out. Combine the meat, onion, bread, salt, and pepper and stuff the cabbage leaves. Cut the bacon strips in half. Lay one on each cabbage roll. Proceed as directed under "Method" or lay the cabbage rolls on top of

49

the sauerkraut, pour over the tomato juice, and cook. Stir in the sour cream just before serving.

9 • HUNGARY

1 large head cabbage
1½ pounds ground pork
1 onion, chopped
1 teaspoon salt
1 teaspoon Hungarian
    paprika

1 cup cooked rice
2 eggs
sauerkraut (optional)
tomato juice (optional)
1 cup sour cream
    (optional)

Prepare the cabbage as directed on page 47. Brown the onion and meat and combine with salt, paprika, rice, and eggs; stuff the cabbage leaves. Either cook as directed under "Method" or lay the cabbage rolls between layers of sauerkraut, pour over the tomato sauce, and cook. Stir in the sour cream just before serving.

Abroad, cabbage is generally cooked from 1 hour to 2 hours. However, the following recipes are good with a shorter cooking time, especially if you like your cabbage crisp and not too strong.

10 • HOLLAND

1 medium head cabbage
2 tablespoons butter
2 tablespoons flour

dash nutmeg
salt

Cook the cabbage and reserve 1 cup of the water. Melt the butter, stir in the flour, and gradually add the cabbage water; cook till thickened. Add a dash of nutmeg and salt to taste. Serve the mixture over the sliced cabbage.

11 • AUSTRIA

1 medium head cabbage
butter
sour cream

caraway seeds
salt
pepper

Shred the cabbage. Cook it gently in butter with a few tablespoons of sour cream, a sprinkling of caraway seeds, salt, and pepper, with the pan covered.

1 medium head cabbage
½ pound bacon
1 onion, sliced
1 carrot, sliced
1 stalk celery, sliced
¼ teaspoon thyme

½ teaspoon chopped parsley
clove garlic, minced
salt
pepper
1 cup bouillon

Quarter the cabbage and remove the hard core. Parboil 10 minutes. Partially cook the bacon, remove from the pan, and drain. Put the bacon in a pan with the onion, carrot, celery, thyme, garlic, parsley, and cabbage. Sprinkle with salt and pepper and pour the bouillon over it. Simmer until tender.

13 • ENGLAND

1 medium head cabbage
butter
salt

3 tablespoons currant jelly
1 tablespoon sugar

Slice the cabbage and cook until tender. Drain and toss with a little butter, salt, and the currant jelly and sugar.

14 • AUSTRIA

1 head red cabbage
fat
½ cup white wine
3 tablespoons sugar

2 apples, sliced, or a few
        chestnuts, parboiled
        and cut up

Shred the red cabbage, salt it, and cook it in a little fat a few minutes. Add the sliced apples or the chestnuts and cook gently until everything is tender.

VIII • CARROTS

Generally, the new small carrots can be cooked whole and the large normal-size carrots are cut up before cooking.

1 • FRANCE

6 medium carrots
1 tablespoon butter
1 onion, sliced
clove garlic, minced

1 tablespoon flour
½ cup white wine
1 egg yolk, beaten

Parboil the carrots about 5 minutes and reserve ½ cup of the water. Melt the butter; sauté the onion and garlic until golden. Stir in the flour and gradually add the carrot water and wine. Season to taste. Add the carrots to this sauce and cook until tender. Just before serving, stir in the egg yolk.

2 • PHILIPPINES

6 carrots   1 tablespoon sugar
1 tablespoon soy sauce

Slice the carrots lengthwise and parboil 5 minutes. Drain and reserve the liquid. To the carrots add the soy sauce, sugar, and the carrot liquid with enough water added to make 1 cup. Cook until carrots are tender.

3 • ENGLAND

carrots   chopped parsley or mint
melted butter

Cook the carrots until tender. To serve, pour over the melted butter and sprinkle with either the chopped parsley or the mint.

IX • CAULIFLOWER

1 • POLAND

1 small head cauliflower or 1   ¼ teaspoon salt
    package frozen   1 tablespoon grated
    cauliflower   Parmesan cheese
4 tablespoons butter   ¼ teaspoon nutmeg
3 tablespoons flour   2 eggs, beaten
2 cups milk

Cook the cauliflower and separate the flowerets. Melt the butter, stir in the flour, and gradually add the milk. Stir in the salt, cheese, nutmeg, and eggs. Combine the sauce with the cauliflower in a buttered casserole. Set in a pan of hot water and bake at 350° for 1 hour. (This can be frozen. Line the casserole with aluminum foil, bake, freeze, and remove from the dish with the foil.)

2 • ITALY

1 small head cauliflower or
   1 package frozen
   cauliflower
oil
minced garlic

chopped parsley
tomato paste (optional)
grated Parmesan cheese
   (optional)

Separate the flowerets; parboil in salted water and drain.
Brown lightly in oil with the garlic and parsley. Serve plain
or with the following addition: Combine equal parts of tomato paste and water, pour over the flowerets, heat through,
and sprinkle with grated cheese.

3 • SWEDEN

1 small head cauliflower or
   1 package frozen
   cauliflower
butter

bread crumbs
hard-boiled eggs, chopped
chopped parsley
dash nutmeg

Cook the flowerets and drain. Brown the bread crumbs in
butter. Sprinkle the cauliflower with the crumbs, chopped
eggs, parsley, and nutmeg.

X • CHICORY

1 • BELGIUM

2 heads chicory
¼ cup olive oil
½ teaspoon salt
pepper
little minced garlic

½ teaspoon sweet basil
½ teaspoon chopped fresh
   mint or ¼ teaspoon
   dried mint
2 cups tomatoes (optional)

Shred the chicory. Combine it with all the other ingredients
and cook, covered, for 1 hour, stirring occasionally.

XI • CUCUMBERS

The first six recipes can also be made with zucchini. General
method: The cucumbers or zucchini may be peeled or not, as
you wish. You can cut them in half lengthwise, hollow the
center out, and place the stuffing in the hollow, or you can
leave them whole and carefully core them with a fruit or
vegetable corer. When they are stuffed, place them in a
baking dish with either (1) 1 cup water or (2) 1 cup stock
or consommé or (3) 1 can tomato paste and 1 can water.
Bake at 325° for 30 minutes or until tender. A little garlic

can be added. These stuffed vegetables may be prepared a day ahead, wrapped in foil, and then baked when ready to use or they may be baked completely, frozen, and then re-heated when ready to serve.

1 • HOLLAND

4 cucumbers or zucchini
1 cup sausage meat
¼ cup chopped dill pickles

1 tablespoon vinegar or
    lemon juice
1 teaspoon nutmeg

Prepare the cucumbers or zucchini for stuffing. Mix together all the other ingredients. Season. Stuff the vegetables and bake at 325° until tender.

2 • FRANCE

4 cucumbers or zucchini
4 strips bacon, diced
4 small onions, chopped
4 tomatoes, chopped

½ cup bread crumbs
salt
pepper
butter

Prepare the vegetables for stuffing. Mix the bacon, onions, tomatoes, bread crumbs, and seasoning with the scooped-out vegetable pulp. Cover the bottom of a buttered baking dish with half of this mixture. Stuff the vegetables with the rest. Lay them in the baking dish and dot with butter. Bake at 325° until done.

3 • AUSTRIA

4 cucumbers or zucchini
½ cup cooked diced meat
½ cup cooked rice or
    bread crumbs
1 small onion, chopped

1 teaspoon chopped parsley
¼ teaspoon thyme
salt
pepper
butter

Prepare the cucumbers or zucchini for stuffing. Mix all the ingredients except the butter with the scooped-out pulp of the vegetables. Stuff the vegetables with this mixture. Dot with butter and bake at 325° for 30 minutes or until tender.

4 • FRANCE

4 cucumbers or zucchini
1 pound mushrooms,
    chopped
1 onion, chopped

¼ cup butter
2 teaspoons chopped parsley
salt
pepper

Prepare the cucumbers or zucchini for stuffing. Cook the mushrooms and onion in butter a few minutes. Combine with the parsley, salt, and pepper and stuff into prepared vegetables. Bake at 325° until done.

5 • ITALY

4 cucumbers or zucchini	2 tablespoons grated
1 slice bread	Parmesan cheese
1 cup ground beef	salt
1 sliced boiled ham, diced	pepper
1 egg	

Prepare the cucumbers or zucchini for stuffing. Soak the bread in water and squeeze out. Combine the bread with the other ingredients and stuff the cucumbers. Bake at 325° until tender.

6 • ITALY

4 cucumbers or zucchini	2 tablespoons chopped
1 slice bread	parsley
1 small can tuna fish, flaked	pepper
1 tablespoon olive oil or	¼ teaspoon oregano
butter	

Prepare the cucumbers or zucchini for stuffing. Soak the bread in water and squeeze out. Combine the bread with all the other ingredients and stuff the cucumbers. Bake at 325° until tender.

7 • AUSTRIA

cucumbers	salt
1 tablespoon butter	pepper
1 tablespoon flour	½ cup sour cream or
little minced garlic	chicken bouillon
1 tablespoon lemon juice	

Cucumbers may or may not be peeled. Slice the cucumbers. Melt the butter; lightly brown the flour and garlic. Add the lemon juice, salt, pepper, and sour cream or bouillon. Add the cucumber slices and simmer until tender.

8 • FRANCE

cucumbers	butter
salt	sugar

Peel the cucumbers; cut them in half and then in strips, removing the seeds. Parboil in salted water about 10 minutes and drain. Sauté them in butter with a little salt and sugar.

XII • EGGPLANT

1 • ALGERIA

1 large eggplant	pepper
oil	¼ cup ripe olives, pitted
½ cup tomato paste	and chopped
¼ teaspoon salt	

Peel the eggplant, cut it into cubes, and sauté it in oil for 15 minutes or until tender. Add the tomato paste, diluted with ½ cup water, and the salt, pepper, and olives. Cook 5 minutes longer.

2 • ITALY

1 large eggplant	1 cup milk
2 tablespoons butter	½ cup grated American
½ teaspoon salt	cheese
1 teaspoon grated onion	2 tablespoons catsup
2 tablespoons flour	2 eggs, separated

Peel the eggplant, dice it, simmer it until tender, and mash it. Melt the butter, add the salt and onion, stir in the flour, and gradually add the milk. Add the cheese, catsup, and egg yolks. Cook until thickened and fold in the beaten egg whites. Combine the sauce with the mashed eggplant. Pour into a buttered baking dish. Bake in a pan of hot water at 350° for 45 minutes or until set.

3 • FRANCE

1 large eggplant	Hollandaise sauce

Slice and steam the eggplant. Serve with Hollandaise sauce (Vegetable Sauce #1, page 180).

4 • ITALY

1 large eggplant	oregano
tomatoes, sliced	1 green pepper, chopped
salt	1 onion, chopped
pepper	tomato juice (optional)
sweet basil	

Cut the eggplant into ½-inch slices. Butter a baking dish and butter both sides of the slices of eggplant. Arrange the eggplant in alternate layers with the tomatoes, sprinkling each layer with salt, pepper, sweet basil, oregano, green pepper, and onion. Bake at 350° for 1 hour, adding a little tomato juice or water if necessary.

5 • ALGERIA ✓

1 large eggplant	salt
2 onions, chopped	pepper
oil	1 egg yolk
little minced garlic	½ cup cottage cheese
2 cups tomatoes	

Peel the eggplant and cut it into cubes. Sauté the onions and garlic in oil until golden. Add the eggplant and cook 10 minutes. Add the tomatoes, salt, and pepper and cook 10 more minutes. Pour into a buttered baking dish. Mix the egg yolk into the cottage cheese and spread on top of the eggplant mixture. Bake at 375° for 40 minutes.

XIII • LETTUCE

1 • FRANCE

2 heads lettuce	pepper
2 tablespoons butter	1 tablespoon lemon juice
2 tablespoons flour	or vinegar
1 cup chicken broth	1 cup sour cream
salt	

Shred the lettuce. Melt the butter, stir in the flour, and gradually add the broth, salt, pepper, lemon juice, and sour cream (which has been warmed slightly). Combine with the lettuce and cook for 10 minutes. Serve hot.

2 • SPAIN

2 heads lettuce	pepper
2 tablespoons butter	bread crumbs
2 tablespoons flour	½ cup chopped or ground
1 cup milk	nuts
1 teaspoon salt	butter

Cut each head of lettuce in half and parboil 5 minutes. Melt the butter, stir in the flour, and gradually add the milk, salt, and pepper, cooking until thickened. Arrange the lettuce in a baking dish. Pour over the sauce. Sprinkle with bread crumbs and ground nuts and dot with butter. Bake at 450° until browned.

XIV • MUSHROOMS

1 • SPAIN

1 pound mushrooms
little minced garlic
1 onion, chopped
butter or olive oil

¼ teaspoon salt
pepper
1 teaspoon oregano

Slice the mushrooms. Cook the garlic and onion in butter until golden. Add the mushrooms, salt, pepper, and oregano and cook a few minutes, until tender. (The garlic and oregano may be omitted and ½ cup heavy cream added instead.)

2 • ITALY

½ pound sliced mushrooms
3 tablespoons butter
3 tablespoons flour
¾ cup milk
salt
pepper
4 eggs, separated

2 tablespoons grated
*   Parmesan cheese*
1 tablespoon minced onion
*   (optional)*
½ cup chopped almonds
*   (optional)*

Cook the mushrooms in butter a few minutes, stir in the flour, and gradually add the milk. Add the beaten egg yolks, salt, pepper, cheese, onion, and almonds. Fold in the stiffly beaten egg whites (use 5 if the eggs are small). Pour into a buttered baking dish, place in a pan of hot water, and bake at 400° for 40 minutes or until set.

XV • MUSTARD GREENS

1 • CHINA

1 pound mustard greens
oil
3 tablespoons vinegar
1 tablespoon soy sauce
1 tablespoon red wine
*   (optional)*
dash powdered ginger

*   (optional)*
3 tablespoons sugar
½ cup chicken broth or
*   bouillon*
1 teaspoon cornstarch
½ teaspoon curry powder
*   (optional)*

Slice the mustard greens and stir-fry for 5 minute in oil. Add the vinegar, soy sauce, wine, ginger, sugar, and broth. Simmer 2 minutes. Dissolve the cornstarch in 1 tablespoon water; add to the greens with the curry powder. Cook 2 more minutes. Serve hot. (Stir-frying is a good method for cooking vegetables quickly and keeping them crisp. If meat is used in a dish of this type, the cubes should be stir-fried first and the vegetables added and cooked as described.)

XVI • ONIONS

1 • BERMUDA

4 Bermuda onions
toast slices
grated cheese
3 eggs, beaten

1 cup milk
½ teaspoon salt
pinch of marjoram

Parboil the onions 5 minutes; cool and slice into ½-inch thick rings. Cover the bottom of a buttered baking dish with slices of toast. Lay the onions on top; sprinkle with grated cheese. Combine the eggs, milk, salt, and marjoram and pour over the onions. Bake at 350° for 30 minutes or until firm.

XVII • HEARTS OF PALM

1 • FRANCE

1 can hearts of palm
butter

Hollandaise sauce

Slice the hearts of palm and sauté in butter until golden. Prepare Hollandaise sauce (Vegetable Sauce #1, page 180). Serve over the hearts of palm.

XVIII • PEAS

When cooking peas, if you use fresh ones, include a few pea pods while cooking; they add to the flavor. A sprig of mint can also be added. Or toss the cooked peas with a little chopped fresh mint or mint sauce or butter and marjoram.

1 • AUSTRIA

1 pound peas
4 tablespoons uncooked rice
1 onion, chopped

butter
½ cup sliced mushrooms
(optional)

Cook the peas in 2 cups salted water until tender. Drain and reserve the water. Cook the rice in the water from the peas until tender; drain excess liquid. Cook the onion and mushrooms in butter until the onion is golden and the mushrooms are done. Add the peas and rice and cook together a few minutes.

2 • FRANCE

4 pounds peas	¼ teaspoon tarragon
1 head lettuce	salt
1 tablespoon sugar	pepper
3 tablespoons flour	chopped chives (optional)
1 tablespoon butter	2 slices bacon, diced and
1 cup pearl onions	cooked (optional)
¼ teaspoon thyme	

Cut the lettuce into eighths and cook with the peas in 1 cup of water with the sugar until tender. Work the butter and flour together with the fingertips and add gradually to the liquid. Put the peas and lettuce into a baking dish with the onions, thyme, tarragon, salt, pepper, chives, and bacon. Heat through.

3 • CHINA

1 package frozen peas or	pinch sugar
fresh peas	1 tablespoon cornstarch
¼ cup soy sauce	⅛ teaspoon powdered
1 tablespoon sherry	ginger (optional)

Cook the peas in a little water with the soy sauce, sherry, and sugar until tender. Dissolve the cornstarch in 2 tablespoons water; add to the peas and cook until thickened. Add the ginger.

4 • FRANCE

2 cups puréed peas or	pepper
4 cups strained peas	½ teaspoon onion juice
¼ cup light cream	4 eggs, beaten
salt	

Mix the peas with cream, salt, pepper, and onion juice. Add the eggs and pour into a buttered ring mold or individual timbales. Place in a pan of hot water and bake at 375° about 30 minutes or until set. For a firmer pudding, use 2 cups medium white sauce instead of the cream. To serve, fill the center of the ring with creamed mushrooms (to which 1 tablespoon red wine has been added) or with warm croutons.

XIX • GREEN PEPPERS

Peppers may be cut in half or left whole, with the top cut off before stuffing. Clean out the seeds and wash the peppers. Place the stuffed peppers in a pan with 2 cups of water or whatever liquid is specified in the recipe. Bake them at 375° or steam them, using the convenient steaming rack that fits all pans. If the peppers are cut in half, they will take about 30 minutes to cook; if they are whole, they will take about 1 hour.

1 • Mexico

6 green peppers
1 onion, chopped
clove garlic, minced
1 pound ground beef

¼ cup tomato paste
1 tablespoon chili powder
1 teaspoon salt
¼ cup chopped almonds

Prepare the peppers for stuffing. Sauté the onion and garlic and combine with all the other ingredients. Cook 5 minutes, adding a little water if necessary. Stuff the peppers and bake at 375° or steam until done.

2 • Hungary

6 green peppers
1 onion, chopped
1 pound ground pork
½ cup cooked rice
1 teaspoon salt

½ teaspoon Hungarian
   paprika
1 egg, beaten
2 cups tomato juice

Prepare the peppers for stuffing. Sauté the onions and combine them with the pork, rice, salt, paprika, and egg. Stuff the peppers. Put them in a baking pan and pour the tomato juice around them. Bake at 375° until done.

3 • Austria

6 green peppers
2 onions, chopped
butter
2 tablespoons flour
1 cup sour cream
2 cups cut-up sausages

4 tomatoes, peeled and
   chopped
½ teaspoon salt
1 teaspoon sugar
1 teaspoon caraway seeds

Prepare the peppers for stuffing. Sauté the onions in butter.

Stir in the flour and blend in the cream. Add all the other ingredients and stuff the peppers. Bake at 375° or steam until done.

4 • CHINA

6 green peppers	1 onion
1 pound fillet of sole	1 tablespoon soy sauce
1 cup crab meat	1 teaspoon Mei Yen, MSG,
¼ cup water chestnuts	or Accent
¼ cup dried Chinese	1 teaspoon salt
mushrooms	1 teaspoon sugar

Prepare the peppers for stuffing. Soak the mushrooms in water about 15 minutes or until soft. Grind together the sole, crab meat, water chestnuts, mushrooms, and onion. Add the soy sauce, Mei Yen, salt, and sugar. Stuff the peppers and bake at 375° or steam until done.

5 • ITALY

6 green peppers	2 tablespoons chopped
2-ounce can anchovy fillets	parsley
12 ripe olives	1 cup olive oil
¼ cup seedless raisins	salt
1 cup bread crumbs	pepper
1 tablespoon basil	½ cup tomato paste

Prepare the peppers for stuffing. Cut up the anchovies and olives and combine them with the raisins, bread crumbs, basil, parsley, olive oil, salt, and pepper. Stuff the peppers and place them in a baking dish. Dilute the tomato paste with ½ cup water and pour a little over each pepper. Bake at 375° until done.

6 • FRANCE

6 green peppers	1 onion, chopped
1 cup chopped cooked	1 cup uncooked rice
chicken, ham, or	5 cups chicken or beef
shrimp	consommé

Prepare the peppers for stuffing. Lightly brown the onion in butter, add the rice and 3 cups of consommé, and bake, covered, at 350° for 20 minutes or until the liquid is absorbed and the rice is cooked. Mix with the meat and season to taste. Stuff the peppers and place in a baking dish. Pour the remaining 2 cups of consommé in the dish around the peppers. Bake at 375° until done.

For other possible stuffings for peppers, see recipes 4 through 17 under Chopped Meats, pages 128-132.

XX • POTATOES

1 • FRANCE

3 potatoes	½ cup bouillon
3 onions	bread crumbs
butter	little prepared mustard
Gruyère, Parmesan, or	(optional)
cottage cheese	dash nutmeg (optional)
salt	sliced tomatoes (optional)
pepper	

Peel the potatoes and onions and slice them thin. Butter a baking dish and arrange in it alternate layers of potatoes, onions, and cheese, seasoning to taste with salt and pepper. Pour the bouillon over the potatoes, sprinkle with bread crumbs, and dot with butter. Cover with a lid or aluminum foil and bake at 350° (about 1 hour to 1½ hours), removing the cover for the last 15 minutes to brown the top. If you use the mustard, add it at the same time as the bouillon. If you use the nutmeg, sprinkle it on with the other seasonings. This is also good made without the onions or with a layer of sliced tomatoes added.

2 • POLAND *similar to scalloped*

5 potatoes	bread crumbs
butter	grated cheese
1 onion, chopped	2 eggs
salt	1 cup sour cream
pepper	

Cook the potatoes, peel and slice them, and lay them in a buttered baking dish. Sauté the onion in butter and add to the potatoes. Sprinkle with salt, pepper, bread crumbs, and grated cheese. Beat the eggs into the sour cream; pour the mixture over the potatoes and bake at 400° until the top is browned.

3 • HUNGARY

6 baking potatoes	¼ pound chopped ham or
½ cup sour cream	dried beef
1 egg, beaten	butter

Bake the potatoes, rubbing the skins with fat to keep them soft. Cut off the tops and scoop out the pulp. Combine the potato pulp with warm sour cream, egg, and chopped ham. Stuff back into the skins, top with butter, and brown under the broiler.

4 • ITALY

6 baking potatoes	little crushed garlic
6 tablespoons warm milk	salt
6 tablespoons butter	pepper
1 egg yolk	grated Parmesan cheese

Bake the potatoes, rubbing the skins with fat to keep them soft. Cut off the tops and scoop out the pulp. Mix the potato pulp with the milk, butter, egg yolk, garlic, salt, and pepper. Stuff back into the skins. Sprinkle with cheese and brown under the broiler.

5 • INDIA

3 potatoes	1 teaspoon salt
¼ cup yogurt or sour cream	½ teaspoon cinnamon
1 tablespoon curry powder	1 teaspoon powdered
4 tablespoons butter	ginger (optional)

Peel the potatoes, cut them into 1-inch cubes, boil them until tender, and drain them. Mix the yogurt and curry powder and toss with the potatoes. Melt the butter in a pan with the salt, cinnamon, and ginger. Brown the potatoes in this mixture.

XXI • SWEET POTATOES

1 • HAWAII

6 sweet potatoes	butter
1 banana	slivered almonds

Cook the sweet potatoes and mash them with the banana and a little butter. Season to taste and sprinkle with slivered almonds.

2 • WEST INDIES

6 sweet potatoes
juice of 1 orange
salt

6 scooped-out halves of
    oranges
6 marshmallows

Cook the sweet potatoes and mash them with the orange juice and salt. Fill the orange-skin halves with the mixture and top each with a marshmallow. Brown lightly under the broiler.

3 • FRANCE

6 sweet potatoes
1½ cups milk
few mint leaves

salt
2 tablespoons butter

Cook the sweet potatoes. Scald the milk with the mint leaves and strain. Mash the sweet potatoes with salt, butter, and the strained scalded milk.

XXII • SPINACH

1 • CHINA

4 pounds fresh or 2 packages
    frozen spinach
little soy sauce

pinch sugar
salt
½ cup chopped peanuts

Cook the spinach until tender. Chop it and toss it in a serving dish with soy sauce, sugar, salt, and peanuts.

2 • HOLLAND

4 pounds fresh or 2 packages
    frozen spinach
4 slices bacon
1 tablespoon butter
½ teaspoon sugar
1 tablespoon flour

salt
pepper
pinch mace
½ cup cream or milk
croutons

Cook the spinach a few minutes—until it is tender but still crisp—and drain. Cook the bacon, crumble it, and mix it with the spinach. Melt the butter; stir in the sugar, flour, salt, pepper, and mace; and gradually add the cream. Simmer until thickened and mix with the spinach. Heat through. Serve with croutons.

3 • ITALY

4 pounds fresh or 2 packages	pepper
frozen spinach	pinch nutmeg
½ cup butter	¼ cup grated Parmesan
salt	cheese

Cook the spinach in the butter until just tender. Add salt, pepper, nutmeg, and cheese. Mix thoroughly over heat and serve.

4 • HAWAII

2 pounds fresh or 1 package	1 teaspoon salt
frozen spinach	1 teaspoon lemon juice
1 cup grated coconut	pepper
1 cup milk	1 onion, chopped

Soak the coconut in the milk 1 hour; then simmer together 10 minutes. Drain and squeeze the milk from the coconut. Add to the milk the salt, lemon juice, pepper, onion, and spinach. Cook 10 minutes.

5 • FRANCE

6 pounds fresh or 3 packages	1 teaspoon salt
frozen spinach	pepper
½ cup butter	pinch nutmeg
6 tablespoons flour	3 eggs, beaten

Cook the spinach and save the water. Purée the spinach through a sieve or in the blender. Melt the butter, stir in the flour, and gradually add 2 cups of spinach water. Add the salt, pepper, nutmeg, and eggs. Mix with the spinach and pour into a buttered 2-quart baking dish or 2 9-inch ring molds. Put in a pan of hot water and bake at 350° for 1 hour or until set. If you want to bake only one mold, cover the other with foil and freeze. If you use a ring mold, fill the center with croutons or cooked carrots and encircle the ring with hot whole baby beets.

XXIII • SQUASH

1 • ITALY

zucchini squash	butter
salt	sweet basil
pepper	

Slice the squash thin. Season with salt and pepper and fry quickly in butter with a little sweet basil.

2 • ITALY

yellow squash   1 egg, lightly beaten
flour   butter
salt

Slice the squash. Dip the slices in flour with a little salt and then in egg. Fry on both sides until golden.

3 • ITALY

yellow crooked-neck squash   powder or garlic salt
butter   1 onion, chopped
salt   grated Parmesan cheese
pepper   1 cup tomato juice
minced garlic or garlic

Slice the squash and put it in a buttered baking dish with salt, pepper and garlic. Sauté the onion lightly and add to the squash. Dot with butter, sprinkle with cheese, and pour over the tomato juice. Bake at 350° until tender.

4 • GREECE

yellow squash
olive oil   ½ teaspoon sugar
minced garlic   1 teaspoon chopped mint
½ teaspoon salt   3 tablespoons vinegar

Slice the squash thin. Sauté it in oil with the garlic until tender. Add the salt, sugar, mint, and vinegar. Cook a few minutes longer.

5 • HUNGARY

4 pounds any small, soft-   1 teaspoon chopped dill
    skinned squash   (optional)
salt   pepper
4 tablespoons butter   ½ cup bouillon
4 tablespoons flour   2 tablespoons vinegar
2 teaspoons minced onion   ½ cup sour cream
¼ teaspoon paprika

Peel the squash, cut it into thin strips, salt it, and set it aside for ½ hour. Melt the butter and add the flour, onion, paprika, dill, pepper, bouillon, squash, and vinegar. Cook 15 minutes. Stir in the sour cream and heat thoroughly.

6 • WEST INDIES

acorn squash   salt
butter   brown sugar

Split each squash in half and scoop out the seeds. Fill with a little butter and add salt and brown sugar to taste. Place in a pan of hot water and bake at 350° for 40 minutes or until tender, depending on the size of the squash.

XXIV • TOMATOES

1 • PHILIPPINES

4 tomatoes, peeled and
    chopped, or 2 cups
    canned tomatoes
4 tablespoons butter
1 onion, chopped
clove garlic, minced
¼ teaspoon chili powder

¼ teaspoon powdered
    ginger (optional)
1 teaspoon salt
1 teaspoon sugar
1 tablespoon grated
    coconut

If you use canned tomatoes, drain them first. Melt the butter; add the onion, garlic, chili powder, ginger, salt, and sugar; and cook together a few minutes. Add the tomatoes and coconut and simmer 10 minutes.

2 • PORTUGAL

2 cups canned or fresh
    tomatoes
1 tablespoon sugar
1 onion, chopped fine

little minced garlic
    (optional)
1 bouillon cube, crushed
chopped parsley

If you use fresh tomatoes, peel and chop them. Simmer the tomatoes with the sugar, onion, garlic, bouillon cube, salt, and pepper. Serve garnished with chopped parsley.

XXV • MIXED VEGETABLES

1 • GERMANY

1 package frozen lima
    beans
1 package frozen green
    beans

1 can kernel corn
1 onion, sliced
½ teaspoon paprika
1 cup tomato juice

Cook the onion in butter until golden. Add all the other ingredients, season to taste, and cook until tender.

4 zucchini or summer	2 green peppers
squash	salt
1 eggplant	pepper
3 tomatoes	clove garlic, minced
1 onion	4 tablespoons olive oil

Peel and chop the zucchini, eggplant, tomatoes, and onion; chop the green peppers; and mix all together with salt, pepper, and garlic. Put in a pan with the olive oil and 1 cup water. Simmer together 45 minutes or until vegetables are soft enough to mash together. (These same vegetables can be sliced, arranged in layers in a pan—with the oil on the bottom—and seasoned to taste. Simmer over very low heat 30 minutes or until tender. Serve hot or cold.)

3 • AUSTRIA

combination of cooked	salt
vegetables, such as:	pepper
peas	paprika or nutmeg
lima beans	sour cream or 1 cup cream
green beans	sauce
cauliflowers	2 egg yolks (optional)
mushrooms	grated cheddar or
little onion juice or lemon	Parmesan cheese
or vinegar	

Combine the cooked vegetables of your choice with onion juice, lemon juice, or vinegar; add salt and pepper and paprika or nutmeg. Thicken with either sour cream or cream sauce (made with 2 tablespoons butter, 2 tablespoons flour, and 1 cup cream milk); add the egg yolks to the sauce for richness, if desired. Cheese may be added. Heat through or until cheese is melted.

4 • CHINA

bamboo shoots	peanut or sesame oil
water chestnuts	soy sauce or butter and salt
bean sprouts	

Slice the bamboo shoots and water chestnuts and drain the bean sprouts. Stir-fry them quickly in the oil until they are tender but still crisp. Serve hot with soy sauce or butter and salt.

• 5 •

SALADS AND
SALAD DRESSINGS

In my experience, salads all over the world have recognizable characteristics. Green, leafy vegetables may either form
the body of the salad or be the base of operations. If there
are other ingredients, they can be almost *anything*. There are
very few restrictions when it comes to making salads. Elements used in salads in various parts of the world (some of
which may be familiar and some of which may not) include:
clams, scallops, shrimp, herring, sardines, smoked fish;
chicken, game; corn, eggplant, avocado, broccoli (raw), bean
sprouts, water chestnuts, raw sliced mushrooms, sauerkraut;
apples, chestnuts, grated coconut, brandied fruit; dill pickles,
chutney, black olives; ginger; sweet potato leaves; poppy
seeds, caraway seeds, celery seeds, or, my favorite, toasted
sesame seeds. Only a lack of imagination or courage can
deter you.

I • VEGETABLE SALADS

Most vegetables—raw or cooked—go well in salads. And
vegetable salads can be fortified with cubes or slivers of meat,

fish, or cheese; cooked and crumbled bacon; olives; pickles; and chopped hard-boiled eggs.

1 • MEXICO

Slice cucumbers (with the peel) and cube avocados. Serve on lettuce. Top with a mixture of equal parts of mayonnaise and chili sauce.

2 • BALKANS

Combine equal amounts of cooked asparagus tips, cubed apples, and cubed cooked or canned beets. Add a little prepared mustard to Salad Dressing #2 (Vinaigrette), page 76, and serve with salad.

3 • ITALY

Cube and cook an eggplant and combine with 6 chopped anchovy fillets, 2 sliced green onions or scallions, and 2 chopped hard-boiled eggs. Toss with mayonnaise.

4 • GERMANY

Combine cubes of hot, cooked potatoes with crumbled cooked bacon. Toss with Salad Dressing #2 (Vinaigrette), page 76.

5 • FAR EAST

Mix a can of drained bean sprouts; a can of drained, sliced bamboo shoots; a bunch of watercress; and shredded lettuce. Toss with Salad Dressing #2 (Vinaigrette), page 76.

6 • FAR EAST

Toss mixed greens with toasted sesame seeds (brown them in a skillet until they crackle). Use any dressing.

7 • INDONESIA

Cook and cool 1 package of frozen French-cut green beans or an equal amount of fresh green beans. Combine the beans with ½ small head of cabbage shredded, 1 can drained bean sprouts, 4 shredded radishes, 1 shredded cucumber, and a few slices of water chestnut (optional). Toss with Salad Dressing #8 (Soy), page 77. This can be made hours ahead of time and kept in the refrigerator. Add the dressing when ready to serve.

8 • FRANCE

Combine 1 chopped green pepper, 4 tomatoes cut up, 2 diced cucumbers, 10 sliced green onions or scallions, ¼ cup chopped parsley, 2 tablespoons chopped fresh mint or 1 tablespoon mint flakes, and 2 cups croutons. Toss with a mixture of ½ cup oil, 4 tablespoons vinegar, and 1 teaspoon salt.

9 • FRANCE

Serve cooked vegetables—such as asparagus, cauliflower, beets, artichoke hearts, green beans, or raw onions—with Salad Dressing #2 (Vinaigrette), page 76.

10 • BALKANS

Arrange a platter with sliced cucumbers, radishes, onions, small whole mushrooms, and cubes or fingers of cantaloupe. Serve with Salad Dressing #1 (Sour Cream), page 76.

11 • SCANDINAVIA

Combine 4 diced boiled potatoes, 2 diced pickled beets, 1 can skinless and boneless sardines cut up, 1 chopped apple, 1 tablespoon chopped onion, and 1 tablespoon pickle relish. Mix ½ cup mayonnaise with 2 tablespoons beet liquid. Toss with vegetables.

12 • FRANCE

Combine lettuce, 2 cups croutons, and 2 beaten egg yolks with any of these salad dressings: #11 (Herb), #13 (Sweet), #25 (Anchovy), pages 77 and 79. Sprinkle with grated cheese. A good dash of Worcestershire sauce may be added to dressing #11.

13 • ITALY

Parboil 1 package of frozen cauliflower or an equal amount of fresh cauliflower. Toss the flowerets with a few pitted and chopped ripe olives and 1 can anchovy fillets. Combine 2 tablespoons oil, 1 tablespoon vinegar, salt, and pepper and toss with salad.

14 • GERMANY

Arrange cooked asparagus spears on leaves of romaine. Sprinkle with chopped hard-boiled eggs and crumbled cooked bacon. Add 2 tablespoons vinegar to 6 tablespoons warm bacon fat and pour over the vegetables immediately before serving. Do not allow dressing to cool, as it will congeal.

15 • FRANCE

Slice 4 hot, cooked potatoes and moisten them with white wine. Mix ¼ cup oil with 2 tablespoons lemon juice or vinegar; add 2 tablespoons minced onion and pour over the potatoes. When the dressing has been absorbed, sprinkle with chopped parsley.

16 • FRANCE

Toss mixed greens with cheese balls: (1) form tiny balls of cream cheese and roll in crushed nuts, (2) mix cream cheese with chopped mint or chives and roll in chopped almonds that have been browned in hot butter, or (3) mix equal parts of cream cheese and Roquefort or bleu cheese with chopped chives or grated onion or chopped parsley or minced chutney, form into balls, and roll in paprika and ground nuts. Chill the cheese balls before tossing with the greens. Toss with any dressing.

17 • ITALY

Cut a raw eggplant, with the skin, into cubes. Chill in a mixture of ½ cup wine vinegar, clove garlic crushed, 1 teaspoon salt, ½ teaspoon pepper, 1 teaspoon sweet basil, and 1 teaspoon oregano. This can keep for days in the refrigerator. Before serving, add a little olive oil.

II • MEAT AND FISH SALADS

1 • FRANCE

Slice 4 oranges and add to 2 cups cooked, cut-up duck. Pour over a mixture of ½ cup oil, 1 tablespoon vinegar, ½ teaspoon salt, pepper, ¼ teaspoon paprika, and ¼ teaspoon tarragon. Serve on lettuce with sprigs of watercress or parsley and additional orange slices.

2 • FRANCE

Combine diced cooked chicken; blanched, salted almonds; and seedless grapes. Whisk together ½ cup mayonnaise and ½ cup whipped cream; mix with the chicken. Serve on lettuce.

3 • ENGLAND

Cook a chicken; remove the meat and dice it. Combine 1 cup mayonnaise, ¼ cup sour cream, 1 tablespoon prepared mustard, 1 tablespoon lemon juice, salt, pepper, paprika, and sugar. Mix with the chicken. Serve on lettuce garnished with quartered hard-boiled eggs.

4 • INDIA

Cook a chicken; remove the meat and dice it. Combine Salad Dressing #5 (Basic French), page 76, with 2 tablespoons minced chutney. Mix with the chicken.

5 • POLYNESIA

Marinate fillet of sole in lime juice, then cook it. Chill and serve on lettuce with mayonnaise or a little olive oil, salt, and pepper.

6 • POLYNESIA

Cut 3 avocados in half and reserve the skins. Cook and shell 1 pound of shrimp. Combine the shrimp with the diced meat of the avocados and 1 chopped onion. Mix ¼ cup oil, 2 tablespoons vinegar, little crushed garlic, ¼ teaspoon dry mustard, ½ teaspoon salt, and pepper. Toss the dressing with the shrimp mixture and fill the avocado shells. Serve on a bed of lettuce.

7 • FAR EAST

Drain bean sprouts and mix them with cooked shrimp, chopped hard-boiled eggs, and blanched almonds. Toss with Salad Dressing #6 (Curry), page 77.

III • FRUIT SALADS

1 • GUATEMALA

Mix together meat from 3 avocados, 2 teaspoons sugar, ¾ cup sour cream, ¼ cup mayonnaise, ½ teaspoon oregano, salt, pepper, and juice of ½ lemon. Force through a strainer or put in the blender. Soften 1 envelope of gelatin in ½ cup cold water and add 1 cup boiling water; add to the avocado mixture and allow to cool slightly. Oil a ring mold or 6 individual molds and sprinkle the bottom with caviar (optional). Carefully spoon the avocado mixture into the mold. Chill for 2 hours or more, until firm. Unmold on a bed of lettuce and fill the center of the ring with salad greens and/or tomatoes or grapefruit or orange sections.

2 • FRANCE

Arrange slices of avocado on romaine or endive and serve with Salad Dressing #3 (Thousand Islands), page 76.

3 • FRANCE

Arrange slices of avocado on chopped raw spinach. Sprinkle with nutmeg and sugar or with chopped hard-boiled egg and minced onion. Serve with Salad Dressing #16 (Tarragon), page 78.

4 • MEXICO

Beat a little Salad Dressing #5 (Basic French), page 76, and 1 teaspoon chili powder into the meat of 3 avocados with a fork. Serve in mounds on a bed of lettuce.

5 • SCANDINAVIA

Arrange slices of orange and cooked or canned beets on lettuce. Pour over Salad Dressing #2 (Vinaigrette), page 76.

6 • PHILIPPINES

Peel bananas and cut them into strips. Roll the strips in chopped peanuts and arrange them on lettuce with tangerine sections. Top with mayonnaise and sprinkle with pomegranate seeds.

7 • ENGLAND

Combine ½ cup chopped cooked or canned cranberries, ½ cup chopped celery, and ¼ cup chopped nuts. Serve with a combination of equal parts of mayonnaise and whipped cream.

8 • FRANCE

Add cheese balls (Vegetable Salad #16, page 73) to fruit salad. Sprinkle with chopped fresh mint.

9 • FRANCE

Sprinkle melon balls or cubes with lemon juice, lime juice, Kirsch, or Cointreau. Arrange on lettuce.

IV • SALAD DRESSINGS

Countries are not designated for salad dressings because so many have been either universally adopted or subtly adapted. Some dressings, of course, have geographically recognized ingredients: the soy, chutney and curry of the East; the sour cream and dill so often found in middle and northern European cooking. But the boundaries have been crossed often. Even our well-known "French" dressing comes from the Roman *Jus Simplex* or Greek Sharp Sauce.

1 • SOUR CREAM

Combine 1 cup sour cream with 2 tablespoons lemon juice or vinegar, ¼ teaspoon salt, and pepper to taste. Add any combination of the following: 1 tablespoon chopped chives, little crushed garlic, 2 tablespoons grated onion, 2 teaspoons horseradish, 1 teaspoon chopped dill, ½ teaspoon paprika. For the sour cream, you can substitute half sour cream, half mayonnaise.

2 • VINAIGRETTE

Combine ¾ cup oil, ¼ cup cider vinegar or wine vinegar, ¼ teaspoon salt, ⅛ teaspoon pepper, 2 teaspoons chopped parsley, 1 teaspoon green olives chopped fine, 1 hard-boiled egg yolk chopped fine, and chopped chives.

3 • THOUSAND ISLANDS

Combine 1 cup mayonnaise, ¼ cup chili sauce, 4 stuffed olives chopped, and any or all of the following: 1 tablespoon pickle relish, 1 tablespoon chopped chives, ½ teaspoon paprika.

4 • COOKED

Cook together 1 cup sour cream, 1 grated onion, 1 3-ounce package cream cheese, ¼ cup vinegar, ½ teaspoon salt, ¼ teaspoon paprika, 2 tablespoons flour, and 2 tablespoons sugar. Stir until smooth. Add the yolk of 1 egg and cook 2 minutes; remove from heat and add 2 tablespoons butter.

5 • BASIC FRENCH

Combine 1½ cups oil, ½ cup vinegar, ½ teaspoon salt, and ¼ teaspoon pepper.

6 • CURRY

Combine 1 cup mayonnaise, 1 teaspoon curry powder, and 1 tablespoon soy sauce.

7 • EGG

Rub 3 hard-boiled egg yolks into ½ cup oil and stir in 2 tablespoons vinegar, 1 teaspoon curry powder, salt, and pepper.

8 • SOY

Combine ½ cup oil, ¼ cup vinegar, 2 teaspoons soy sauce, 1 teaspoon sweet basil, 1 teaspoon sugar, and 1 teaspoon salt.

9 • RUSSIAN

Combine ¼ cup mayonnaise, 2 tablespoons catsup, 1 table-spoon chili sauce, 1 tablespoon tarragon vinegar, 2 teaspoons chopped parsley, 1 teaspoon minced onion, and ⅛ teaspoon paprika.

10 • TOMATO

Combine ¼ cup mayonnaise, 1 tablespoon chili sauce, 1 tablespoon Worcestershire sauce, 1 tomato peeled and chopped fine, and 1 teaspoon chopped chives.

11 • HERB

Combine ¼ cup oil; 1 tablespoon wine vinegar; ⅛ teaspoon each onion powder, thyme, basil, and garlic powder; ½ teaspoon salt; and ¼ teaspoon pepper. You can substitute a small amount of grated onion and minced or crushed garlic for the powders.

12 • DILL

Combine ½ cup oil, 3 tablespoons lemon juice, 2 teaspoons salt, 1 teaspoon dill seeds, and ¼ teaspoon pepper.

13 • SWEET

Combine 1 cup oil, ½ cup vinegar, 6 tablespoons sugar, 1 teaspoon dry mustard, 1 teaspoon paprika, 1 tablespoon Worcestershire sauce, 2 teaspoons salt, ¼ teaspoon pepper, 1 teaspoon celery seeds, and ⅛ teaspoon garlic powder or a little crushed garlic.

14 • MOLASSES

Combine ¼ cup molasses, ½ cup vinegar, and ½ teaspoon pepper.

15 • BASIC

Combine ½ cup oil, ¼ cup lemon juice, and 1 teaspoon salt.

16 • TARRAGON

Combine ½ cup oil, 2 tablespoons tarragon vinegar, 1 teaspoon salt, ½ teaspoon pepper, 2 tablespoons grated onion, 1 teaspoon chopped chives, 2 teaspoons chopped parsley, and ½ teaspoon sugar.

17 • CREAM

Mash the yolks of 2 hard-boiled eggs. Work in ¼ cup cream; a little salt, pepper, and sugar; and 2 tablespoons lemon juice.

18 • ONION

Combine ¼ cup oil, ¼ cup vinegar, 1 minced onion, ⅛ teaspoon chopped dill, ¼ teaspoon chopped parsley, and ¼ teaspoon salt.

19 • PICKLE

Combine ½ cup sesame (or other) oil, 2 tablespoons lemon juice, 1 tablespoon pickle relish, ½ teaspoon salt, and pepper.

20 • SESAME

Combine ½ cup oil, 2 tablespoons vinegar, 2 tablespoons soy sauce, 2 tablespoons sugar, and 4 tablespoons sesame seeds that have been browned in a skillet.

21 • CHUTNEY

Mash the yolks of 2 hard-boiled eggs; work in 6 tablespoons oil and add 2 tablespoons lemon juice, 2 tablespoons finely chopped chutney, ¼ teaspoon salt, and pepper.

22 • COTTAGE CHEESE

Combine 1½ cups oil, ½ cup vinegar, ½ teaspoon salt, ½

teaspoon pepper, ½ cup cottage cheese, and 2 tablespoons chopped parsley.

23 • JELLY

Blend smoothly 1 3-ounce package cream cheese, 4 tablespoons currant jelly, 1 tablespoon lemon juice, and ¾ cup whipped cream. Chill.

24 • BEET

Combine 1½ cups oil, ½ cup vinegar, ½ teaspoon salt, ¼ teaspoon pepper, 6 chopped hard-boiled eggs, ¼ cup chopped olives, ¼ cup chopped pickled beets, 2 tablespoons grated onion, and 2 tablespoons chervil (optional).

25 • ANCHOVY

Combine ½ cup oil, ½ cup wine vinegar, ¼ teaspoon salt, little crushed garlic or ⅛ teaspoon garlic powder, 3 tablespoons dry mustard, ¼ cup lemon juice, ½ cup Worcestershire sauce, ½ cup chopped anchovies, and 1 teaspoon pepper.

26 • MUSTARD

Mash the yolk of 1 hard-boiled egg; work in 1 teaspoon prepared mustard, 1 teaspoon A-1 sauce, 4 drops Worcestershire sauce, and 1 tablespoon vinegar. Stir in 3 tablespoons oil, ¼ teaspoon salt, pepper, and 1 egg white chopped fine.

The following are suggestions for using some of the above dressings:
For tossed green salad: 4, 5, 7, 8, 11, 12, 13, 14, 15, 18, 19, 20, 21, 25.
For any cooked vegetable (asparagus, cauliflower, beets, etc.): 2.
For chilled sliced cucumbers, radishes, onions, mushrooms: 1.
For lettuce quartered: 3, 9, 17, 24.
For shellfish: 6, 10.
For fruit: 2, 3, 4, 5, 13, 16, 22, 23.
For avocado: 2, 13, 16, 26.
For bean sprouts, bamboo shoots, cooked green beans, etc.: 19, 20.
For tomatoes: any of the suggestions for tossed salads, 3, 9, 22.

• 6 •

MEAT

Meat is used universally, although the quantity and type varies considerably. The kind of meat is very much determined by geographical limitations: where there is land for grazing there are cattle. But the variety of meat, and how it is handled, is also affected by religious taboos. Amounts used are also determined by the availability of the product. Pork is widely used: it is a favorite in China, appears frequently in Japan, but is seldom eaten in the Near East because of religious restrictions. Mutton and lamb are used in the Near East and, of course, in Australia, where sheep-raising is a main industry. European recipes make use of all the meats we have available and so offer us a great variety of practical suggestions. But Asia and the Pacific areas offer us fresh and delightful ideas for meat cookery. Meat in their recipes is usually in small pieces, sometimes combined with vegetables or wrapped in leaves. It is obviously intended to be eaten with chopsticks or fingers. Cooks in these regions also roast whole animals, usually in pits, as, for instance, in the Hawaiian *luau*. Try *that* some time instead of the usual barbecue!

I • BEEF

These recipes may be prepared ahead of time and frozen. Reheat when you are ready to serve. Always cook these dishes in a covered pot. If you don't have sour cream on hand, substitute 1 cup milk with 1 tablespoon lemon juice.

1 • HUNGARY

4 pounds round steak (1½ inches thick)
flour

4 fresh tomatoes, cut up
2 #2 cans tomatoes
2 cups sour cream

Pound the flour into the steak; season the meat to taste and brown it on both sides in hot fat. Add the fresh and the canned tomatoes. Bake at 350° about 3 hours or until meat is tender. Add the sour cream to the sauce. Bake 30 minutes longer.

2 • HOLLAND

4 pounds round steak (1½ inches thick)
4 onions, sliced

generous sprinkling nutmeg
2 bay leaves
little water

Pound the steak. Season to taste. Brown on both sides in hot fat. Add all the other ingredients. Cover and simmer 2 to 3 hours or until tender.

3 • RUSSIA

4 pounds round steak (1½ inches thick)
salt
pepper
2 onions, chopped
2 cups chopped celery

2 cups mushroom pieces
1 large can tomatoes
2 cups catsup
1 cup water
2 tablespoons flour

Brown the meat on both sides in hot fat. Season with salt and pepper. Cover with the vegetables. Combine the catsup, water, and flour and pour over the meat. Bake at 350° for 3 hours or until tender.

4 • SWITZERLAND

4 pounds round steak (1½ inches thick)
flour
2 onions, chopped

oregano
marjoram
2 cups sour cream
2 cups water

Pound the flour into the steak; season the meat to taste and brown it on both sides in hot fat. Sprinkle the meat with the onions and herbs. Add the sour cream and water. Bake at 350° for 3 hours or until tender.

5 • WEST INDIES

4 pounds round steak (1½ inches thick)
clove garlic, minced
½ teaspoon thyme
½ teaspoon mace
½ teaspoon nutmeg
2 teaspoons salt

pepper
2 tablespoons chopped parsley
3 onions, sliced
2 tomatoes, chopped
¼ cup vinegar

Marinate the steak in a combination of all the other ingredients for 2 hours. Remove the steak from the marinade, wipe it dry, and brown it in butter. Add ½ cup boiling water to the marinade and pour it over the steak. Cover and bake at 350° about 3 hours.

6 • DENMARK

4 pounds round steak (1½ inches thick)
4 onions, chopped
2 tablespoons prepared

mustard
¼ cup red wine
2 tablespoons flour

Season the steak and brown it in butter. Add onions, mustard, wine, and enough water just to cover. Cover and simmer 3 hours or until tender. Brown the flour slightly in a tablespoon of butter and stir it into the pan juices. Simmer a minute or two longer.

4 pounds round steak (1½
    inches thick)
salt
pepper
2 truffles (optional)

½ pound bacon
1 onion, chopped
2 cups stock or consommé
2 tablespoons flour
3 tablespoons red wine

Pound the meat with salt and pepper. Lard it with truffles and pieces of bacon (or have your butcher do it). Fry the onion; add the meat to the pan and cover it with stock. Bake at 350° for 3 hours or until tender. Remove the meat from the pan. Lightly brown the flour in 1 tablespoon butter and stir it into the pan juices (adding a little stock or water if necessary). Add the wine. Serve the sauce with the meat.

8 • HOLLAND

4 pounds round steak (1½
    inches thick)
6 slices bacon
1 teaspoon thyme

1 teaspoon basil
1 bay leaf
6 cloves
½ cup sherry

Season the steak. Place it in a baking dish and arrange the slices of bacon over it. Add the remaining ingredients. Bake at 350° for 3 hours or until tender.

9 • YUGOSLAVIA

4 pounds round steak (1½
    inches thick)
½ cup red wine
2 lemons, peeled and
    sliced thin
2 egg yolks
2 tablespoons bread crumbs

2 tablespoons horseradish
2 teaspoons sugar
2 teaspoons salt
½ teaspoon pepper
¼ cup flour
4 tablespoons sour cream

Brown meat on both sides in butter. Add the wine and 1 cup water. Bake at 350° for 1½ hours. Make about 20 slits in the meat and insert a lemon slice in each one. Beat the egg yolks; add the crumbs, horseradish, and seasonings and spread the mixture on the steak. Bake 1 hour more or until the meat is tender. Remove the steak from the pan. Blend the flour with the sour cream and add it to the pan juices. Heat through.

Cooking time for beef tenderloin varies with the thickness of the meat. One of the safest methods for roasts is to use a meat thermometer.

10 • CZECHOSLOVAKIA

3 pounds beef tenderloin
salt
pepper
2 tablespoons butter
strips of bacon
1 stalk celery

1 whole carrot
rind 1 lemon
sprig parsley
bay leaf
2 tablespoons flour
1 cup medium cream

Salt and pepper the beef and place it in a roaster with the butter. Lay bacon strips over the top. Add the celery, carrot, lemon rind, parsley, and bay leaf. Roast at 350° until done. Remove vegetable pieces and excess fat from pan. Combine the flour and the cream and stir into the remaining pan juices.

11 • ITALY

3 pounds beef tenderloin
2 teaspoons salt
pepper
¼ teaspoon thyme
2 onions, chopped
¼ pound ham, chopped
½ truffle, chopped
   (optional)

2 tablespoons chopped
   parsley
1 carrot, sliced
flour
1 cup stock or consommé
1 cup red wine
1 jigger cognac (optional)

Rub salt, pepper, and thyme into the beef. Brown the onions and remove from the pan. Brown the meat. Return the onions to the pan and add the ham, truffle, parsley, and carrot; sprinkle flour on top. Add the stock and wine. Roast at 350°. Remove the meat from the pan and force the gravy through a sieve. Return the gravy to the pan with the cognac added. Reheat and serve with the roast.

12 • SOUTH AMERICA

3 pounds beef tenderloin
4 slices bacon
2 hard-boiled eggs, chopped
½ cup chopped mushrooms
2 tablespoons parsley
1 tablespoon olive oil
1 cup white wine
bay leaf

½ cup stock or consommé
4 peppercorns
1 onion, chopped
¼ teaspoon thyme
salt
¼ cup bread crumbs
¼ cup Parmesan cheese
flour

Brown beef on all sides. Put bacon on the bottom of a roasting pan and place beef on top. Mix the eggs, mushrooms, parsley, and oil and spread on the beef. Add wine, bay leaf, stock, peppercorns, onion, thyme, and salt. Roast at 350° until done. Garnish the top of the meat with bread crumbs and cheese and brown under broiler a few minutes. For gravy, add flour to the skimmed pan juices and simmer 5 minutes.

13 • HUNGARY

3 pounds beef tenderloin
2 slices bacon
3 onions, sliced
1 teaspoon Hungarian
*   paprika*

1 tablespoon vinegar
1 cup tomato paste
1 cup water
1 cup sour cream

Brown beef on all sides and season. Add bacon, onions, paprika, vinegar, and tomato paste combined with water. Roast at 350°. Blend sour cream into the gravy and heat through before serving.

14 • FRANCE

3 pounds beef tenderloin
½ cup tarragon vinegar
¼ teaspoon thyme
¼ teaspoon nutmeg
¼ teaspoon ground cloves

bay leaf
1 onion, sliced thin
½ lemon, sliced thin
1 teaspoon salt

Marinate the beef in a mixture of all the other ingredients. Let it stand 3 hours (longer in the refrigerator, if you wish). Remove the meat from the marinade and roast it at 350° until done. Add the marinade to the pan juices, heat through, and pour over the meat.

15 • ITALY

3 pounds beef tenderloin
flour
1 egg, beaten
bread crumbs
butter
1½ cups stock or undiluted
*   consommé*

salt
pepper
2 tablespoons grated
*   Romano cheese*
2 tablespoons chopped
*   parsley*

Cut the beef into 12 slices; dip each slice in flour, egg, and bread crumbs and sauté in butter till done. Keep warm. Melt 2 tablespoons butter; blend in 2 tablespoons flour; add stock, salt, and pepper; and simmer 5 minutes. Add cheese and parsley. Pour over the beef.

16 • FRANCE

3 pounds beef tenderloin	*½ teaspoon pepper*
1 cup brandy	*sliced truffles (optional)*
2 cups stock or consommé	*½ pound butter*
1½ teaspoons salt	

Cut the beef into 12 slices; sauté the slices in butter till done. Combine the brandy and stock with the salt and pepper and boil till reduced to half. Cook the truffles in this liquid a few minutes until they are just done; remove them. Add the butter to the liquid and cook until blended. Pour this over the beef and garnish with truffle slices.

17 • FRANCE

3 pounds beef tenderloin	*Vegetable Sauce # 1, page*
12 slices bacon	*180, made with tarra-*
dry bread, cut in rounds	*gon vinegar instead*
and fried in butter	*of lemon juice*

Cut the beef into 12 slices; wrap each slice in a strip of bacon and secure with a toothpick. Sauté in butter till done. Remove the toothpicks, place on croutons, and serve with a generous amount of sauce.

18 • FRANCE

3 pounds beef tenderloin	*pepper*
butter	*2 cups stock or consommé*
salt	

Rub the meat with butter, salt, and pepper. Add the stock and roast at 350° until done.

For stews, ragouts, and pot roasts the cuts of beef most suitable are round steak, chuck, brisket, cross rib, and flank steak. The meats should cook slowly and be well covered. More liquid may be added during cooking if necessary. If you like your gravy thickened, blend 2 tablespoons flour with a little water, stir the mixture into the almost finished dish, and cook a little while longer. Stews can be frozen and reheated to serve. In fact, many are even better when reheated. Such vegetables as peas, beans, and carrots may be cooked separately and added before serving, if you wish.

19 • ECUADOR

4 pounds round or flank steak	2 teaspoons salt
4 onions, chopped	½ teaspoon pepper
2 green peppers, chopped	6 tablespoons peanut butter
4 tomatoes, chopped	1 quart milk
2 teaspoons paprika	8 potatoes, diced

Season the meat and bake at 350° with a little water for 2 hours or until tender. Fry the onions and peppers; add the tomatoes, seasonings, peanut butter, and then the milk slowly. Meanwhile, boil or pressure-cook the potatoes. Place the meat on a warm platter, surround it with the potatoes, and cover it with the sauce.

20 • HUNGARY

4 pounds stewing beef	2 onions, chopped
3 teaspoons salt	clove garlic, minced
½ teaspoon pepper	1 can tomato sauce
3 tablespoons Hungarian paprika	1 cup sour cream

Cut beef into 1½-inch cubes and roll in a mixture of salt, pepper, and paprika. Fry the onions in butter; remove from the pan. Brown the meat in the pan. Add the onions, garlic, and tomato sauce with an equal amount of water. Simmer 3 hours. Stir in the sour cream a few minutes before serving.

21 • ITALY

4 pounds beef	¼ teaspoon marjoram
4 slices bacon	2 teaspoons salt
1 teaspoon garlic powder or minced garlic	½ teaspoon pepper
3 onions, chopped	6 tomatoes, quartered
½ teaspoon fennel seed (optional)	1 cup red wine

Cut the bacon in bits and sprinkle with garlic powder; insert the pieces in slits cut in the beef. (If you have the butcher lard the meat, rub it all over with garlic before browning.) Brown the meat in hot oil; add the onions and brown lightly. Add the remaining ingredients and simmer gently 2 hours or until tender.

22 • RUSSIA

4 pounds beef
10 gingersnaps
1 cup vinegar
2 onions, sliced

few peppercorns
2 cups water
6 bay leaves
2 teaspoons sugar

Soak the gingersnaps in the vinegar. Cut the meat into thin, bite-size pieces and season to taste. Brown the meat with the onions. Combine all the ingredients. Simmer gently 30 minutes or until tender.

23 • MEXICO

4 pounds stewing beef
2 teaspoons sugar
4 tablespoons flour
2 tablespoons chili powder
2 teaspoons salt
few peppercorns

1 bay leaf
¼ teaspoon thyme
4 tomatoes, quartered
4 green peppers, chopped
2 cups stock or consommé

Cut the beef into 1½-inch cubes. Combine the sugar, flour, and chili powder and sprinkle over the meat. Brown the meat in hot fat. Add all the remaining ingredients. Simmer gently 2 hours or until tender.

24 • DENMARK

4-pound piece of beef
4 onions, chopped
¼ cup red wine
2 teaspoons salt

½ teaspoon pepper
¼ cup prepared mustard
water to cover
2 tablespoons flour

Season the meat and brown it in butter. Add the remaining ingredients, except the flour, and simmer gently 2 hours or until tender. Blend the 2 tablespoons flour into a little water and stir into the gravy. Cook a few minutes longer.

25 • GERMANY

4 pounds round steak,
    sliced ½-inch thick
4 slices bacon
1 onion, sliced
1 tablespoon dark corn
    syrup
beer

water
½ cup vinegar
4 cloves
bay leaf
few peppercorns
1 teaspoon caraway seed
    (optional)

Pound the beef slices flat, season, and roll up and tie. Lay in layers on the bottom of the pan first the bacon strips, then the onion rings, and then the beef rolls. Add the remaining ingredients, using equal parts of beer and water to cover the meat. Bake at 350° for 3 hours or until tender. If there is too much fat in the gravy, cool it, skim the fat, and reheat before using.

26 • BELGIUM

4 pounds stewing beef
4 onions, chopped
¼ cup vinegar
1 teaspoon sugar

½ teaspoon marjoram
½ teaspoon thyme
½ teaspoon rosemary
1 can beer

Cut the meat into 16 pieces and brown it with the onions. Add the remaining ingredients and simmer gently 2 hours or until tender.

27 • YUGOSLAVIA

4 pounds stewing beef
4 potatoes, diced
4 tomatoes, quartered
1 cup small white onions
4 bay leaves
1 cup diced celery

4 tablespoons chopped
    parsley
2 teaspoons salt
few peppercorns
2½ teaspoons Hungarian
    paprika
6 cups stock or consommé

Cut the beef into 1-inch cubes. Combine all the ingredients and bake at 350° for 3 hours or until tender.

28 • CHILE

4 pounds stewing beef
2 cups stock or consommé
2 teaspoons salt

few peppercorns
3 dozen small stuffed olives
1 cup raisins

Cut the meat into 1½-inch cubes and brown. Add the remaining ingredients and simmer 1½ hours or until tender.

29 • BURMA

4 pounds stewing beef
5 onions
3 teaspoons turmeric
1 teaspoon chili powder
3 teaspoons powdered ginger

oil, preferably sesame or
   peanut
2 teaspoons salt
2 cups tomatoes
2 cups stock or consommé

Chop the onions very fine; stir in the turmeric, chili and ginger powders, and salt. Cut the beef into 1½-inch cubes, sprinkle with the onion mixture, and let stand 2 hours, turning occasionally. Brown the meat in hot oil. Add the remaining ingredients. Simmer gently 2 hours or until tender.

30 • FRANCE

4 pounds stewing beef
4 cups small white onions
24 whole button mushrooms
6 tablespoons flour
2 tablespoons tomato paste
2 cups stock or consommé
¼ teaspoon marjoram

¼ teaspoon rosemary
¼ teaspoon thyme
2 teaspoons salt
½ teaspoon pepper
2 cups red wine
chopped chervil or parsley

Cut the beef into 2-inch cubes and brown the cubes in butter. Remove the meat and brown the onions. Add the mushrooms and cook for 2 minutes. Stir in the flour and tomato paste till smooth. Stir in the stock. Add the browned beef and all the other ingredients except chervil, using only 1 cup of the wine. Bake at 350° for 3 hours or until tender, adding the rest of the wine as needed. Garnish with chopped chervil or parsley.

31 • AUSTRIA

4 pounds stewing beef
2 onions, sliced
3 tablespoons tomato sauce
clove garlic, minced
¼ teaspoon marjoram
2 teaspoons caraway seeds

2 teaspoons salt
½ teaspoon pepper
2 cups stock or consommé
1 large head cabbage,
   shredded
2 tablespoons flour

Cut beef into 1½-inch cubes and brown together with the onions. Add the tomato sauce, garlic, marjoram, caraway seeds, salt, pepper, and stock. Simmer gently 1½ hours. Add the shredded cabbage to the meat and simmer until the cabbage is tender. Mix the flour with a little water and stir into the gravy. Simmer a few minutes longer.

32 • CHILE

4 pounds stewing beef	1 cup diced squash
1 onion, chopped	½ cup peas
2 teaspoons paprika	½ cup kernel corn
3 cups boiling water	3 egg yolks, beaten
½ cup uncooked rice	

Brown the meat in butter with the onion and paprika. Add the water and simmer 1 hour. Add the rice, squash, peas, and corn and simmer 1 hour more. Put the beaten egg yolks into a serving dish; pour the stew over them, stirring all the while.

Casserole dishes like the following are practical to prepare and easy to serve. For other casseroles, you can start with the basic stew recipes (#19 through #32) or the hash recipes (#38 through #44). To serve those recipes as casseroles, sprinkle the top with crumbs or grated cheese and dots of butter and brown in the oven or under the broiler. Or top with mashed potatoes or mix with cooked noodles, rice, or diced potatoes.

33 • GERMANY

2 pounds round steak	2 cloves
4 slices bacon	2 bay leaves
1 onion, sliced	few peppercorns
1 tablespoon dark corn	1 teaspoon caraway seeds
syrup	beer
½ cup vinegar	water

Have the beef cut in 4 slices. Season each slice, roll it up, and tie it securely. Place the strips of bacon in the bottom of a casserole; on top of them place the slices of onion and then the rolls of beef. Add the other ingredients, using equal parts of beer and water to cover the meat. Cover and bake at 350° for 2 hours or until tender. If you want to remove excess fat, cool the gravy until the fat rises to the top, skim off the fat, and reheat the sauce to serve. Or, if you prefer, cook the bacon before it is placed in the casserole.

34 • RUSSIA

2 pounds round steak
1 onion, chopped
salt
pepper

2 bay leaves
cinnamon (optional)
1 cup sour cream

Cut the beef into cubes and brown. Place it in a casserole, sprinkle it with the onion and seasonings, and pour the sour cream over it. Cover and bake at 350° about 1½ hours or until tender.

35 • FRANCE

2 pounds round steak or
    chuck
1 teaspoon tomato paste
2 cups small white onions
12 whole mushrooms
3 tablespoons flour
1 cup red wine

1 cup stock or consommé
1 teaspoon salt
¼ teaspoon pepper
¼ teaspoon marjoram
¼ teaspoon rosemary
¼ teaspoon thyme

Cut meat into 2-inch cubes and brown in butter; remove from pan. Brown the onions slightly; add the mushrooms and sauté together 2 minutes. Combine the tomato paste and flour and stir until smooth. Add the remaining ingredients with the meat, using only ½ cup of the wine. Cover and bake at 350° for 2 hours or until tender, adding the rest of the wine as necessary.

36 • GERMANY

½ pound dried beef,
    shredded
2 tablespoons butter
2 tablespoons flour
1 cup milk
¼ teaspoon pepper

1 teaspoon celery seeds
1 egg, slightly beaten
½ package noodles, cooked
bread or zwieback crumbs
grated Parmesan cheese

Melt the butter; stir in the flour and then the milk and cook until thickened. Add the pepper, celery seeds, egg, and beef. Put the noodles in a buttered casserole and place the beef mixture on top. Sprinkle with crumbs and cheese. Bake at 350° for 30 minutes.

2 pounds round steak or chuck	1½ tablespoons Hungarian paprika
1 onion, chopped	½ can tomato paste
clove garlic, minced	½ can water
1 teaspoon salt	1 cup sour cream
¼ teaspoon pepper	noodles (optional)

Sauté the onion and garlic lightly in butter. Remove them from the pan. Cut the meat into bite-size cubes; roll them in salt, pepper, and paprika and brown them. Combine the onion and garlic with the meat. Combine the tomato paste and water and add to the meat with half the sour cream. Cover and bake at 350° for 1½ hours or until tender. Stir in remaining sour cream and heat for a moment more. Serve on egg noodles.

Cooked meat should not be recooked because it loses flavor and gets tough. Warm the following dishes just long enough to heat through and serve immediately. For a good hash, you can use any cooked meat combined with cooked potatoes, a bit of onion, seasoning, herbs, and gravy. When potatoes are not included in the recipe, they are a good accompaniment.

38 • FRANCE

2 cups diced cooked beef	½ cup gravy or canned tomatoes or both
1 onion, chopped	
3 potatoes, cooked and diced	bread crumbs
2 teaspoons chopped parsley	butter

Sauté the onion in butter till golden. Combine all the ingredients in a buttered baking dish and season to taste. Sprinkle with bread crumbs and dot with butter. Bake at 400° until brown. (In England people add ½ cup cooked chestnuts to this dish. They chop the chestnuts and sauté them with the onion.)

39 • CUBA

2 cups minced cooked beef	dash cumin
½ cup seedless raisins	dash oregano
1½ cups blanched almonds	1 cup red wine
bay leaf	

Combine all the ingredients, season to taste, and brown in a skillet.

2 cups diced cooked beef
1 tablespoon chopped onion
2 teaspoons chopped parsley
butter
few mushrooms, chopped
2 slices bread

milk
salt
pepper
1 egg yolk
4 fried eggs

Cook the onion, parsley, and mushrooms in butter. Soak the bread in the milk and squeeze out; add it to the pan with the meat, salt, pepper, and egg yolk. Stir together and cook a few minutes. Serve garnished with the fried eggs.

41 • GERMANY

2 cups diced cooked beef
2 slices bacon

1 onion, chopped
2 eggs, beaten

Cook bacon until crisp; remove and drain. Cook the onion and beef in the bacon fat until the onion is golden. Pour off the excess fat. Add the eggs and crumbled bacon to the pan; season to taste. When the hash is brown, fold over like an omelet and serve.

42 • DENMARK

2 cups diced cooked beef
4 slices apple, peeled

1 cup gravy
1 tablespoon sugar

Simmer the apple slices in the gravy until tender. If you have no gravy, melt 2 tablespoons of butter, add 2 tablespoons of flour, and stir in 1 can consommé gradually; simmer about 5 minutes. Add the meat and sugar and season to taste. Heat through and serve immediately.

43 • ENGLAND

2 cups diced cooked beef
1 onion, chopped
1 cup sliced cooked potatoes
2 tablespoons vinegar

1 tablespoon Worcestershire
   or A-1 sauce
2 tablespoons chopped
   parsley

Cook the onion in butter until golden. Add all the other ingredients and heat through. Serve immediately. Garnish with more chopped parsley if desired.

2 cups diced cooked beef
1 cup cooked rice
1 egg

2 strips bacon, cooked and
    crumbled
1 tablespoon lemon juice
½ cup sour cream

Combine the meat, rice, egg, and crumbled bacon and season to taste. Shape into patties, brown on both sides, and remove from the pan. Add the lemon juice and sour cream to the pan, stir well, simmer a moment, and pour over the patties.

The following dishes are particularly suited to informal entertaining, whether luncheons, late suppers, or buffets.

45 • ITALY

2 pounds ground beef
    (or beef and pork)
1 onion, chopped
clove garlic, minced
2 tablespoons chopped
    parsley
2 large cans tomatoes

2 cans tomato paste
1 teaspoon basil
bay leaf
1 teaspoon salt
½ teaspoon pepper
1 pound spaghetti
grated Parmesan cheese

Brown the meat in oil with the onion, garlic, and parsley. Add the tomatoes, tomato paste, basil, bay leaf, salt, and pepper and simmer 1 hour. Boil the spaghetti in salted water, drain, and serve with the sauce and grated Parmesan cheese.

46 • MALAYA

2 pounds beef sirloin
1 teaspoon powdered ginger
1 teaspoon chili powder
1 teaspoon garlic powder or
    2 cloves garlic, crushed

grated rind ½ lemon
butter
1 teaspoon sugar
2 tablespoons plum jam
3 tablespoons lemon juice
1½ teaspoons salt

Cut the meat into strips 2 inches long and ½ inch wide. Mix the ginger, chili powder, garlic, and lemon rind. Dip the meat in this mixture and brown it in butter. Combine the sugar, plum jam, lemon juice, salt, and 1½ cups water. Add the meat and simmer 20 minutes or until tender. (This is fairly typical of Malayan flavoring, without being too strange for an American palate. Curry powder may be used instead of chili powder, if you wish. The plum and lemon combination is our best substitute for Eastern tamarind flavor. Serve with rice.)

47 • JAPAN

2 pounds beef sirloin
2 tablespoons peanut or salad oil
½ cup soy sauce
½ cup sugar
1 tablespoon sherry

1 cup consommé
2 onions, sliced
½ pound mushrooms, sliced
1 cup sliced celery
1 can bamboo shoots, sliced

Cut the beef into strips 2 inches long and ½ inch wide. Brown the meat in the oil. Combine the soy sauce, sugar, wine, and consommé. Add half to the pan with the meat. Make room in the pan for the vegetables; add them and simmer all together for 3 minutes. Add the remaining sauce and simmer 3 more minutes. Serve immediately. (This can be cooked right on the table in a chafing dish or an electric skillet or on an electric hot plate. There are many other vegetables that may be added, such as strips of green pepper, scallion, spinach, and watercress. Serve this with rice and Japanese tea.)

48 • MEXICO

1 pound ground beef
1 onion, chopped
salt
pepper
½ teaspoon marjoram
¼ teaspoon thyme

1 tablespoon chili powder
2 tablespoons chopped parsley
¼ cup tomato paste
loaf French bread

Brown the onion in hot oil; add the meat and brown. Add the seasoning, herbs, parsley, tomato paste, and ¼ cup water. Simmer together 10 minutes. Cut off one end of the French bread and scoop out the center. Add half of this bread to the meat mixture and pack into the bread shell. Replace the end and secure with a skewer. Bake at 350° for 15 minutes.

II • BEEF TONGUE

Method for boiling tongue: cover the tongue with salted water and add any or all of the following: 1 onion, a bay leaf, a few peppercorns, a pinch of thyme, a pinch of basil, 2 stalks celery, 2 whole carrots, a clove of garlic. Simmer for

2 hours or until tender. When done, remove the skin and hard root end of the tongue and proceed with the recipes. When the broth from the tongue is used in the preparation, strain out the vegetables. Tongue may be garnished with parsley, olives, quartered hard-boiled eggs, anchovy fillets coiled on slices of hard-boiled egg, sour pickles, or lemon slices.

1 • SOUTH AMERICA

1 boiled beef tongue
½ cup bouillon
clove garlic, minced
1 tomato, chopped

½ cup ground almonds
salt
pepper
bread crumbs

Simmer the bouillon with the garlic, tomato, almonds, salt, and pepper for 10 minutes. Thicken with bread crumbs and pour over slices of tongue.

2 • FRANCE

1 boiled beef tongue
1½ cups broth from tongue
    or consommé
1½ envelopes gelatin

¼ cup cold water
½ cup red wine
stuffed olives (optional)

Line the bottom of a ring mold with sliced stuffed olives. Slice the tongue and lay it in the mold. Bring the broth to a boil. Dissolve the gelatin in the cold water; add it to the broth with the wine. Pour over the tongue. Chill until set. (When you unmold the tongue, try filling the center of the ring with cottage cheese mixed with chopped chives.)

3 • ITALY

1 boiled beef tongue
1 onion, sliced
clove garlic, minced
1 can anchovy fillets,
    chopped
2 tablespoons vinegar

2 tablespoons red wine
1 cup broth from tongue
    or consommé
½ teaspoon prepared
    mustard
½ teaspoon pepper

Sauté the onions and garlic lightly in butter. Combine with the other ingredients and pour over slices of tongue.

4 • CHINA

1 boiled beef tongue
1 cup soy sauce
1 cup broth from tongue
    or consommé

2 tablespoons sugar
salt
½ teaspoon Mei Yen pow-
    der, MSG, or Accent

Combine all the ingredients and simmer the whole cooked tongue in this liquid for 20 minutes, basting or turning frequently.

5 • POLAND

1 boiled beef tongue
¼ cup sugar
¼ cup water
1 tablespoon flour
1 tablespoon butter
2 cups broth from tongue
    or consommé

¼ cup red wine
1 tablespoon lemon juice
grated rind ½ lemon
½ cup raisins
½ cup chopped blanched
    almonds

Cook sugar and water until caramelized; blend the flour and butter and stir in; add the broth gradually. Add the wine, lemon juice and rind, raisins, and almonds. Slice the tongue and add it to the sauce. Bring to a boil.

6 • HUNGARY

1 boiled beef tongue
2 eggs, lightly beaten

flour
butter

Slice the tongue. Dip the slices in egg, then in flour. Brown in butter.

III • VEAL

1 • ITALY

4 veal cutlets or chops
flour
4 tablespoons butter
½ cup red wine

¼ cup stock or water
¼ cup grated Parmesan
    cheese

Season the meat and dip in flour. Brown on both sides in butter. Add the wine and cook until it evaporates. Add the stock, cover the pan, and cook 10 minutes or until the meat is done. Sprinkle with cheese, cover, and cook until the cheese melts.

2 • ITALY

4 veal cutlets or chops
flour
1 egg yolk, lightly beaten

bread crumbs
butter
lemon wedges

Pound the veal cutlets or scaloppine until they are very

thin. Dip meat in flour, in seasoned egg yolk, and then in bread crumbs. Fry in butter until golden. Garnish with lemon wedges. Serve with crisp fried potatoes.

3 • AUSTRIA

4 veal cutlets or chops	*1 tablespoon Hungarian*
flour	*paprika*
2 onions, sliced	*1 cup sour cream*

Dip cutlets in flour. Brown onions lightly in butter; stir in paprika. Add the meat to the pan. Season, add the sour cream, and simmer till done.

4 • GERMANY

4 veal cutlets or chops	*½ teaspoon salt*
1 egg, beaten	*¼ teaspoon pepper*
2 tablespoons flour	*¼ teaspoon nutmeg*
¼ cup grated Parmesan	*¼ teaspoon chopped parsley*
cheese	*butter*
½ cup milk	*juice 1 lemon*

Pound the cutlets very thin. Combine all the ingredients except flour, butter, and lemon juice. Dip meat in flour, then in egg mixture. Fry in butter until golden. Remove from the pan and keep warm. Brown 2 tablespoons of butter in a pan, add lemon juice, and pour over the cutlets.

5 • GERMANY

4 veal cutlets or chops	*2 cloves*
1 cup beef stock or	*1 bay leaf*
consommé	*¼ cup caviar*
½ cup red wine	*juice 1 lemon*

Combine the stock, wine, cloves, bay leaf, add seasoning and simmer the cutlets in this for 30 minutes or until done. Mix the caviar and lemon juice and place some on each cutlet. Simmer a few minutes longer.

7 • FRANCE

4 veal cutlets or chops	*1 bay leaf*
flour	*¼ teaspoon thyme*
butter	*¼ teaspoon chopped*
4 onions, sliced	*parsley*
4 carrots, sliced	

Season the meat and sprinkle with flour. Cook in butter until golden. Add the remaining ingredients and a little water. Simmer 1 hour or until done.

8 • POLAND

4 veal cutlets or chops	3 tablespoons red wine
2 onions, sliced	1 teaspoon salt
½ pound mushrooms	1 teaspoon Hungarian
1 cup sour cream	paprika

Brown the cutlets on both sides and place in a baking dish. Lightly brown the onions and mushrooms and add them to the meat with the other ingredients. Bake at 375° for 1 hour or until tender.

TIPS: There are many attractive garnishes for veal: slices of lemon either sprinkled with chopped parsley or topped with a pitted olive wrapped in an anchovy fillet; fried eggs, one for each cutlet; parsley; paprika; anchovy fillets; capers; sliced truffles; and hard-boiled eggs with the whites chopped and the yolks sieved.

9 • ITALY

4 veal fillets or pieces veal round	4 anchovy fillets
	¼ cup butter
4 pieces mozzarella or other Italian cheese	½ cup stock or bouillon

Place a finger-shaped piece of cheese and an anchovy on each fillet; roll up and secure each fillet. Sprinkle with salt and pepper and brown in butter. Add the stock to the pan. Simmer gently or bake at 350° until done.

10 • ITALY

4 veal fillets or pieces veal round	chopped parsley
	salt
4 chicken livers, chopped	pepper
2 slices bacon, cooked and crumbled	½ cup red wine

Combine the chicken livers, bacon, parsley, salt, and pepper. Place some of the filling on each fillet; roll up and tie or skewer each piece. Brown the rolls in oil. Add the wine and simmer gently or bake in oven at 350° until tender. Add more wine if necessary.

11 • HUNGARY

4 veal fillets or pieces veal round	2 chopped hard-boiled eggs
½ pound mushrooms, chopped	1 egg
	salt
4 slices bread, soaked in milk and squeezed	pepper
	Hungarian paprika
	1 cup sour cream

Mix the mushrooms, bread, chopped cooked eggs, raw egg, salt, and pepper. Place some of the filling on each fillet; roll up and tie or skewer each piece. Sprinkle with paprika and brown on all sides. Pour over the cream. Either simmer gently or bake in the oven at 350° until tender. (You may substitute a prepared herb stuffing if you wish.)

12 • WEST INDIES

4 veal fillets or pieces veal round	Worcestershire sauce
2 onions, chopped	salt
1 cup chopped cashew nuts	pepper
small clove garlic, minced	½ can tomato paste
	1 cup water

Mix the onions, nuts, and garlic and moisten with a dash of Worcestershire sauce. Place a little of the filling on each fillet; roll up and secure each piece. Sprinkle with salt and pepper and brown in butter. Mix tomato paste and water; pour into pan around rolls. Simmer gently or bake at 350° until tender.

13 • SWEDEN

4 veal fillets or pieces veal round	chopped parsley
4 pitted prunes or 4 table- spoons butter blended with ½ teaspoon	salt
	pepper
	½ cup stock or bouillon
	½ cup cream or milk

Place either a prune or 1 tablespoon of the blended butter and parsley on each fillet. Roll and secure each piece. Sprinkle with salt and pepper and brown in butter. Add the stock and simmer gently or bake at 350° until done. Stir the cream into the pan juices. (A similar dish is made in Holland. But the Dutch use pieces of veal fat instead of the butter or prune and place a lemon slice on each roll before baking. They also omit the cream.)

4 veal fillets or pieces veal
  round
½ pound mushrooms,
  chopped
1 onion, chopped
4 teaspoons chopped parsley
½ teaspoon thyme

1 tablespoon grated
  Parmesan cheese
¼ cup red wine
clove garlic, minced
salt
pepper
1 cup stock or bouillon

Cook the mushrooms, onion, and garlic in butter a few minutes without browning. Add the parsley, thyme, cheese, and wine. Place some of the filling on each fillet; roll up and secure each piece. Sprinkle with salt and pepper. Place in a baking dish with the stock and bake at 350° until tender.

TIPS: If veal round steak is used, have it sliced thin and flattened by pounding. (The butcher can do this for you or you can do it yourself.) The pieces should be about 3 inches by 5 inches. Cooking time will vary: for fillets about 20 minutes, for round steak about 1 hour. To serve, pour whatever pan juices there are over the meat. If juices have cooked away, add water or stock, turn heat high, scrape the pan, and simmer a minute or two.

Veal is excellent for ragouts and casseroles: think of the famous Hungarian gulyas, for instance. Dishes that are also delicious when made with veal are the recipes from #27 through #31 under Pork, pages 122-123.

15 • ENGLAND

4 veal cutlets, sliced thin
4 potatoes
4 slices ham or Canadian
  bacon
salt
pepper

2 tablespoons chopped
  parsley
1 teaspoon thyme
butter
stock or consommé
pie pastry
egg yolk (optional)

Butter a casserole or ovenproof dish. Slice the potatoes and parboil them 5 minutes. Place the veal, ham, and potatoes in alternate layers in the casserole, sprinkling the meat with salt, pepper, parsley, and thyme and dotting the potatoes with butter. End with a layer of potatoes. Add enough stock to fill the casserole two-thirds of the way. Cover the dish with the piecrust, which can be brushed with egg yolk if desired. Bake at 350° for 1 hour. (The English often serve this dish cold. If you wish to do so, add 1 tablespoon gelatin softened in ¼ cup cold water to the stock, bake, and chill before serving.)

The following is an unusual recipe for a very special potato salad that is good for informal but festive suppers and buffets.

16 • LATVIA

2 pounds cold roast veal
6 potatoes, boiled
4 sour pickles
2 large beets, cooked
1 onion, chopped
6 hard-boiled eggs

3-ounce can herring fiillets
   in salt
½ small jar pickled
   cocktail mushrooms
2 cups sour cream
1 cup mayonnaise

Cut the veal, potatoes, pickles, and beets into small pieces. Add the onion, 5 chopped hard-boiled eggs, and cut-up herring. Cut up the mushrooms and add them to the meat with the combined sour cream and mayonnaise. Stir well. Slice the remaining hard-boiled egg and use as a garnish.

IV • LAMB

In the following recipes for leg of lamb, if you want to keep your meat on the pink side, allow 18 to 20 minutes per pound. A meat thermometer is very useful in helping you to control the finish of your roast. Be sure to skim the fat from the pan juices before going on to make any of the gravies suggested. You might try a dash of nutmeg with or without a little lemon juice in your lamb gravy.

1 • ENGLAND

4-5 pound leg of lamb
salt pork

salt
pepper

Have the butcher bone the lamb and lard it with salt pork. Season the meat and roast it at 325°, adding water as needed and basting frequently. Allow 25 minutes per pound.

2 • ARABIA

4-5 pound leg of lamb
salt
pepper
1 onion, chopped

¼ pound butter
fat or shortening
½ cup water

Have the butcher bone the lamb. Put the salt, pepper, onion, and butter in the cavity. Tie or skewer the meat and rub it well with fat. Roast at 325° with the water, allowing 25 minutes per pound. Baste frequently and add more water if necessary.

3 • ENGLAND

4-5 pound leg of lamb
fresh mint
salt
pepper

garlic salt or fresh garlic
    (optional)
1 cup water

Have the butcher bone the lamb. Fill the cavity with sprigs of mint. Rub the meat with salt, pepper, and garlic. Roast at 325° with 1 cup of water until done. Allow 25 minutes per pound. (The Arabs do this with a whole animal roasted on a spit.)

4 • ITALY

4-5 pound leg of lamb
1 teaspoon salt
1 teaspoon pepper
garlic
½ cup olive oil
2 onions, sliced
2 carrots, sliced

2 cups white wine
¼ pound salt pork, diced
⅔ cup tomato paste
2 tablespoons chopped
    parsley
½ teaspoon oregano
1 cup water

Rub the meat with salt, pepper, and garlic. Brown in hot oil with the onions and carrots. Add the wine and cook until it evaporates. Add the remaining ingredients and simmer, covered, 1½ hours or until done. Strain the gravy and serve over the lamb.

5 • SWEDEN

4-5 pound leg of lamb
1 tablespoon salt
½ teaspoon pepper
2 onions, sliced
2 carrots, sliced

1 cup strong coffee
¼ cup cream
1 tablespoon sugar
4 tablespoons flour

Rub the meat with salt and pepper and roast at 400° until brown. Add the onions, carrots, and water and reduce the heat to 325°. Allow 25 minutes to the pound and baste occasionally. When the meat is half done, add the combined coffee, cream, and sugar. When the meat is done, skim the fat from the pan juices. Add the flour to 4 tablespoons of the fat and combine again with the skimmed juices.

4-5 pound leg of lamb   *pepper*
garlic   *vinegar (about 1 pint)*
salt   *cream (optional)*

Rub the lamb with garlic, salt, and pepper. Pour hot vinegar over the lamb and let stand 1 hour to 2 hours. Roast at 325°, allowing 25 minutes per pound. If the cream is used, remove the roast from the oven when it is half done, pour the cream around it, and finish cooking over low heat in a covered pan.

7 • FRANCE

4-5 pound leg of lamb   *½ teaspoon thyme*
garlic salt or fresh garlic   *2 teaspoons chopped*
lard or butter   *   parsley*
1 cup water   *1 onion, sliced thin*
1 bay leaf   *1 carrot, sliced thin*

Rub the lamb with salt, pepper, and garlic salt (or insert slivers of fresh garlic in slits cut into the lamb). Rub the meat with lard or butter. Roast with the water, bay leaf, thyme, parsley, onion, and carrot at 325°, allowing 25 minutes per pound.

8 • AUSTRIA

4-5 pound leg of lamb   *1 tablespoon butter*
¼ pound salt pork   *1 cup sliced mushrooms*
salt   *½ cup sour cream*
1 cup water

Have the butcher bone and lard the lamb. Rub the meat all over with salt. Sear it in hot fat. Roast it in a 325° oven, with the water in the pan. Add more water if necessary as it roasts and baste frequently. Allow 25 minutes per pound. Remove the roast. Skim the fat from the pan juices. Knead the butter and flour together and stir them into the juices. Add the mushrooms, which have been sautéed in butter. Add the sour cream and serve hot with the roast.

There are many ways to prepare and serve lamb chops. One of the simplest, if you like cheese, is to spread the top of each chop with Roquefort cheese before broiling. (Warning: This is pungent while cooking!) Appropriate garnishes are hard-boiled eggs, mushrooms, lemon slices, mint sprigs, mint sauce or jelly, and currant jelly. Lamb chops, especially the

Eastern versions, are good served with rice or with a baked potato—the skin of which has been rubbed with butter before baking to keep it soft—with melted butter and chopped chives poured into the slit.

9 • SOUTH AFRICA

12 lamb chops
1 small can tomato sauce
½ cup vinegar
1 onion, minced

2 tablespoons Worcestershire sauce
1 teaspoon dry mustard
1 teaspoon salt

Combine all the ingredients and marinate the chops 1 hour. Remove the chops; wipe dry. Pan-fry them, turning frequently, until done. Serve with the heated marinade.

10 • HUNGARY

12 lamb chops
1 egg, beaten

1½ cups grated cheese
1 cup bread crumbs

Dip the chops in the egg, which has been beaten with a little water. Dip the chops in a mixture of the cheese and bread crumbs. Broil them 10 minutes on each side.

11 • AUSTRALIA

12 lamb chops
salt
pepper
1 onion, chopped

1 cup sliced mushrooms
4 carrots, chopped
3 cups stock
piecrust

Sprinkle the chops with salt and pepper and brown them in butter. Add the onion, mushrooms, carrots, and stock. Simmer 10 minutes. Place the chops and vegetables in a baking dish. Pour in stock two-thirds of the depth of the dish. Cover with piecrust, pricked to let out steam, and bake at 375° for 40 minutes.

12 • MOROCCO

12 lamb chops
salt

pepper
chopped fresh mint

Season the chops and broil them 10 minutes on each side. Serve with the mint sprinkled on top.

13 • TURKEY

12 lamb chops
1 cup vinegar
¼ cup oil
1 onion, chopped

2 tablespoons chopped
  parsley
few whole cloves
pepper

Marinate the chops in a mixture of all the other ingredients for 1 hour. Remove them from the marinade and broil them 10 minutes on each side or until done. (The Turks use generous amounts of cloves and pepper.)

14 • ITALY

12 lamb chops
2 tablespoons olive oil
1 teaspoon oregano
1 clove garlic, minced
1 teaspoon salt

½ teaspoon pepper
1 tablespoon lemon juice
1 tablespoon prepared
  mustard
6 anchovy fillets, chopped

Combine the oil, oregano, garlic, salt, pepper, and lemon juice. Spread this mixture on the chops. Let them stand 2 hours. Mix the mustard and anchovies. Spread this mixture on the chops. Broil them 10 minutes on each side.

15 • AUSTRALIA

12 lamb chops
1 onion, chopped
1 apple, chopped
2 tablespoons flour
1 tablespoon curry powder

1 teaspoon sugar
½ teaspoon prepared
  mustard
1 teaspoon salt
2 cups water

Brown the chops in fat; remove them from the pan. Add the onion and apple to the pan and sauté. Replace the chops. Add the other ingredients. Simmer 10 minutes or until done. (If you like curry, a very simple method is to mix 1 tablespoon curry powder with 1 teaspoon sugar and to spread the chops with the mixture and broil them.)

16 • IRAQ

6 double or 12 single lamb
    chops
1 onion, sliced
½ chopped green pepper
2 tomatoes, quartered

½ teaspoon oregano
1 teaspoon chopped parsley
1 teaspoon salt
3 cups water

Arrange the chops in a buttered baking dish. Combine all the remaining ingredients and pour over the chops. Bake at 400° for 30 minutes. (If you use 6 double chops—the better choice—bake the dish about 20 minutes longer.)

17 • FRANCE

6 double or 12 single lamb
    chops
bacon
garlic (optional)
2 cups sliced mushrooms

butter
½ teaspoon chopped chives
½ teaspoon tarragon
1 teaspoon chopped parsley

Bone the chops and wrap each one in a strip of bacon secured with a toothpick. Rub the chops with a cut clove of garlic, if you wish. Broil 10 minutes on each side. Serve with the mushrooms, which have been sautéed in butter with the herbs.

18 • FRANCE

12 lamb chops
1 teaspoon salt
½ teaspoon pepper
clove garlic or ½ teaspoon
    garlic powder

2 cups white wine
2 onions, chopped
2 tablespoons chopped
    parsley
3 tablespoons flour

Rub the chops with the salt, pepper, and garlic. Brown them in butter and arrange them in a baking dish. Add a little more butter to the pan if necessary, stir in the flour, add the wine and other ingredients, and stir until thickened. Pour over the chops. Cover and bake at 350° for 20 minutes; uncover and bake 10 minutes longer.

You can add flavor to a stew by browning the meat and vegetables before proceeding with the recipe. In addition, by adding a little sugar to the pan you can help the browning process and enhance the flavor even more. Cook stews slowly, but do not overcook. However, stews hold well at warming temperature. Stews can also be served in a baking dish and finished off with a pastry crust or a topping of mashed potatoes: these variations are particularly festive in individual casseroles. Stews can also be frozen and reheated just before serving.

2 pounds lamb, cut up
1 teaspoon chili powder
¼ teaspoon saffron
½ teaspoon garlic powder
    or minced fresh garlic
1 teaspoon powdered ginger
1 teaspoon salt

1 cup vinegar
oil
1 teaspoon coriander
    (optional)
1 teaspoon cumin seed
    (optional)

Blend the chili powder, saffron, garlic, ginger, and salt. If you wish to use the coriander and cumin seed, pound them and add them to the mixture of spices. Roll the meat in this mixture. Pour over the vinegar and marinate 1 hour. Drain the meat and brown it well in oil. Add enough water to cover, and simmer 1 hour.

20 • FRANCE

2 pounds stewing lamb
salt
pepper
clove garlic, minced
2 tablespoons flour
1 cup tomatoes
1 cup pearl onions
2 carrots, diced

4 potatoes, diced
2 stalks celery, diced
bay leaf
¼ teaspoon thyme
½ teaspoon chopped parsley
½ cup green beans
½ cup peas

Sprinkle cubes of meat with salt and pepper and brown well. Pour off the fat. Sprinkle the garlic and flour over the meat and cook for a few minutes. Add the tomatoes and enough water to cover. Simmer ½ hour. Brown the onions and carrots lightly and add to the meat with the potatoes. Add the celery, bay leaf, thyme, and parsley. Simmer another ½ hour. Add the green beans and peas and cook 15 minutes longer.

21 • SOUTH AMERICA

2 pounds stewing lamb
clove garlic, minced
1 onion, chopped
1 carrot, chopped
2 stalks celery, chopped
1 teaspoon chopped parsley
½ teaspoon marjoram
½ teaspoon mint

2 potatoes, diced
1 can kernel corn
½ cup lima beans
½ cup peas
2 tablespoons milk
1 egg
1 cup uncooked rice
    (optional)

Place the meat in a heavy pot; sprinkle with salt, pepper, and garlic; add water to cover. Simmer ½ hour. Sauté the onion in butter until it is golden and add it to the meat with the carrot, celery, parsley, marjoram, mint, and potatoes. Simmer another ½ hour. Add the corn, beans, and peas and simmer 20 minutes. Beat the egg with the milk and add to the stew at the very end. Sometimes 1 cup of uncooked rice is added to this dish at the same time as the corn, beans, and peas. The rice may be used with or instead of potatoes.

22 • RUSSIA

2 pounds ground lean
   lamb, neck or leg
2 onions, chopped
1 eggplant, peeled and
   sliced thin

1 can tomato paste
bread crumbs
grated Parmesan cheese

Sauté the onions lightly in oil and mix with the ground lamb. Season mixture to taste and place in a casserole. Lay the slices of eggplant on top of the meat. Dilute the tomato paste with an equal amount of water and pour over the eggplant. Sprinkle the top with bread crumbs and grated cheese, cover, and bake at 350° for 1 hour. Add more liquid or tomato juice if necessary. (In Egypt they add 1 teaspoon cinnamon to the meat and bake the lamb in alternating layers with the eggplant and 2 cups cooked rice.)

23 • HUNGARY

2 pounds stewing lamb
¼ pound bacon or salt
   pork, diced
2 onions, sliced
1 teaspoon Hungarian
   paprika

1 tablespoon lemon juice
   or vinegar
1 teaspoon salt
1 cup water
1 cup sour cream
2 tablespoons tomato paste

Cook the bacon until it is almost crisp; add the onions and sauté them until they are golden. Pour off the fat. Add the paprika, lemon juice, and salt and cook for a few minutes. Add the water and meat and simmer 1 hour or until tender. Mix the sour cream and tomato paste and stir into the stew. Bring to a boil. Serve immediately.

24 • FRANCE

2 pounds boned lamb, neck
   or leg
1 teaspoon crushed celery
   seeds
salt

pepper
2 cups tiny white onions
1½ cups red wine
6 cloves
2 bay leaves

110

Cut meat into 1-inch cubes. Blend the celery seeds with salt and pepper and roll the meat in this mixture. Place it in a casserole in layers with the onions. Add the remaining ingredients, cover, and bake at 350° for 2 hours or until meat is tender. Add more wine while cooking, if necessary.

25 • IRELAND

2 pounds stewing lamb
4 potatoes, sliced thin
4 onions, sliced thin

½ cup chopped carrots
    (optional)
½ cup chopped turnips
    (optional)

In a pot lay alternate layers of potatoes, onions, meat, carrots, and turnips, seasoning each layer. Finish with a layer of potatoes. Cover with boiling water. Simmer 1 hour or until tender.

26 • INDIA

2 pounds boned lamb,
    neck or leg
1 onion, sliced
clove garlic, minced
1 tablespoon curry powder
    (optional)

2 teaspoons salt
½ teaspoon pepper
1 tomato, peeled and
    chopped
2 cups water

Cut lamb into 1-inch cubes; brown in butter and place in a casserole. Sauté the onion and garlic lightly; stir in the curry powder, salt, pepper, and tomato. Add to the casserole. Pour over the water, cover, and bake at 350° for 2 hours or until tender. Serve with rice and chutney.

Hash and various hashlike dishes are excellent places for leftover cooked lamb. This meat can also be served surrounded by broiled tomatoes or mushrooms or with cooked sausages. And there are no limits to the seasonings you can try—thyme; oregano; basil; Mei Yen, MSG, or Accent; garlic; soy sauce; chili powder; nutmeg; ginger, curry powder; Worcestershire sauce; and, of course, onion. If you don't want to mix your hash with potatoes or rice, try it with noodles. The following four recipes (#27 through #30) can also be done with pork.

111

2 cups cooked diced lamb
1 onion, chopped
few mushrooms, chopped
1 green pepper, chopped
½ clove garlic, minced
butter

2 boiled potatoes, diced
½ cup gravy or bouillon
salt
pepper
dash nutmeg

Sauté the onion, mushrooms, green pepper, and garlic in butter until the onion is golden. Add the meat, potatoes, gravy or bouillon, and seasonings. Heat through.

28 • ITALY

2 cups cooked lamb
1 onion, chopped
½ clove garlic, minced
butter
2 teaspoons chopped parsley
pinch thyme
pinch sugar

salt
pepper
1 cup gravy
¼ cup tomato paste
¼ cup water
bread crumbs
grated Parmesan cheese

Sauté the onion and garlic in butter. Add the meat, parsley, thyme, sugar, salt, pepper, gravy, tomato paste, and water. Pour into a buttered baking dish, sprinkle with bread crumbs and cheese, and bake at 375° until heated through and browned on top.

29 • INDONESIA

2 cups diced cooked lamb
2 tablespoons oil
1 teaspoon ground coriander
   (optional)
½ teaspoon chili powder
¼ teaspoon crushed cumin
   seed (optional)

¼ teaspoon saffron
¼ teaspoon powdered
   ginger
½ teaspoon salt
clove garlic, minced
½ cup cooked rice
½ cup water

Heat the oil in a skillet, add all the seasonings, add the meat, and toss until lightly browned. Add the rice and water and heat through.

2 cups diced cooked lamb
2 onions, chopped

2 hard-boiled eggs,
    chopped
½ cup cooked rice

Brown the onions slightly, add the remaining ingredients, and season to taste. Heat through.

Curries in the East are quite different from our packaged powder; there they are many and varied. The spices, seeds, and herbs are dried, freshly ground, and combined—in blends of a few to a few dozen—according to the dish they are to season.

31 • INDIA

2 pounds boned lamb
1 onion, chopped
butter
1 tablespoon curry powder
1 tablespoon flour

1 teaspoon salt
1 teaspoon powdered ginger
    (optional)
2 cups water or consommé
1 teaspoon sugar

Cut the lamb into 1-inch cubes. Sauté the onion in butter; add the curry powder, flour, salt, and ginger; and cook until dark brown. Add the liquid gradually. Brown the meat in butter with the sugar and add to the spice mixture. Simmer 1½ hours or until the meat is tender.

32 • ENGLAND

2 pounds boned lamb
1 onion, chopped
1 cup chopped celery
butter
4 tomatoes, peeled and
    chopped

1 tablespoon curry powder
1 teaspoon salt
1 tablespoon Worcester-
    shire sauce
2 cups consommé

Cut the lamb into 1-inch cubes. Brown the onion and celery together in butter. Add the remaining ingredients and simmer 1½ hours or until the meat is tender.

2 pounds boned lamb
flour
butter
1 teaspoon sugar
1 onion, chopped
1 tomato, peeled and
    chopped

¼ cup chopped celery
½ eggplant, peeled and
    chopped
clove garlic, minced
1 tablespoon curry powder
2 teaspoons salt
1 teaspoon pepper

Cut the lamb into 1-inch cubes. Dip the cubes in flour and brown in butter with the sugar. Combine the meat with all the other ingredients, add 1 cup water, and simmer 1½ hours or until tender.

34 • HAWAII

2 pounds boned lamb
3 cups grated coconut
3 cups milk
½ onion, chopped
clove garlic, minced
butter
1 tablespoon curry powder

1 teaspoon salt
1 teaspoon powdered
    ginger
2 tablespoons flour
2 tablespoons water
1 tablespoon lemon juice

Cut the lamb into 1-inch cubes. Soak the coconut in the milk for 1 hour. Sauté the onion and garlic in butter. Add the curry powder, salt, and ginger; blend the flour and water and add. Stir over the fire a few minutes. Strain the coconut milk and add to this mixture. Add the meat and simmer 1½ hours or until tender. Add the lemon juice before serving.

V • PORK

1 • MEXICO

6 pork chops
1 cup water
¼ cup vinegar
1 teaspoon salt

½ teaspoon oregano
2 tablespoons chili powder
    (or to your taste)
clove garlic, minced

Marinate the chops in a mixture of all the other ingredients for at least 1 hour. Broil them slowly. (Or marinate the chops, brown them, and bake them in the marinade at 350° for 20 minutes or until done.)

2 • PHILIPPINES

6 pork chops   *lemon*
salt   *grated sharp cheese*

Sprinkle the chops with salt and lemon juice and let them stand 30 minutes. Sprinkle with cheese and broil or bake at 350° for 20 minutes or until done.

3 • HAWAII

6 pork chops   *flour*
salt   *6 slices pineapple*
pepper   *6 prunes*
6 whole carrots   *water, stock, or bouillon*

Dust the chops with salt, pepper, and flour. Arrange them in a buttered baking dish with the carrots; on each chop place a pineapple slice with a prune in the center. Add enough water or stock to cover the bottom of the pan. Cover the pan and bake at 325° about 1 hour or until the chops are tender. Thicken the gravy and serve it over the chops.

4 • HUNGARY

6 pork chops   *2 tablespoons sherry*
salt   *1 onion, chopped*
pepper   *1 cup sour cream*
1 tablespoon Hungarian   *12 slices bacon, cooked*
     paprika

Brown the chops and sprinkle them with salt, pepper, and paprika. Add the sherry, onion, and enough water to cover the bottom of the pan. Cook the chops 30 minutes or until done. Remove the chops from the pan. Stir the sour cream slowly into the pan juices. Pour over the chops. Serve with crisp bacon. (The Hungarians also like this dish with sauerkraut. For this variation, omit the sherry and water. Drain the liquid from 2 cans sauerkraut and reserve it. Brown the sauerkraut by tossing it in hot fat with the onion. Replace the juice. Brown the chops slightly and place them on top of the sauerkraut; cook slowly 1 hour. When done, remove the chops, stir the sour cream into the sauerkraut, and replace the chops. Garnish each chop with a dill pickle.)

5 • ITALY

6 pork chops   *½ teaspoon fennel seeds*
1 cup red wine   *2 tablespoons tomato sauce*
clove garlic, minced

Season the chops and brown them in butter, cooking them about 30 minutes or until done. Remove the chops from the pan and keep warm. Add the wine, garlic, fennel seeds, and tomato sauce to the pan. Cook about 5 minutes and pour over the chops.

6 • AUSTRIA

6 pork chops	1 tablespoon caraway seeds
flour	1 cup sour cream

Season the chops, dust with flour, and brown 10 minutes on one side. Turn them, sprinkle with caraway seeds, and cook 10 minutes more or until done. Remove the chops. Add the sour cream to the pan, stir, heat through, and pour over the chops.

7 • FRANCE

6 pork chops	1 cup stock or bouillon
1 onion, chopped	1 teaspoon prepared
1 teaspoon flour	mustard
½ cup white wine	

Brown the chops and cook until done (about 30 minutes). Serve with the following sauce: Sauté the onion in butter till yellow and transparent; stir in the flour and slowly add the wine and stock. Season to taste and simmer 20 minutes. Stir in the mustard.

8 • SWEDEN

6 pork chops	6 potatoes, sliced
salt	1 tablespoon sherry
pepper	water, stock, or milk
flour	1 onion, chopped

Sprinkle the chops with salt, pepper, and flour. Arrange the potato slices on the bottom of a buttered baking dish. Barely cover them with the sherry mixed with the water, stock, or milk. Add the onion and lay the chops on top. Bake at 350° for 30 minutes or until done.

TIPS: As a garnish for pork chops, try mushrooms, parsley, dill pickles, apple sauce, sautéed apple rings, tomatoes, green peppers, cucumbers, prunes, or pineapple slices. You might also try serving the chops with a spinach ring with whole baby beets or kernel corn in the center.

9 • ITALY

6 thick pork chops	6 tablespoons tomato paste
oil (olive, preferably)	(optional)
1 onion, chopped	½ teaspoon oregano
(optional)	1 teaspoon rosemary
1 cup white wine	pinch garlic powder or
1 cup water or stock	fresh minced garlic

Season the chops and brown them in oil with the onions. Pour off the fat. Add the wine to the pan; cook till it is almost evaporated, turning the chops occasionally. Add the stock or water and tomato paste and then the herbs and garlic; cook 30 minutes or until done. Serve with the sauce.

10 • ITALY

6 double chops with	salt
pockets	pepper
¼ pound mozzarella	¼ teaspoon nutmeg
cheese, diced	1 egg, beaten
6 slices Italian prosciutto	½ cup bread crumbs
or Virginia ham,	
minced	

Stuff the cheese and ham—which has been seasoned with salt, pepper, and nutmeg—into the pockets cut into the chops. Dip the chops in egg and in crumbs and brown them in oil for 20 minutes on each side or until done.

11 • INDONESIA

6 pork chops	soy sauce

Dip the chops in soy sauce and broil them, using the soy sauce to baste.

12 • SOUTH AMERICA

6 pork chops	1 teaspoon cumin seeds
2 tablespoons red wine	(optional)
2 tablespoons vinegar	salt
clove garlic, minced	pepper
½ green pepper, chopped	cayenne pepper

Marinate the chops in a mixture of all the ingredients with enough water added to cover the meat. Remove the chops from the marinade. Brown them under the broiler and then cook them in the oven, basting with the marinade, for about 30 minutes or until done.

13 • PHILIPPINES

6 pork chops
2 tablespoons flour
1 small can of figs,
    chopped, with the juice

1 cup cooked rice
paprika

Trim the fat from the chops and melt it in the pan; remove the particles. Brown the chops in the clear fat, season, and remove to a baking dish. Pour off the fat except for 2 tablespoons; stir in the flour and then the juice from the figs with ½ cup water added. Bring this sauce to a boil and pour it over the chops. Cover the chops with the rice and figs; sprinkle with paprika. Bake at 350° for 30 minutes or until chops are done.

14 • NEAR EAST

6 pork chops
6 slices onion
6 tablespoons uncooked
    rice

1 can tomato soup
1 can water

Brown the chops and arrange them in a baking dish. Place a slice of onion and a tablespoon of rice on each chop. Pour the soup and water around the chops. Bake at 350° until done.

15 • AUSTRIA

6 double chops with pockets
1 apple, chopped
1½ cups cubed stale
    bread
¼ cup seedless raisins

¼ cup melted butter
½ teaspoon powdered
    ginger
¼ teaspoon cinnamon

Stuff into the pocket of each chop a filling made of all the ingredients combined and seasoned to taste. Arrange the chops in a buttered baking dish. Pour in ¼ cup water and bake at 350°, adding more water if necessary, until done.

16 • HOLLAND

6 pork chops
flour
¼ cup sherry

½ cup water
6 lemon slices

Cut most of the fat from the chops and melt it in a skillet; remove the particles. Flour the chops and brown them in the clear fat. Remove the chops from the pan, add the sherry and water, and stir. Replace the chops, lay a lemon slice on each, and season to taste. Cover and simmer 1 hour or until done, adding more water if necessary.

17 • GERMANY

6 pork chops	3 tablespoons honey
1 cup stock	3 tablespoons sugar
3 tablespoons Worcestershire sauce	salt
	pepper

Marinate the chops 1 hour in a combination of all the other ingredients, with enough water added to cover the meat. Remove the chops and arrange them in a buttered baking dish. Bake them at 350° for 1 hour or until done. Baste them with the marinade while they are baking and turn them to brown both sides.

Pork must be thoroughly cooked. It is a good idea when making a roast to use a meat thermometer. Roasting time can vary depending on the length and thickness of the pork loin; you cannot judge exactly by weight. In making gravies for either roasts or spareribs, skim off most of the fat before adding flour, if it is used in the recipe, and simmer a little before adding water or whatever liquid is called for.

18 • WEST INDIES

6-pound pork loin roast	2 teaspoons grated orange rind
salt	cayenne pepper
pepper	clove garlic, minced
butter	¼ teaspoon oregano
2 cups orange juice	

Rub salt and pepper into the pork. Melt butter and cover the bottom of the pan; place the meat in it. Pour over the roast a mixture of the orange juice and rind, cayenne pepper, 1 teaspoon salt, pepper, garlic, and oregano. Bake at 325° for 2½ hours or until thoroughly cooked, basting with the pan juices.

19 • CENTRAL AMERICA

6-pound pork loin roast
1 teaspoon salt
½ teaspoon pepper
1 teaspoon powdered
    saffron
½ teaspoon marjoram
1 teaspoon basil

½ teaspoon cumin seeds
clove garlic, minced
¼ cup minced onion
2 tablespoons chopped
    parsley
2 tablespoons wine vinegar
¼ teaspoon chili powder

Rub the roast with a mixture of the salt, pepper, saffron, marjoram, basil, cumin, and garlic. Wrap it in wax paper and leave it in the refrigerator overnight. Roast it, with a little water in the pan, at 325° for 2½ hours or until done. Skim most of the fat from the pan. Heat the remaining juices with the onion, parsley, vinegar, chili powder, and ½ cup water.

20 • EAST INDIES

1 onion, chopped
3 cups diced roast pork
6 slices boiled ham, diced
3 tablespoons pork or
    bacon fat

1 teaspoon salt
½ teaspoon chili powder
3 cups cooked rice
1 egg
1 tablespoon milk

Brown the onion in the fat. Add the pork, ham, salt, and chili powder and cook till pork is browned. Add the rice and keep it warm. Beat the egg with the milk and fry in butter like an omelet; cut into strips and use as a garnish on top of the rice and meat mixture.

21 • SWEDEN

6-pound pork loin roast
12 prunes
salt
pepper

¼ teaspoon powdered
    ginger
1 cup prune juice

Soak the prunes for ½ hour, pit them, and insert them into deep slits in the roast. Rub the meat with salt, pepper, and powdered ginger. Roast it at 325° for 2½ hours or until done, basting occasionally. Skim most of the fat from the pan. Stir in the prune juice.

120

22 • MEXICO

6-pound pork loin roast
olive oil
4 onions, chopped
clove garlic, minced
4 Spanish-type sausages,
    diced

4 tomatoes, chopped
2 teaspoons salt
1 teaspoon pepper
2 cups chicken stock
6 green peppers, sliced

Brown the roast in oil with the onions, garlic, and sausages. Add the tomatoes, salt, pepper, and stock. Cover and roast at 325° for 2½ hours or until done. Garnish with the pepper slices, which have been sautéed in oil.

23 • AUSTRIA

6-pound pork loin roast
salt

crushed caraway seeds

Rub the roast with salt and caraway seeds. Roast at 325° for 2½ hours or until done.

24 • SOUTH AMERICA

6 pounds spareribs
2 cups vinegar
2 teaspoons salt
1 teaspoon pepper
2 teaspoons paprika
1 teaspoon marjoram

6 eggs
2 tablespoons flour
1 cup bread crumbs
½ cup parsley flakes
    (or fresh parsley)

Cut the ribs into serving pieces and marinate 2 hours in a mixture of the vinegar, salt, pepper, paprika, and marjoram. Roast, covered with the marinade, at 325° for 1 hour. When cool, dip the ribs in a mixture of the eggs, flour, crumbs, and parsley. Fry in deep fat 10 minutes or until well browned.

25 • CHINA

6 pounds spareribs
1 onion, chopped
clove garlic, minced
2 tablespoons vinegar
2 tablespoons lemon juice

1 tablespoon prepared
    mustard
2 teaspoons salt
pepper
¼ cup soy sauce
1 cup water

Cut the ribs into serving pieces. Brown the onion and garlic in oil, combine with the other ingredients, and pour over the ribs. Bake at 325° for 1½ hours, basting frequently.

6 pounds spareribs
salt
caraway seeds
1 onion, chopped
clove garlic, minced
   (optional)

2 tablespoons chopped
   parsley
½ teaspoon thyme
½ teaspoon marjoram
1 cup water or chicken stock

Rub the ribs with salt; sprinkle with caraway seeds. Sauté the onion and garlic with the parsley; add the thyme and marjoram and spread over the ribs. Place in a roasting pan with the water or stock. Bake at 325° for 1½ hours, basting frequently.

Stews and ragouts are very flexible dishes. The following five recipes—#27 through #31—are equally good made with either pork or veal. Stews are generally economical and easy to make; you can even use a pressure cooker if you wish. Try serving stews with dumplings.

27 • AUSTRIA

2 pounds pork (or veal)
2 onions, sliced
2 stalks celery, diced
2 carrots, sliced
1 teaspoon salt

½ teaspoon caraway seeds
pepper
bay leaf
¼ cup freshly grated
   horseradish

Cut the meat into cubes and brown lightly in butter. Add the onions and sauté until golden. Add the celery, carrots, salt, caraway seeds, pepper, bay leaf, and enough water to cover. Simmer 1 hour or until tender. Remove the meat to a serving dish, pour over the liquid, and sprinkle with the horseradish. Serve with croutons or boiled or mashed potatoes.

28 • SPAIN

2 pounds pork (or veal)
4 onions, sliced
4 pimientos, cut in strips
4 tomatoes, peeled and
   chopped

2 or 3 vegetable marrows
   or squash, cut up
stock (chicken bouillon or
   broth)

Cut the meat into cubes and brown lightly in fat with the onions and pimientos. Add the tomatoes, marrows, salt, pepper, and enough stock to cover. Simmer 1 hour or until tender and the stock is absorbed. (In Spain this stew is served with scrambled eggs.)

2 pounds pork (or veal)
2 onions, chopped
salt
pepper

Hungarian paprika
1 pound sauerkraut
1 pint sour cream

Cut the meat into cubes. Sprinkle the meat and onions with the salt, pepper, and paprika and cook in fat until the onions are golden. Add a little water and simmer 1 hour or until tender, adding small amounts of water as needed. Add the sauerkraut and heat through. Stir in the cream and serve.

30 • ITALY

2 pounds pork (or veal)
clove garlic, minced
bay leaf
½ teaspoon rosemary
½ teaspoon marjoram

2 teaspoons chopped parsley
1 cup white wine
1 1-pound can tomatoes
chicken broth or bouillon

Cut the meat into cubes and sprinkle with salt and pepper. Sauté the garlic in oil (olive oil, if you have it); add the cubes of meat and brown them. Add the bay leaf, rosemary, marjoram, parsley, and wine. Cook until the wine evaporates. Add the tomatoes and enough stock to cover the meat. Simmer 1 hour or until the meat is tender.

31 • RUSSIA

2 pounds pork (or veal)
1 onion, sliced
salt
pepper
1 teaspoon chopped parsley

bay leaf
1 cup pearl onions
3 cups stock
3 tablespoons flour

Cut the meat into cubes and brown it with the onion in hot fat. Pour off the excess fat. Season with salt and pepper; add the parsley, bay leaf, onions, and stock. Simmer 1 hour or until the meat is tender. Blend the flour with a little of the liquid, stir it into the stew, and cook a few minutes longer before serving.

Leftovers of pork can be used to great advantage in this sturdy peasant dish:

2 cups diced cooked pork
1 pound sauerkraut
½ cup sliced mushrooms
2 strips of bacon, diced
    and cooked
2 teaspoons chopped
    parsley

1 onion, chopped
2 Polish-style sausages,
    sliced
1 cup red wine
½ teaspoon sugar

Combine all the ingredients except the wine; season to taste and heat through. Add the wine and bring to a boil. Serve.

Pork is a great favorite in the East and is used there with considerable imagination.

33 • CHINA

2 pounds pork, diced
peanut or sesame oil
salt
2 onions, sliced
2 green peppers, sliced
2 tablespoons cornstarch

2 tablespoons soy sauce
1 tablespoon lemon juice
4 cups chicken broth
2 tablespoons curry powder
    (optional)

Cook the pork in the oil with salt, stir-frying for 2 minutes. Add the onions and green peppers and stir-fry 2 minutes more. Combine the cornstarch, soy sauce, lemon juice, and chicken broth. Pour over the meat and simmer 15 minutes or until the meat is cooked and the sauce is thickened. (For a different effect, you can add curry powder after stir-frying the green peppers and then cook 5 minutes, stirring as before.)

34 • PHILIPPINES

2 pounds pork, diced
2 onions, chopped
2 green peppers, chopped
peanut or sesame oil
1 teaspoon salt
½ teaspoon thyme
2 cloves

½ teaspoon pepper
2 tablespoons curry powder
2 cups chicken broth
4 cups cooked rice
2 egg yolks
2 tablespoons cream

Sauté the onions and peppers in peanut or sesame oil. Combine with the meat, seasoning, thyme, cloves, curry powder, and broth. Simmer 45 minutes or until the meat is well cooked. Combine with the rice, which has been mixed with the egg yolks and cream.

Ham is an adaptable meat and is particularly good for unusual late-supper and buffet dishes like these:

35 • SOUTH AMERICA

8 slices boiled ham
4 sweet potatoes or 1 package frozen asparagus or fresh asparagus
oil
1 tablespoon flour
½ cup orange juice

grated rind ½ orange (optional)
½ cup seedless raisins (optional)
1 tablespoon honey
salt
pepper

Cook the sweet potatoes or asparagus spears. (If you use sweet potatoes, peel them and cut them in half. If you use asparagus spears, separate them into 8 bunches.) Wrap each potato half or bunch of asparagus in a slice of ham and secure with a toothpick or skewer. Brush the ham rolls with oil and broil until browned. Meanwhile, stir the flour into 2 tablespoons hot oil until it is browned. Add the remaining ingredients and simmer together a few minutes. Serve over the ham rolls.

36 • HUNGARY

12 Hungarian pancakes
12 tablespoons deviled ham or minced ham mixed with a little sour cream

1 egg, beaten
bread crumbs
fat for deep frying

Make 12 pancakes, following pancake recipe #1, page 195. Spread 1 tablespoon deviled ham on each pancake and roll up, tucking in the ends. Dip each pancake in egg, in flour, in egg again, and then in bread crumbs. Fry in deep fat until golden brown.

VI • VENISON

1 • AUSTRIA

4 servings venison (fillets,
    steaks, or chops)
larding fat
clove garlic, minced
2 onions, sliced
2 carrots, sliced
½ teaspoon chopped
    parsley

¼ teaspoon rosemary
¼ teaspoon thyme
½ cup red wine
½ cup water
few strips lemon peel
½ cup sour cream

Lard the venison. Combine the garlic, onions, carrots, parsley, rosemary, thyme, wine, and water; season to taste and simmer 10 minutes. Pour over the venison and add the strips of lemon peel. Cover and roast in 325° oven 1 hour or until almost tender. Add the cream to the juices and cook 30 minutes longer. Strain the gravy and pour over the meat to serve. (If you wish, venison can be marinated before proceeding with this recipe. Use equal parts of vinegar and water and marinate at least 1 hour.)

2 • NORWAY

4 servings fillet of venison
vinegar

larding fat
1 cup sour cream

Marinate the meat in equal parts of vinegar and water for 2 hours. Dry and lard with thin strips of fat by threading the strips through the meat with a larding needle or laying them between the slices. Brown in butter, season to taste, and place in a buttered casserole. Pour over enough sour cream to cover and bake at 350° for 2 hours or until tender. Add more cream while baking, if necessary.

VII • CHOPPED MEATS

1 • SOUTH AMERICA

2 pounds ground beef,
    lamb, or pork or a
    combination of these
2 onions, chopped
2 tablespoons butter
2 tablespoons lemon juice
1 tablespoon curry powder
    or chili-powder

4 tablespoons ground nuts
    (optional)
1 teaspoon salt
½ teaspoon pepper
1 egg, beaten
4 bay leaves

Brown the onions in the butter and combine with all the other
ingredients except the bay leaves. Butter a casserole and place
the meat mixture in it. Lay the bay leaves on top of the meat.
Bake at 350° for 1½ hours.

2 • YUGOSLAVIA

2 pounds ground cooked
    meat or 1 pound meat
    plus 2 cups cooked rice
gravy or water

2 tomatoes, sliced
4 slices eggplant
bread crumbs
butter

Season the meat and add enough gravy or water to moisten.
Sauté the tomato and eggplant slices in a little oil. Butter a
casserole. Place half the meat in the dish, make a layer of
tomato slices and then a layer of eggplant, and top with the
remaining meat. Sprinkle with bread crumbs and dot with
butter. Bake at 400° until brown.

3 • AUSTRIA

2 cups diced sausages
2 onions, sliced
1 cup sour cream
2 tablespoons flour
4 green peppers, sliced

4 tomatoes, peeled and
    chopped
½ teaspoon salt
1 teaspoon sugar

Sauté the onions in butter until golden. Brown the sausage
lightly and drain off fat. Mix the flour into the sour cream.
Combine all the ingredients and place in a buttered casserole.
Bake at 350° for 30 minutes.

Meatballs and meat loaves are always popular. Meatballs may
be served with spaghetti, noodles, rice, or potatoes or in their
own gravy. Made very tiny, they can be served hot or cold as
an hors d'oeuvre. Left over, they are wonderful dropped into
consommé. Make a generous supply and freeze some. Meat
loaf also is good either hot or cold. It can be used in sandwiches or taken, cold and sliced, on a picnic and served with
potato salad. For entertaining, you can prepare these ground-
meat mixtures in individual servings. Butter small jelly jars, fill
with the meat mixture, and bake in a pan of hot water for 1
hour at 350°. Turn out the timbales onto a hot serving platter, pour over a flavorful sauce, and garnish with parsley. Or,
for an ideal buffet dish, surround with rice or mashed potatoes and serve extra sauce on the side.

¾ pound pork sausage
    meat
¾ pound ground veal
¾ pound ground beef
1 egg

½ cup milk
1 teaspoon salt
pepper
1 cup beef stock or 1 can
    consommé

Combine all the ingredients except the stock. Shape into balls. Simmer in the stock 15 minutes. To make a loaf, shape the meat in a buttered pan and bake 1 hour at 350°, basting with stock.

5 • SWEDEN

1½ pounds beef
½ pound pork or ¼
    pound pork and ¼
    pound veal
2 tablespoons minced onion
½ cup bread crumbs
2 eggs

1½ teaspoons salt
½ teaspoon pepper
¼ teaspoon nutmeg
    (optional)
2 tablespoons flour
2 cups milk or water

Have the butcher grind the meat together 3 times. Sauté the onion lightly in butter. Combine the meat, onions, bread crumbs, eggs, salt, pepper, and nutmeg and shape into balls. Brown in butter over low heat. Remove from the pan. Stir in the flour and milk or water to make the gravy. Return the meatballs to the pan. Simmer gently 15 minutes for medium-size, less for tiny, meatballs. To make a meat loaf, shape the mixture in a buttered pan, brush with egg, sprinkle with bread crumbs, and add 1 cup water. Bake 1 hour at 350°, basting occasionally.

6 • CHINA

2 pounds ground beef
oil
2 teaspoons salt
¼ teaspoon pepper
½ cup chopped onion
clove garlic, minced
2 cups stock or consommé

¼ cup cornstarch
2 tablespoons soy sauce
2 teaspoons powdered ginger
    or a little grated fresh
    ginger root
½ cup water

Shape the meat into balls the size of walnuts. Put the oil into a pan with the salt, pepper, onion, and garlic; brown the meatballs in it. Add the stock and simmer 20 minutes. Mix the cornstarch, soy sauce, ginger, and water; add to the pan and stir until thickened. To make a loaf, add the salt, pepper, onion, and garlic to the meat and shape in a buttered pan. Bake 1 hour at 350°, basting with the stock. Add the cornstarch, soy sauce, ginger, and water mixture to the pan juices; simmer until thickened and serve with the meat.

7 • MEXICO

2 pounds ground beef
4 slices bread
2 eggs
1 teaspoon marjoram
dash chili powder
clove garlic, minced, or ½
    teaspoon garlic powder

1 onion, chopped
¼ cup tomato paste
1 quart water.
salt
pepper

Soak the bread in water and squeeze out. Mix with the meat, eggs, marjoram, chili powder, and garlic and shape into balls. Sauté the onion lightly; add the tomato paste and water and salt and pepper to taste. Simmer the balls in this sauce for 20 minutes. Serve with the sauce. To make a loaf, shape the meat in a buttered pan and bake at 350° for 1 hour, basting with the sauce.

8 • ITALY

2 pounds ground beef
1 onion, chopped
2 eggs, lightly beaten
2 slices bread
water or tomato juice
1 teaspoon salt
¼ teaspoon pepper
dash powdered cloves

dash cinnamon
dash nutmeg
2 teaspoons chopped parsley
½ teaspoon basil
clove garlic, minced
4 tablespoons olive oil
2 cans tomato paste
grated Parmesan cheese

Combine the meat with the onion, eggs, bread (which has been soaked in water or tomato juice and squeezed out), salt, pepper, cinnamon, cloves, nutmeg, parsley, and basil. Shape into balls the size of walnuts. Brown gently in oil with the garlic. Add the tomato paste with an equal amount of water and simmer 10 minutes. Sprinkle with Parmesan cheese and serve. To make a loaf, prepare the meat mixture as above but add the garlic to it. Shape in a buttered pan. Pour the tomato paste and water over the loaf. Bake at 350° for 1 hour, basting occasionally. Sprinkle with cheese before serving.

9 • JAPAN

2 pounds ground beef, *¼ cup cornstarch*
    pork, or chicken *¼ cup soy sauce*
1¼ cups water *1 tablespoon sugar*

Blend the cornstarch with ¼ cup water and combine with the meat. Shape into balls the size of walnuts. Simmer 10 minutes in a sauce made of 1 cup water and the soy sauce and sugar. To make a loaf, shape the meat in a buttered pan and bake at 350° for 1 hour, basting with the sauce. Serve with carrots (recipe #2, page 52) and rice with mushrooms.

10 • RUSSIA

2 pounds ground beef *¼ teaspoon pepper*
3 onions, chopped *1 cup cooked rice*
1 green pepper, chopped *1 can tomato paste*
1 teaspoon salt

Combine the meat, onions, green pepper, salt, pepper, and rice. Shape into balls and simmer gently in equal parts of tomato paste and water for 15 minutes. To make a loaf, shape the meat mixture in a buttered pan and bake at 350° for 1 hour, basting occasionally with the tomato paste and water.

11 • NORWAY

2 pounds ground beef *1 tablespoon powdered*
½ cup medium cream   *ginger*
1 cup minced suet *1 egg*
1 tablespoon cornstarch *1 teaspoon salt*
    ¼ teaspoon pepper

Mix all the ingredients together; shape into balls and brown gently in butter. Simmer 15 minutes, adding more butter if necessary. To make a loaf, shape in a buttered pan, add 1 cup water, and bake at 350° for 1 hour, basting occasionally.

12 • POLAND

2 pounds ground beef *2 eggs, separated*
1 onion, chopped *flour*
1 teaspoon salt *1 cup sour cream*
¼ teaspoon pepper *1 cup mushrooms*
3 slices bread

Sauté the onion lightly and mix with the meat, salt, pepper, bread (which has been soaked in milk and squeezed out), and egg yolks. Beat the egg whites stiff and fold into the meat. Shape meat into balls; roll balls in flour and brown them gently in butter. Add the cream and mushrooms and simmer 15 minutes. To make a loaf, shape the meat mixture in a buttered pan, brush with butter, sprinkle with flour, and add 1 cup water. Bake at 350° for 1 hour, basting occasionally. Add the cream and mushrooms for the last 10 minutes.

13 • AUSTRIA

1 pound beef	*1 teaspoon salt*
1 pound pork	*¼ teaspoon pepper*
3 slices bread	*¼ teaspoon marjoram*
1 egg	*½ cup stock or consommé*
1 onion, chopped	*1 cup sour cream*
1 tablespoon chopped	
parsley	

Have the meat ground together. Soak the bread in a little water and squeeze dry. Add to the meat with the egg, onion, parsley, salt, pepper, marjoram, and stock. Form into balls, dredge in flour, and brown slowly in butter. Add the sour cream and simmer gently 5 minutes. To make a loaf, shape the meat mixture in a buttered pan, add 1 cup stock or water, and bake 1 hour at 350°, basting occasionally. Add the sour cream to the pan juices 15 minutes before the meat is done.

14 • WEST INDIES

1¼ pounds beef	*¼ cup chopped green*
¼ pound bacon	*pepper*
½ pound veal	*1 tablespoon chopped*
½ cup bread crumbs	*parsley*
½ cup red wine	*1 teaspoon salt*
¼ teaspoon thyme	*¼ teaspoon pepper*

Have the butcher grind all the meat together. Soak the crumbs with the wine; add to the meat with the thyme, green pepper, parsley, salt, and pepper. Shape into balls the size of walnuts and brown gently in butter about 15 minutes. To make a loaf, shape in a buttered pan, add 1 cup water, and bake 1 hour at 350°, basting occasionally. (For a further West Indian touch, serve with Beef Sauce #7, page 182.)

15 • AUSTRIA

1 pound beef	*1 teaspoon salt*
1 pound pork	*½ teaspoon pepper*
3 slices bread	*1 egg*
milk	*1 cup sour cream*

131

Have the meat ground together. Soak the bread in the milk and squeeze out. Season and mix together with the egg. Shape into balls and brown gently in butter. Add the sour cream and simmer 15 minutes. To make a loaf, shape the meat mixture in a buttered pan, add a little water, and bake at 350° for 1 hour, basting occasionally. Add the cream for the last 15 minutes.

16 • DENMARK

1½ pounds beef
½ pound pork
1 egg, beaten
1 onion, chopped
3 tablespoons red wine
1 cup bread crumbs
¼ teaspoon thyme

¼ teaspoon chopped
    parsley
¼ teaspoon basil
1 teaspoon salt
1 cup stock or consommé
2 tablespoons flour

Have the meat ground together. Combine with the egg, onion, wine, bread crumbs, herbs, and seasoning. Shape into balls and brown gently in butter. Add the stock and simmer 15 minutes. Combine the flour with a little water and stir into the pan juices; cook a few minutes more. To make a loaf, shape the meat mixture in a buttered pan and bake 1 hour at 350°, basting occasionally with the stock.

17 • FRANCE

2 pound (4 cups) cooked
    beef, ground or minced
1 onion, chopped fine
1 cup bread crumbs or
    1 cup cooked rice
milk

1 tablespoon chopped
    parsley
1 tablespoon lemon juice
½ teaspoon thyme
¼ teaspoon sage
2 eggs, slightly beaten

If you use bread crumbs rather than rice, soak them in milk first. Mix all the ingredients together; shape into balls and cook gently in butter 15 minutes. Drain. To make a loaf, shape the mixture in a buttered pan, place a few strips of bacon on top if you wish, and add 1 cup water. Bake at 350° for 1 hour, basting occasionally.

• 7 •

POULTRY

There is one thing we have noted in the thousands of miles we have motored on all five continents: chickens (regardless of nationality) always dash across the road right in front of a car. The fact that there seem to be chickens wherever there are human beings gives the chicken enthusiast (and I am one) a glorious array of dishes to choose from: France's *Poularde au Riz Sauce Suprême* with its exquisite sauce; Chicken Sesame made with Chinese vegetables and sesame seeds; Eastern chicken curries; Hungarian chicken smothered in sour cream and paprika; Arabian chicken with ginger, black cherries and pistachio nuts; and so on. Duck is widely used and is a specialty in China, viz., their Peking duck. Goose is a special favorite for Christmas feasts in central and northern Europe. Game birds and turkeys are also used throughout Europe. And there was the dinner of roast peacock served to us one evening in Lucknow, India.

I • CHICKEN

1 • RUSSIA

2 young chickens
12 green onions or
    scallions, sliced
salt

6 tomatoes, peeled and
    chopped
½ cup white wine
¼ cup chopped parsley
1 cup sour cream

Cut up the chicken and brown the pieces. Add the green onions and salt and simmer a few minutes. Add the tomatoes. Cover and cook until chicken is tender. Remove chicken pieces. Stir in the wine and parsley and then the cream slowly. Heat but do not boil. Pour over the chicken.

2 • CHINA

2 young chickens
soy sauce
1 tablespoon Mei Yen,
    MSG, or Accent
½ teaspoon salt
2 eggs

½ cup flour
oil
1 cup vinegar
1 cup sugar
2 tablespoons cornstarch
1 cup diced sweet pickles

Cut the chicken into 1-inch cubes. Sprinkle it with soy sauce, Mei Yen, and salt. Beat the eggs and flour together. Dip the pieces of chicken in this batter and fry in a generous amount of oil. Drain the pieces. Cook the sugar with the vinegar and 1 cup water until it is dissolved. Stir the cornstarch with ½ cup water and add to the sweet-sour liquid, stirring till it is clear. Add the pickles and chicken. Serve with rice.

3 • CHINA

1 stewing chicken
oil
2 cans chop suey vegetables
2 cans bamboo shoots
2 cans water chestnuts
1 teaspoon powdered ginger
    or grated fresh ginger
    root (optional)

1 cup consommé
soy sauce
1 tablespoon red wine
    (optional)
3 tablespoons cornstarch
2 teaspoons sugar
1 tablespoon Mei Yen,
    MSG, or Accent

Cook the chicken; remove the meat and shred it. Stir-fry the chicken in oil for 2 minutes. Add the chop suey vegetables, sliced bamboo shoots, sliced water chestnuts, and ginger; then add the consommé, 2 tablespoons soy sauce, and wine and simmer 5 minutes. Stir the cornstarch into 1 cup water with 1 tablespoon soy sauce, sugar, and Mei Yen. Add to the chicken mixture and simmer, stirring, for 2 more minutes. Serve with additional soy sauce on the side and with boiled rice.

4 • SPAIN

2 young chickens
lard
¼ cup grape jam
1 onion, chopped

1 cup mushroom pieces
1 tomato, diced
1 bay leaf

Cut the chicken into pieces and brown in the lard. Season to taste and add all the other ingredients. Cover and cook gently until tender. Serve with fried bread.

5 • HUNGARY

2 young chickens
4 onions, chopped
2 tablespoons Hungarian
     paprika

1 teaspoon salt
2 cups sour cream
noodles (optional)

Cut the chicken into pieces. Brown the onions in fat; add the paprika, chicken pieces, and salt. Cover and simmer until chicken is tender. Pour over the cream and heat without boiling. Serve on boiled noodles.

6 • SOUTH AMERICA

2 young chickens
1 cup dried peas
flour
salt
pepper
olive oil
4 onions, diced

4 tomatoes, chopped
1½ cups sliced mushrooms
2 green peppers, sliced
1½ cups red wine
¼ teaspoon chili powder
¼ teaspoon oregano
bay leaf

Soak the peas; cook in water and drain. Cut the chicken into pieces; dust pieces with flour, salt, and pepper and brown in oil. Add the peas and all the other ingredients and simmer gently, covered, until chicken is tender. Remove the bay leaf before serving.

135

7 • AUSTRIA

2 young chickens
6 onions, sliced
1 tablespoon paprika
2 egg yolks

½ pint sour cream
salt
pepper

Cut the chicken into pieces. Brown the onions and chicken. Remove the onions. Sprinkle the chicken with paprika and cook until tender. Mix the egg yolks with the sour cream, salt, and pepper and pour over the chicken; also return the onions to the pot. Heat gently a few minutes.

8 • ARABIA

2 broilers
honey
salt
pepper

powdered ginger
1 cup pitted black cherries
¼ cup chopped pistachio
    nuts

Split the broilers in half. Rub them with a combination of honey, salt, pepper, and a pinch of ginger. Broil them. Sprinkle with the cherries and nuts and serve.

9 • GREECE

2 young chickens
olive oil
1 teaspoon salt
¼ cup lemon juice

¼ cup butter
2 teaspoons oregano
2 cups canned tomatoes

Cut the chicken into pieces. Combine the oil with 1 teaspoon salt and the lemon juice. Rub this over the chicken pieces and brown them in the oven. Meanwhile, simmer the butter, oregano, and tomatoes together about 5 minutes. Pour the tomatoes over the chicken and bake at 350° until tender, basting frequently.

10 • ITALY

2 young chickens
½ cup olive oil
½ cup lemon juice
½ teaspoon salt
pepper

2 tablespoons chopped
    parsley
flour
1 egg, beaten

Cut up the chicken. Marinate the pieces in a mixture of the

oil, lemon juice, salt, pepper, and parsley for 2 hours. Wipe the pieces dry. Dip them in flour and then in beaten egg and fry, preferably in olive oil.

11 • SANTO DOMINGO

2 young chickens	1 teaspoon salt
½ cup vinegar	pepper
1 green pepper, chopped	½ teaspoon oregano
2 tomatoes, chopped	2 tablespoons tomato paste
1 onion, chopped	½ cup sliced stuffed olives
clove garlic, minced	

Cut up the chicken and marinate the pieces 2 hours in a mixture of the vinegar, green peppers, tomatoes, onion, garlic salt, pepper, and oregano. Wipe chicken pieces dry and brown in oil. Pour the marinade over the chicken; stir in the tomato paste and olives. Cover and simmer 30 minutes or until tender.

12 • POLAND

2 young chickens	1 egg, beaten
salt	1 cup bread crumbs
pepper	¼ cup butter
flour	1 cup heavy cream

Cut the chicken into pieces. Dust with salt, pepper, and flour and dip in egg, which has been beaten with a little water. Dip in bread crumbs and brown in butter. Pour over the cream and bake at 350° for 1 hour or until tender.

13 • HAWAII

2 young chickens	2 cups shredded coconut
salt	1 cup milk
2 packages frozen chopped spinach or fresh spinach	

Cut the chicken into pieces; brown the pieces in butter. Add salt and enough hot water to cover halfway. Simmer until tender. Meanwhile, cook the spinach and simmer the shredded coconut in the milk. Squeeze the coconut through a cheese cloth or put it in the blender. Add the spinach and the coconut milk to the chicken and simmer a few minutes longer.

14 • AFRICA

2 young chickens	½ cup chopped almonds
1 package frozen peas	1 teaspoon salt
1 cup diced celery	1 tablespoon sherry
2 cups stock	

Cook the chickens and save the stock. Cut them up and remove the bones. Meanwhile, cook the peas. Brown the chicken pieces in hot oil. Combine them with the celery, cooked peas, 2 cups of the stock the chicken was cooked in, almonds, salt, and sherry. Simmer together 10 minutes. (This can be served with noodles.)

The following nine recipes—#15 through #23—are especially good for festive luncheons, late suppers, and buffets.

15 • ENGLAND

8 slices cooked chicken
    or turkey
1 onion, chopped
1 cup mushroom pieces
½ teaspoon salt

1 tablespoon paprika
dash nutmeg
heavy cream
grated Parmesan cheese

Cook the onion and mushrooms in butter 5 minutes; do not let the onion brown. Add the salt, paprika, and nutmeg. Spread on the bottom of a casserole. Lay the meat slices on top and add enough cream to cover. Sprinkle with cheese and bake at 400° until bubbly and brown on top.

16 • FRANCE

1 large stewing chicken
6 servings asparagus
    or broccoli
¼ cup butter
¼ cup flour
2 cups milk or chicken stock
¼ cup red wine

salt
pepper
½ cup heavy cream,
    whipped
½ cup grated Parmesan
    cheese

Cook the chicken and slice the meat. Cook the asparagus or broccoli. Melt the butter, stir in the flour, and gradually add the milk or stock. Simmer a few minutes until thickened; add the wine, salt, and pepper and fold in the whipped cream. Arrange the asparagus or broccoli on the bottom of an ovenproof dish, pour over half the sauce, and lay the slices of meat on top. Add the cheese to the remaining sauce and pour over the meat. Place under the broiler until lightly browned. (When ½ cup Hollandaise sauce is added to the cream sauce, this is called "chicken Divan." In Norway people add a dash of nutmeg and Worcestershire sauce to the mixture of sauces and whipped cream.)

17 • CHINA

2 pounds chicken
½ cup soy sauce
1 tablespoon red wine
1 teaspoon Mei Yen,
    MSG, or Accent

1 teaspoon sesame seeds
1 pound bacon
¾ cup flour
4 eggs
fat for frying

Cut the chicken into 1-inch cubes and marinate in a combination of the soy sauce, wine, Mei Yen, and sesame seeds for 10 minutes. Wrap each cube in a bit of bacon and dip in a batter made from the flour and lightly beaten eggs. Fry in deep fat until golden brown. (Shrimp can be handled in the same way.)

18 • RUSSIA

4 chicken breasts
½ teaspoon garlic powder
    or minced garlic
¼ pound butter
¼ teaspoon basil
¼ teaspoon thyme
¼ teaspoon marjoram

¼ teaspoon tarragon
salt
pepper
flour
1 egg, beaten
bread crumbs
fat for frying

Split the breasts in half and remove the meat from the bones in one piece. Wrap each of these pieces in wax paper and beat with a mallet until very thin. Remove the paper. Blend the garlic with the butter and place a small finger-shaped stick (2 teaspoons) of the mixture in the center of each piece of chicken. Sprinkle each with herbs, salt, and pepper. Roll each piece up neatly, tucking in the ends so that the butter is completely enclosed. Dip pieces in flour, egg, and then bread crumbs, being sure they are thoroughly coated so that the butter cannot run out. Fry quickly in deep fat until golden brown. (When eating this, make the first knife incision carefully, as the melted butter tends to squirt out.)

19 • SCANDINAVIA

6 chicken breasts, cooked
2 lobsters, cooked
2 slices bread
milk

4 egg yolks
½ pint heavy cream,
    whipped

Hold aside a few chunks of the chicken and lobster meats; chop the rest fine or grind together. Soak the bread in a little milk; mix it with the meat and egg yolks. Season and fold into the whipped cream. Put mixture into a buttered baking dish, garnish with the chunks of meat, set in a pan of hot water, and bake at 350° for 1 hour or until set. (Unbaked, this makes a delectable hors d'oeuvre spread.)

20 • FRANCE

1 stewing chicken	*1 tablespoon red wine*
¼ cup butter	*(optional)*
¼ cup flour	*salt*
2 cups chicken stock	*pepper*
	6 artichokes

Cook the chicken and cut it up. Melt the butter, stir in the flour, and gradually add the stock. (You can use the stock that the chicken was cooked in.) Simmer 10 minutes. Add the wine, salt, pepper, and pieces of chicken. Meanwhile, cook the artichokes and remove the choke from each one. To serve, pour the chicken mixture into the center of the artichokes.

21 • CHINA

4 chicken breasts	*4 cups chicken broth or*
1 head cauliflower	*bouillon*
1 egg white	*salt*
1 cup cold water	*2 tablespoons deviled ham*

Separate the cauliflower into buds and cook. Mince the raw chicken and add to the egg white, which has been beaten with the water. Bring the chicken broth to a boil. Stir in the chicken mixture. Add the cauliflower. Simmer 2 minutes more. Pour into soup bowls and garnish with bits of ham. (For a luncheon, serve this with watercress sandwiches or a tossed salad.)

22 • RUSSIA

cooked chicken or turkey	*½ teaspoon thyme*
for 4 people	*½ teaspoon marjoram*
1 cup canned Bing cherries	*¼ cup butter*
with juice	*2 tablespoons brandy*
6 tablespoons red wine	*(optional)*
½ teaspoon basil	

Simmer the cherries with juice, wine, and herbs for 15 minutes. Meanwhile, slice the meat and heat it in butter. Remove

140

the cherries from the liquid, chop them fine, and return them to the sauce. Lay the slices of meat on a platter; pour sauce over it. Just before serving, pour over the brandy and ignite.

23 • ITALY

*1 pound fresh or 2 packages
    frozen chicken livers*
6 large onions
½ teaspoon salt
¼ teaspoon pepper

¾ cup butter
2 tablespoons flour
2 cups stock or consommé
*grated Parmesan cheese
    (optional)*

Cut the onions in half and scoop out the centers. Chop the chicken livers fine and combine with the salt, pepper, and half the butter, melted. Fill the onion shells with the chicken livers and place them in a buttered baking dish. Cover and bake at 375° for 15 minutes. Melt the remaining butter, stir in the flour, and gradually add the stock. Stir until thickened. Pour over the onions and continue to bake 15 minutes longer. The stuffed onions may be sprinkled with grated Parmesan cheese before baking if you wish.

For the following recipes you can use either young, tender chickens or stewing hens. Cooking time will vary accordingly from approximately 45 minutes to 2 hours. The chicken can be simmered with seasonings and served with boiled rice, noodles, or mashed potatoes and its own hot broth. When you are cooking chicken like this, prepare an extra chicken for salads, sandwiches, hash, or croquettes. If you don't use all the broth in the recipe, save it for your stock supply.

24 • INDONESIA

3- to 4-pound chicken
1 teaspoon nutmeg

¼ cup soy sauce
4 cloves

Cut up the chicken, put it into a pot with the other ingredients, and barely cover it with water. Simmer gently 1 hour or until tender. Serve with the broth.

25 • CENTRAL AMERICA

3- to 4-pound chicken
¼ cup butter
1 onion, chopped
clove garlic, minced
1 green pepper, chopped
¼ teaspoon chili powder
1 cup hard cider

1 tablespoon vinegar
*1 cup prunes, pitted
    and soaked*
1 cup stuffed olives
1 cup small white onions
2 potatoes, cubed
3 sausages

Cut up chicken; rub pieces with salt and pepper and brown in butter. Add the chopped onion and cook for a few minutes; then add the garlic, cider, and vinegar and simmer, covered, for 1 hour or until chicken is almost done. Add the prunes, olives, onions, and potatoes and cook 10 minutes. Meanwhile, fry the sausages and cut them up. Add to the chicken and cook 10 more minutes or until chicken is tender.

26 • JAPAN

3- to 4-pound chicken
2 cups stock

¼ cup soy sauce
1 can bamboo shoots

Cut up the chicken; pour over the stock and soy sauce. Simmer, uncovered, until stock is evaporated and meat is tender. Serve with sliced bamboo shoots that have been heated in their own liquid.

27 • BULGARIA

3- to 4-pound chicken
2 onions, chopped
2 tablespoons flour
½ teaspoon paprika
salt

2 tablespoons tomato paste
1 cup water
½ pound shelled uncooked
    chestnuts

Cut up the chicken and brown it in butter with the onions. Mix the flour, paprika, salt, and tomato paste with the water; pour over the chicken and add the chestnuts. Simmer, covered, for 1 hour or until meat is tender. Add water if necessary while cooking.

28 • ITALY

3- to 4-pound chicken
olive oil
1 cup red or white wine
clove garlic, minced

½ teaspoon marjoram
2 slices prosciutto (Italian
    ham) or Virginia ham,
    diced

Cut up the chicken, season it to taste, and brown it in oil. Pour over the wine and add the other ingredients. Cover and cook slowly 1 hour or until tender, adding a little water while cooking if necessary.

29 • HUNGARY

3- to 4-pound chicken
1 cup white wine
1½ teaspoons salt
1 onion, chopped

1 small head cabbage,
    chopped
1 tablespoon lemon juice
½ teaspoon pepper

Cut up the chicken and simmer it in the wine and salt for 45 minutes or until tender. Brown the onion and cabbage in butter or fat; add the lemon juice and pepper. Lay the chicken pieces on top of the cabbage. Cover and simmer together 15 minutes.

30 • AFRICA

3- to 4-pound chicken
1 onion
1 carrot
salt
clove garlic, minced

1 teaspoon crushed
    coriander seed
3 packages frozen chopped
    spinach or 2 pounds
    Swiss chard

Cut up the chicken; put it in a pot with the onion and carrot and enough water to cover. Simmer until tender. Remove the chicken from the liquid and brown it in another pan in butter with the salt, garlic, and coriander. Take chicken from pan, put in spinach or Swiss chard, and return chicken, laying the pieces on top of the greens. Cover and simmer about 10 minutes or until spinach is done.

31 • MEXICO

3- to 4-pound chicken
2 onions, chopped
clove garlic, minced
1 tablespoon flour
2 tablespoons tomato sauce
1 cup water, chicken
    broth, bouillon, or
    sherry

3 cloves
1 tablespoon vinegar
1 green pepper, sliced
½ cup raisins
½ cup stuffed olives

Cut the chicken into pieces and brown. In another skillet brown the onions and garlic with the flour. To the onions add the tomato sauce and the liquid (water, stock, or sherry). Bring to a boil; add the cloves, vinegar, and green pepper; and season to taste. Pour over the chicken. Simmer until the meat is tender. Add the raisins and olives and cook 10 minutes more.

3- to 4-pound chicken
2 tablespoons butter
1 tablespoon chopped
    onion
1 tablespoon flour
1 cup boiling water
6 small white onions
1 small bay leaf
2 teaspoons chopped parsley

1 teaspoon celery flakes
pinch thyme
½ teaspoon salt
pepper
6 cooked or canned
    mushrooms
1 egg yolk
2 tablespoons cream or milk

Cut up the chicken and sauté without browning in butter for
5 minutes. Add the chopped onion, which has been mixed
with the flour, and continue to cook a few minutes. Add the
water slowly, stirring continually. Add the white onions, bay
leaf, parsley, celery flakes, thyme, salt, and pepper. Simmer
45 minutes or until tender. Add the mushrooms. Combine
the egg yolk and cream and stir into the sauce until thoroughly blended. Heat through without allowing to boil again.

33 • HAWAII

3- to 4-pound chicken
¼ cup oil
1 cup shredded cabbage
    and celery combined
½ cup coarsely chopped
    mixed nuts

1 teaspoon salt
pepper
1 teaspoon sugar
1 teaspoon soy sauce
1¾ cups pineapple chunks

Barely cover the chicken with water and simmer until tender.
Hold the stock. Remove the skin from the chicken and cut
it up. Heat the oil; add the cabbage, celery, and nuts; and
stir-fry a few minutes. Add the pieces of chicken, 2 cups of
the stock that the chicken was cooked in, salt, pepper, sugar,
and soy sauce. Simmer all together for 10 minutes and garnish with pineapple chunks before serving.

34 • ITALY

3- to 4-pound chicken
flour
1 onion, chopped
clove garlic, minced
few sprigs parsley
1 bay leaf

4 cups strained canned
    tomatoes
salt
pepper
¼ cup sherry, chicken
    stock, or bouillon

Cut up the chicken; dust the pieces with flour and salt and

brown in olive oil. Remove the chicken from the pan. Sauté the onion, garlic, parsley sprigs, and bay leaf. Add the tomatoes, 1 teaspoon salt, and pepper and bring to a boil. Add the chicken to the sauce, add the wine, and simmer, covered, for 45 minutes or until tender. (This recipe can be varied by omitting the tomatoes and substituting 1 cup coarsely chopped green pepper or 1 cup each pitted ripe and green olives and 2 chopped anchovy fillets.)

35 • INDIA

3- to 4-pound chicken	*1 cup buttermilk*
3 onions, sliced	*1 tomato, chopped*
clove garlic, minced	*¼ cup ground almonds*
½ teaspoon powdered	*and cashew nuts*
ginger	*2 teaspoons salt*
⅛ teaspoon chili powder	*¼ cup cream*

Sauté the onions and garlic in butter; add the ginger and chili powder and cook together a couple of minutes. Add the buttermilk and tomatoes and simmer 10 minutes. Add the cutup chicken, ground nuts, and salt and simmer, covered, for 1 hour or until chicken is tender. Stir in the cream and serve.

If, in the following recipes, you do not choose to use stewing chickens, simply allow less time for cooking.

36 • ITALY

2 stewing chickens	*¼ teaspoon pepper*
½ cup butter	*¼ teaspoon nutmeg*
2 tablespoons flour	*1 package elbow macaroni*
3 cups milk	*¼ cup grated Parmesan*
½ teaspoon salt	*cheese*

Stew the chickens. Make a cream sauce by melting the butter, stirring in the flour, gradually adding the milk, and stirring until the mixture thickens slightly. Season with salt, pepper, and nutmeg. Meanwhile, cook the macaroni. Mix half the sauce with the cooked macaroni and pour inside the chickens. Place the chickens in a casserole, pour the remaining sauce over them, and sprinkle the top with grated cheese. Bake at 400° for 14 minutes until golden brown.

37 • HUNGARY

2 stewing chickens	*¼ cup flour*
prepared mustard	*2 cups cream or milk*
¼ cup butter	*½ teaspoon salt*

Cook the chickens and cut them up. Spread the pieces very lightly with mustard and arrange them in a casserole. Make a sauce by melting the butter, stirring in the flour, adding the milk and salt, and cooking till thickened. Pour the sauce over the chicken and bake at 350° for 20 minutes. If you use the milk but prefer a richer sauce stir a tablespoon or two of powdered cream into the hot sauce.

38 • SCOTLAND

2 stewing chickens	4 onions, sliced
salt	⅛ pound butter
pepper	2 cups chicken stock or
6 potatoes, cubed	consommé

Cut up the chickens and rub the pieces with salt and pepper. Place the pieces in alternate layers in a casserole with the potatoes and onions, dotting the vegetables with butter and seasoning them. Pour over the stock. Bake at 325° for 2½ hours or until chicken is tender.

39 • BELGIUM

2 stewing chickens	4 cups red wine
2 onions, chopped	½ cup tarragon vinegar
4 strips bacon, cooked	1 cup prunes
and crumbled	½ cup raisins
½ teaspoon rosemary	

Cut up the chickens and brown them with the onions in butter. Put them in a casserole with all the other ingredients. Cover and bake at 350° for 1 hour; uncover and bake 30 minutes more or until tender.

40 • INDIA

2 stewing chickens, skinned	1 teaspoon black pepper
2 onions, chopped	½ teaspoon powdered ginger
1 teaspoon salt	2 crushed cardamom seeds
2 cloves garlic, minced	or powdered cardamom
½ teaspoon ground cloves	¼ cup melted butter
½ teaspoon chili powder	

Prick the skinned chickens all over with a fork. Combine all the remaining ingredients with enough water to make a paste and rub well over the chickens inside and outside. Place the

146

chickens in a buttered casserole and bake at 350° for 2 hours or until tender, adding water to the dish when necessary.

41 • SOUTH AMERICA

2 stewing chickens	1 teaspoon pepper
2 onions, chopped	2 teaspoons nutmeg
2 cups canned tomatoes	6 raw potatoes, grated or
2 stalks celery, diced	cut very fine
1 tablespoon salt	½ cup orange juice

Cut up the chickens and brown them in butter. Add the onions and cook together a few minutes. Add the tomatoes, celery, salt, pepper, and nutmeg. Simmer 1 hour. Remove the chickens and take the meat off the bones. Mix the tomato sauce with the potatoes and orange juice. Combine with the chicken in a casserole and bake at 350° for 1 hour.

42 • CHINA

2 stewing chickens	2 cups pineapple juice
flour	¼ cup lemon juice
salt	¼ cup soy sauce
pepper	pineapple chunks

Cut the chickens into small pieces; dust pieces with flour, salt, and pepper and brown in fat. Place pieces in a casserole. Combine the juices with the soy sauce and pour over the chicken. Bake at 350° for 1½ hours. Garnish with pineapple chunks that have been floured and fried.

43 • WEST INDIES

2 stewing chickens	1 onion, chopped
¼ cup melted butter	unripe bananas
salt	chopped parsley
pepper	

Cut up the chickens and lay the pieces in a casserole. Pour over the butter and sprinkle with salt and pepper. Brown over a moderate flame. Add the onion; cover and bake at 350° for 1 hour or until tender, adding a little water as needed. Peel the bananas, cut them in quarters, and par-boil them. Lay them on top of the chicken and cook 10 minutes longer. Serve garnished with chopped parsley.

147

2 stewing chickens
flour
salt
pepper

2 eggs, beaten
1½ cups bread crumbs
¼ pound butter
3 cups sour cream

Cut up the chickens; dust the pieces with flour, salt, and pepper. Beat the eggs with a little water. Dip the chicken pieces in egg and then in bread crumbs and brown them in butter. Lay the pieces in a casserole and bake at 350° for 30 minutes. Add half the sour cream and continue baking 30 minutes more. Add the remainder of the cream and bake another 30 minutes or until tender.

45 • FRANCE

2 stewing chickens
flour
oil
1 cup pearl onions
clove garlic, minced
1 cup mushrooms

2 tablespoons tomato
    purée
½ cup veal or chicken
    stock or bouillon
½ cup white wine

Cut up the chickens. Dust pieces with flour, brown in oil, and place in a casserole. Sauté the onions, garlic, and mushrooms lightly in oil. Add to the chicken with all the other ingredients. Bake at 350° for 1½ hours or until tender. Garnish with extra onions and mushrooms if desired.

46 • FRANCE

2 stewing chickens
¾ cup chicken fat or
    butter
¾ cup flour
2 tablespoons salt
½ pound mushrooms

¼ cup red wine
2 packages frozen aspara-
    gus or fresh asparagus
grated Parmesan or
    Romano cheese
½ cup slivered almonds

Stew the chickens and hold the broth. Take the meat off the bones and cut into bite-size pieces. Melt the fat and stir in the flour; gradually add 6 cups of the chicken broth and simmer 10 minutes. Add the salt, mushrooms, wine, and cut-up chicken. Cook the asparagus and arrange in a flat baking dish. Pour the chicken mixture over the asparagus. Sprinkle with grated cheese and the almonds, which have been browned in the oven or in butter in a skillet. Bake at 400° until bubbly and cheese is melted. (This freezes well and can be reheated at 400° for 1 hour or until piping hot.)

TIP: When freezing a casserole recipe, line the casserole dish with aluminum foil before putting the meat into the dish. After the food is frozen, it can be removed from the dish, covered securely with the foil, and labeled. To reheat, slip the whole thing back into the casserole dish and place in the oven.

47 • JAVA

1 stewing chicken	½ teaspoon powdered ginger
1 onion, sliced	½ cup flour
clove garlic, minced	½ cup butter
1 teaspoon salt	1 cup chicken broth
2 tablespoons curry powder	1 cup milk

Cook the chicken and cut it up. Sauté the onion and garlic in butter with salt, curry powder, and ginger. Remove the onion; add the flour and, gradually, the broth and milk. Return the onion to the pot. Add the pieces of chicken to the sauce and simmer 10 minutes. This can be kept over hot water until ready to serve. (This is a basic curry. The original is known as *Rijsttafel*. It is a "Ten Boy Curry Dish" because it takes that many—or more—servants lined up at the table to serve it. The curry is accompanied by rice, chutney, chopped browned peanuts, chopped or thinly sliced raw onion, pickles, crumbled bacon, chopped hard-boiled egg yolks and egg whites served separately, grated coconut, India relish or piccalilli, fried bananas, dried fish, chopped cooked beets, chopped green pepper, olives, plain or pickled pineapple chunks, almonds, cashews, and raisins, all or some of which may be eaten with it.)

48 • INDIA

1 stewing chicken	1 teaspoon chili powder
3 cups grated coconut	2 tablespoons flour
3 cups milk	2 tablespoons water
½ onion, chopped	1 cup cottage cheese
clove garlic, minced	1 tomato, peeled and
1 tablespoon curry powder	chopped
1 teaspoon powdered	1 tablespoon lemon juice
ginger	

Soak the coconut in the milk for 1 hour; strain and press the milk out of the coconut. Cook the chicken and cut it into pieces. Sauté the onion and garlic in butter. Add the curry powder, salt, ginger, chili powder, and flour, which has been

149

blended with the water. Cook togeether a few minutes; then add the milk from the coconut, the cottage cheese, and the tomato. Add the pieces of chicken. Simmer 15 minutes. Stir in the lemon juice.

49 • CHINA

1 stewing chicken	½ teaspoon powdered gin-
½ onion, chopped	ger or grated fresh
clove garlic, minced	ginger root
1 teaspoon salt	1 cup chicken broth
soy sauce	1 teaspoon sugar
1 tablespoon sherry	1 tablespoon cornstarch
2 tablespoons curry powder	1 teaspoon Mei Yen, MSG,
	or Accent

Cook the chicken and cut it into small pieces. Sauté the pieces in oil with the onion, garlic, and salt for 5 minutes. Add 1 tablespoon soy sauce, sherry, curry powder, ginger, and then broth and simmer 15 minutes. Combine soy sauce with the sugar, cornstarch, and Mei Yen powder. Stir into the sauce and continue to stir until it thickens.

50 • INDIA

2 young chickens	few whole cloves
1 cup buttermilk	1 teaspoon salt
2 cloves garlic, crushed	1 tablespoon curry powder
2 onions, minced	1 teaspoon finely chopped
¼ cup butter	almonds
½ teaspoon powdered	
ginger	

Cut the chicken into pieces. Add half the garlic to the buttermilk and marinate the chicken pieces in it for 2 hours. Sauté the onions in butter; add the rest of the garlic, ginger, cloves, salt, curry powder, and almonds. Cook together 5 minutes. Combine with the chicken and buttermilk and simmer 1 hour or until tender. Serve with rice.

51 • ENGLAND

1 stewing chicken	2 cups chicken broth
1 onion, chopped	1 cup cream or milk
1 apple, chopped	¼ cup currant jelly
2 tablespoons curry powder	2 tablespoons chutney, cut up
1 teaspon salt	½ cup red wine
½ teaspoon pepper	

Cook the chicken and cut it up. Sauté the onion and apple in butter. Add the pieces of chicken, curry powder, salt, pepper, and broth (which the chicken was cooked in) and simmer 10 minutes. Stir in the cream and jelly and cook a few more minutes. Add the chutney and wine before serving.

TIP: Use curry powder according to your taste. One tablespoon is mild. If you are a curry lover, you will want at least two tablespoons in these recipes. Curry loses some of its strength when frozen in a dish. If you plan to freeze any of these recipes, double the amount of curry.

II • DUCK

1 • CHINA

2 ducks	2 whole cloves
¼ cup honey	2 tablespoons soy sauce
2 quarts water	2 teaspoons powdered
1½ cups brown sugar	ginger
1 tablespoon cinnamon	

Soak the ducks in the honey and water for at least 1 hour. Let them dry without wiping them. Melt the brown sugar with 1 cup water, salt, and cinnamon and cook until thick. Add the cloves, soy sauce, and ginger. Put the ducks in a roasting pan and pour the syrup over them. Roast at 325° for 2 hours or until tender, basting frequently. Add water to the pan if necessary while roasting.

2 • ITALY

2 ducks	clove garlic, minced
salt	1 onion, chopped
pepper	2 teaspoons chopped parsley
olive oil	1 cup white wine

Dust the ducks inside and out with salt and pepper and brown them in oil with garlic, onion, and parsley. Add the wine and cook until it evaporates. Add enough water to cover and simmer 1 hour or until tender. Skim the fat from the liquid before serving.

3 • SPAIN

2 ducks	2 tomatoes, sliced
oil	1 tablespoon paprika
2 onions, chopped	1 cup consommé

Cut the ducks into pieces and brown in oil. Add the onions and fry until golden. Add salt to taste, add the remaining ingredients, and simmer 1 hour or until tender.

III • PHEASANT

1 • GERMANY

2 pheasants	1 pound sauerkraut
2 slices bacon	1 cup white wine
butter	

Season the birds and tie a strip of bacon over the breast of each. Brown the pheasants well in butter, place them in a baking dish, and surround them with sauerkraut. Add wine and roast at 325° for 1 hour or until tender.

2 • AUSTRIA

2 pheasants	1 cup chicken broth
salt	1 cup sour cream
2 slices bacon	1 tablespoon flour
½ onion, minced	

Salt the pheasants inside and out and tie a strip of bacon over the breast of each. In a roasting pan cook the onion in butter until it is browned. Lay the birds in the pan and pour over the broth. Cover the pan and roast at 325° for 1 hour or until almost done. Blend the flour into the sour cream and add to the pan. Roast 30 minutes more.

3 • FRANCE

2 pheasants	1 tablespoon minced onion
butter	2 teaspoons chopped parsley
4 slices bacon	½ cup chicken broth
pinch nutmeg	1 cup red wine
pinch thyme	

Split the birds in half, dot them with butter, and broil them 5 minutes. Place in a roasting pan with a strip of bacon on each half; season with salt and pepper and sprinkle with nutmeg, thyme, onion, and parsley. Pour over the broth and wine. Cover and roast at 325° for 45 minutes. Uncover and roast 30 minutes more, basting frequently.

FISH AND SHELLFISH

Of all types of food, seafood probably offers the greatest variety. First there is the difference between salt- and fresh-water fish. Then there are differences within geographical areas. And local usage has created individual styles of fish cookery. In many areas of the world fish is a major item of diet, simply because it's available; anyone can go out and catch his own. In most places, too, it is relatively inexpensive. But some seafood also ranks among the world's rarities and delicacies: the sharks' fins of China, the squid (cooked in its own ink) and octopus of the Mediterranean, the unlovely ray, so lovingly cooked in France, and, of course, the imperially elegant caviar of Russia. But in spite of its diversity fish may be handled in remarkably similar culinary ways: it may be cooked whole, or filleted, or in pieces. The recipes in this section have been arranged according to these methods. Whatever your best local types of fish, they can be prepared as suggested under these divisions. Do particularly note the section on Poached Fish. This is a method often neglected in America, and one well worth practicing. Types of shellfish may vary slightly throughout the world, but the recipes given here are good whether made with Irish prawns, Chilean crayfish, or good old Maine lobsters.

I • FISH

When frying fish, do it quickly but carefully. Attractive garnishes are chopped parsley, lemon slices, and hard-boiled eggs. The greatest good fortune, of course, is to be able to pull your fish directly from a stream and drop it into a skillet with hot bacon fat. Lacking this opportunity, the following might be tried:

1 • INDIA

6 fillets of sole or 6 servings trout, halibut, or other white fish
1 teaspoon salt
½ teaspoon garlic powder or minced fresh garlic
½ teaspoon black pepper

¼ teaspoon chili powder
pinch of ground cumin (optional)
butter
½ cup buttermilk
1 tablespoon lemon juice

Rub the pieces of fish with a mixture of the salt, garlic, pepper, chili powder, and cumin. Brown them in butter. Add the buttermilk and lemon juice and simmer until the liquid is absorbed.

2 • AUSTRIA

6 fillets of sole or 6 servings trout, halibut, or other white fish
½ cup oil

3 onions, sliced
6 slices lemon
3 tomatoes, quartered

Heat the oil in a skillet. Add the onions and cook until they are yellow. Salt the fish and lay it in the skillet with a lemon slice on each piece. Add the tomatoes to the pan. Cook 10 minutes or until fish is done.

3 • CHINA

6 fillets of sole or 6 servings trout, halibut, or other white fish
sesame or peanut oil
¼ cup soy sauce
6 tablespoons sherry
½ teaspoon powdered ginger

¼ cup finely chopped onion
1 tablespoon Mei Yen, MSG, or Accent
pepper
½ cup chicken stock or bouillon

Rub the fish with salt and brown in oil. Combine all the other

154

ingredients and pour over the fish. Cook 10 minutes or until the fish is done.

4 • KOREA

6 fillets of sole or 6 servings trout, halibut, or
  other white fish
2 tablespoons sesame seeds
¼ cup soy sauce

1 tablespoon oil
3 green onions or scallions
  with greens, chopped
pepper

Put the sesame seeds in a skillet and toast until brown and crackling. Crush them. Combine the soy sauce, sesame seeds, oil, green onions, and pepper. Dip the pieces of fish in this mixture. Brown the fish in additional oil.

5 • PHILIPPINES

6 fillets of sole or 6 servings trout, halibut, or
  other white fish
1 onion, chopped

1 green pepper, chopped
clove garlic, minced
¾ cup vinegar
¼ cup brown sugar

Brown the fish in oil; remove from the pan and keep warm. Sauté the onion, green pepper, and garlic lightly. Add the vinegar and brown sugar and simmer a few minutes. Pour over the fish and serve.

6 • JAPAN

6 fillets of sole or 6 servings trout, halibut, or
  other white fish
1 cup soy sauce

½ teaspoon powdered
  ginger
½ cup sugar

Mix the soy sauce, ginger, and sugar. Marinate the fish in this mixture 1 hour. Remove the fish from the marinade and brown in oil.

7 • ITALY

6 fillets of sole or 6 servings trout, halibut, or
  other white fish
flour
salt

olive oil
¼ cup raisins
¼ cup chopped nuts
2 onions, chopped
1 cup vinegar

Sprinkle the fish with flour and salt and brown in oil with the raisins and nuts. Remove the fish from the pan, brown the onions, and return the fish with the vinegar. Let stand 1 hour. The fish may be reheated before serving if you prefer it hot.

6 fillets of sole or 6 serv-
    ings trout, halibut, or
    other white fish

¼ cup slivered blanched
    almonds
butter

Brown the fish in a generous amount of foaming butter. Remove the fish from the pan. Brown the slivered almonds in the butter and pour over the fish. (Instead of almonds, you can use sesame seeds: first toast them in a skillet, shaking the pan until they are brown and crackling.)

6 fillets of sole or 6 serv-
    ings trout, halibut, or
    other white fish
1 cup drained canned
    tomatoes

clove garlic, minced
¼ teaspoon tarragon

Brown the fish in butter and remove from the pan. Sauté the tomatoes, garlic, and tarragon a few minutes and pour over the fish.

6 fillets of sole or 6 serv-
    ings trout, halibut, or
    other white fish
butter

juice 1 lemon
2 tablespoons chopped
    parsley

Brown the fish in butter and remove from the pan. Add ¼ pound butter to pan; cook until it is light brown. Add the lemon juice and parsley. Pour over the fish.

Poached fish has a delicate texture and subtle flavor. Its success depends on handling. The fish should be slipped carefully into a seasoned bath and poached gently. It should be removed from the bath with the same kind of care. The result will be well worth the bit of trouble. Appropriate and colorful garnishes are lemon slices, chopped parsley, capers, hard-boiled eggs, and mint. There are many good sauces for poached fish: melted butter with lemon juice and a dash of herbs, a little chopped cucumber in melted butter, 2 tablespoons of flour worked with 2 tablespoons of butter into 4 cups of stock and strained before serving, and Hollandaise, Béarnaise, and tartar sauces.

11 • RUSSIA

2 pounds fish (like had-
    dock)
4 onions, chopped
¼ cup tomato sauce

2 bay leaves
few olives, chopped
1 pickle, sliced
few capers (optional)

Sauté the onions lightly in butter; add the tomato sauce and
simmer a few minutes. Add the bay leaves, olives, sliced
pickle, and capers, then carefully slip in the fish. Poach gently
until the fish is cooked, adding water if necessary. Garnish
with lemon.

12 • HUNGARY

1 large pike or similar fish
2 cups milk
1 teaspoon salt

3 tablespoons flour
3 tablespoons butter

Gently poach the fish in milk with salt about 10 minutes or
until cooked. Remove the fish from the liquid. Work the butter and flour together and stir into the milk, cooking until
thickened. To serve, pour sauce over fish.

13 • HUNGARY

2 to 4 trout
2 cups water
½ cup wine vinegar
½ teaspoon salt

bay leaf
few peppercorns
1 onion, sliced

Combine the water, vinegar, salt, bay leaf, peppercorns, and
onion. Poach the fish gently in this liquid for 10 minutes or
until cooked. Cool the fish in the liquid. Serve with mayonnaise or tartar sauce.

14 • WEST INDIES

2 to 4 fish or swordfish
    steaks
lemon
2 cups water
1 teaspoon salt

few whole cloves
2 teaspoons chopped parsley
¼ teaspoon thyme
½ teaspoon cinnamon
few peppercorns

If you are in an area where it is available, try flying fish for
this. Rub the thick slices of fish with lemon. Combine all the
other ingredients and poach the fish slices in this liquid for
10 minutes or until they are done.

15 • INDIA

4 to 6 servings of halibut,
  pike, or whitefish
2 cups water
1 teaspoon salt
juice 1 lemon
bay leaf
2 peppercorns

1 tablespoon chopped
  onion
2 tablespoons butter
2 tablespoons flour
2 teaspoons curry powder
¼ cup milk

Gently poach the fish in the water with salt, lemon juice,
bay leaf, and peppercorns. When fish is cooked, remove and
keep warm. Brown the onion in butter, add the flour, and
gradually stir in 1 cup of the fish stock. Simmer a few minutes until thickened. Add the curry powder and milk; stir
well and pour over the fish.

16 • GERMANY

6 servings halibut, pike, or
  whitefish
¼ pound butter
1 cup boiling water

1 small head cabbage, cut
  up
4 potatoes, sliced
2 tablespoons caraway
  seeds

Put butter, water, cabbage, potatoes, caraway seeds, and salt
in a pan and simmer 20 minutes. Season the fish with salt
and pepper and place it on top of the vegetables in the pan.
Cover and simmer gently 30 minutes or until done.

17 • GERMANY

2 pounds carp
2 cans beer
1 lemon, sliced
few peppercorns
bay leaf

1 onion, chopped
1 tablespoon flour
1 tablespoon butter
1 tablespoon sugar

Cut the carp into serving pieces; sprinkle with salt and let
stand for a while. Put the fish into a pan with the beer,
lemon slices, peppercorns, bay leaf, and onion. Simmer 10
minutes or until done. Remove the fish and keep warm.
Strain the liquid. Work the flour and butter together and add
to the liquid with the sugar. Cook, stirring, until thickened.
Serve over the fish.

18 • JAPAN

4 fillets of fish like bream
    or carp, if available
1/4 cup soy sauce
2 tablespoons sherry or
    sake

salt
pepper
1 package frozen cauli-
    flower
1 package frozen peas

Cut each fillet into 4 pieces. Poach gently in enough water to cover with soy sauce, sherry, salt, and pepper for 10 minutes. Remove the fish. Add the vegetables to the liquid (you may use fresh vegetables if you prefer) and cook 10 minutes or until they are tender. Return the fish to the pan just long enough to heat through. Strain off the liquid and serve the fish and vegetables with rice.

19 • FRANCE

6 servings of sole or similar
    fish
2 cups water
2 cups wine, white or red
1 teaspoon salt
1 onion, sliced
1 whole clove

bay leaf
1/2 teaspoon thyme
1 teaspoon chopped parsley
1 teaspoon chopped celery
    leaves
few peppercorns

Instead of the wine and water, you can use 3 cups of water combined with 1/2 cup vinegar. Combine the liquids (whichever you decide to use) with the salt, onion, clove, bay leaf, thyme, parsley, celery leaves, and peppercorns and simmer together 20 to 30 minutes. Gently poach the fish in this liquid until done.

Baking is one of the easiest ways to prepare fish in large quantities. And aluminum foil makes a good cover for your baking dish.

20 • FRANCE

1 whole salmon
salt
pepper
1/4 cup butter
1/4 teaspoon thyme
clove garlic, minced

1 cucumber, sliced with
    skin
1 small onion, sliced
bay leaf
2 tablespoons chopped
    parsley
2 cups cream

Melt the butter in a baking dish. Lay the salmon in it and sprinkle the fish with salt, pepper, thyme, and garlic. Lay the slices of cucumber and onion on top. Add the bay leaf and parsley and pour over the cream. Cover and bake at 350°. The meat will easily lift away from the bones for serving. A 3-pound salmon will take about 45 minutes. This is good either hot or cold.

21 • FRANCE

6 fillets of sole or 2 pounds
  of any white fish
juice of ½ lemon
½ cup white wine
bay leaf (optional)

1 teaspoon basil (optional)
onion, sliced thin and
  sautéed (optional)
bit of minced garlic

Sprinkle the fish with salt and pepper and place it in a buttered baking dish. Sprinkle with lemon juice; add the wine and other seasonings. Cover and bake at 350° until done.

22 • ALASKA

1 whole salmon, boned
2 cups bread crumbs
3 tablespoons minced
  onion
2 tablespoons chopped
  parsley

salt
pepper
1 teaspoon sage
1 cup stock
6 slices bacon

Split the fish down the center. Make a stuffing of all the other ingredients except the bacon. Tie or skewer the fish closed. Lay it in a buttered baking dish with the strips of bacon on top. Bake at 350° until done. A 3-pound salmon will take about 45 minutes. This is good hot or cold.

23 • SOUTH SEA ISLANDS

6 slices any white-meat fish
1½ cups cream

2 cups grated coconut
salt

Combine the cream and coconut and bring to a boil. Allow to cool. Strain, reserving the liquid and discarding the squeezed-out pulp. Sprinkle the fish with salt and place it in a buttered baking dish. Pour the coconut cream over it and bake at 350° for 30 minutes or until done. (A whole fish may be used and baked longer.)

6 fillets of any white-meat
    fish
2 onions, chopped
½ pound butter
2 cups bread crumbs

3 egg yolks, beaten
½ cup sherry
2 tablespoons cream
¼ teaspoon nutmeg

Brown onions in half the butter; add the crumbs and stir to-gether. Remove from heat; stir in the egg yolks, half the sherry, the cream, and the nutmeg; and season to taste. Place a spoonful of this stuffing on each fillet; roll each up and secure with a toothpick. Melt the remaining butter in a baking dish, place the rolled-up fillets in it, and add the rest of the sherry. Bake at 350° for 30 minutes or until done.

25 • INDIA

6 fillets of any white-meat
    fish
½ teaspoon powdered ginger
¼ teaspoon chili powder

pinch turmeric (optional)
½ cup grated coconut
salt

Place the fillets in a greased baking dish. Add all the other ingredients and bake at 350° for 30 minutes or until done. Serve this with curried rice: stir 2 tablespoons melted butter blended with 1 tablespoon curry powder into 2 cups cooked rice.

26 • POLAND

1 whole white-meat fish
    large enough for 6
    servings
2 onions, chopped
4 stalks celery, chopped
1 cup chopped mushrooms

1 large loaf bread
3 apples, chopped
1 teaspoon sugar
½ teaspoon thyme
¼ cup butter

Sauté the onions, celery, and mushrooms together in butter. Moisten the bread with water and squeeze out. Combine it with the sautéed vegetables, chopped apples, sugar, thyme, butter, salt, and pepper. Stuff the fish lightly with this mix-ture and tie or skewer it. Brush it with melted butter and bake at 350° for 1 hour or until done.

27 • SPAIN

2 pounds fish fillets
½ pound butter
2 tablespoons flour
3 onions, chopped and
    sautéed
½ cup white wine
1 cup water

2 teaspoons grated baking
    chocolate
salt
pepper
1 cup whole cooked mush-
    rooms

Melt the butter in a baking dish. Stir in the flour; add the onions and fish. Add wine, water, chocolate, salt, and pepper. Cover and bake at 350° for 30 minutes or until done. Add the mushrooms 10 minutes before the fish is done.

28 • AUSTRIA

3 to 4 pounds of fish fillets
    (like sole)
2 cups milk
1 tablespoon lemon juice

salt
anchovy fillets (optional)
butter

Soak the fillets in milk. Dry them and sprinkle with lemon juice and salt. Lay the anchovies on the fish fillets. Melt the butter in a baking dish, add the fillets, and bake at 350° for 30 minutes or until done. (The Viennese serve this with anchovy butter: rub 2 anchovies through a strainer and add to 4 tablespoons lightly browned butter mixed with 1 teaspoon water.)

Casserole dishes are economical and wonderful for using leftover fish. They are also the answer to what to do when your fisherman brings a heterogeneous catch. These casserole dishes freeze well; in fact, they are even better when reheated.

29 • CHILE

2 pounds fish
3 potatoes, boiled and
    sliced
3 tomatoes, sliced
croutons

3 onions, sliced and
    sautéed
butter
1 cup milk
3 hard-boiled eggs,
    chopped

(In Chile eels are popularly used for this dish.) Season the fish and place it in layers in a casserole with the potatoes, tomatoes, croutons, onions, and dots of butter. Pour over the milk; cover and bake at 350° for 30 minutes or until fish is cooked. Garnish with chopped eggs.

2 pounds fish
3 cups sauerkraut
3 onions, sliced
salt
1 small can tomato sauce
2 cups sliced mushrooms

few stuffed olives
bread crumbs
capers (optional)
grated Parmesan cheese
butter

(This is especially good with salmon, either canned or fresh.)
Butter a casserole and make a layer of the sauerkraut on the
bottom. Toss together the broken-up fish, onions, salt, tomato
sauce, mushrooms, olives, bread crumbs, and capers. Make
a layer of this on top of the sauerkraut. Sprinkle with cheese
and dot with butter. Bake at 350° for 30 minutes. If leftover
fish is used, bake just until top is browned and dish is heated
through.

31 • PHILIPPINES

2 pounds fish
flour
salt
oil
clove garlic, minced
1 teaspoon powdered ginger
6 green onions or scallions,
    sliced

2 green peppers, shredded
⅓ cup vinegar
3 tablespoons sugar
2 tablespoons soy sauce
½ cup water
1 tablespoon cornstarch
lime slices

(You might try making this with red snapper.) Dust the fish
with flour and salt and sauté lightly in oil. Place in a baking
dish. Combine the garlic, ginger, green onions, green peppers,
vinegar, sugar, soy sauce, and water and simmer together a
few minutes. Dissolve the cornstarch in 2 tablespoons water
and stir into the sauce, cooking until clear. Pour over the fish.
Chill and serve cold with slices of lime.

32 • FRANCE

2 pounds fish
1 onion, chopped
minced garlic (optional)
¼ cup butter
2 tablespoons flour
½ cup white wine
½ cup medium cream

1 teaspoon mixed herbs
    (thyme, parsley, and
    crushed bay leaf)
6 tomatoes, chopped
1 eggplant (optional)
½ cup sliced mushrooms
    (optional)
bread crumbs
grated cheese

(Sole is good for this recipe.) Sauté the onions and garlic in butter until yellow, stir in the flour, and gradually add the wine. Stir in cream slowly and simmer 5 minutes. Add the herbs and tomatoes. Meanwhile, slice the eggplant, soak in salted water, drain, and sauté. Butter a casserole. Lay the eggplant and mushrooms on the bottom. Lay the fish in next, season to taste, and pour over the sauce. Sprinkle with bread crumbs and grated cheese and dot with butter. Cover and bake at 350° for 30 minutes, uncovering for last few minutes to brown top.

33 • HUNGARY

2 pounds fish	1 cup sour cream
3 potatoes, sliced very thin and parboiled	2 cups sliced mushrooms

(You might try brill for this if it is available.) Butter a casserole and line it with half the potatoes. Pour over half the sour cream. Continue with a layer of mushrooms, the rest of the potatoes, and then the fish. Season to taste and add the rest of the cream. Cover and bake at 350° for 45 minutes or until done.

34 • SPAIN

2 pounds fish	¼ teaspoon saffron
4 tomatoes, chopped	(optional)
clove garlic, minced	bay leaf
olive oil	½ teaspoon chili powder
2 green peppers, shredded	2 cups white wine
2 onions, sliced	1 cup water
2 teaspoons salt	1 cup uncooked rice
1 tablespoon paprika	

(If you can get fresh tuna, try it for this.) Sauté the tomatoes and garlic in oil a few minutes. Add the green peppers, onions, salt, paprika, and saffron and simmer 20 minutes. Sauté the fish in oil; add the bay leaf, chili powder, wine, water, tomato mixture, and rice. Cover and simmer 30 minutes or bake in a casserole at 350° until rice is cooked.

35 • RUSSIA

2 pounds fish	pepper
pastry dough	nutmeg
4 cups cooked rice	½ cup sour cream
salt	

(Russians like this made with very thin slices of smoked fish. You might try salmon.) Butter a casserole and line with pastry dough. Fill with alternate layers of rice and fish sprinkled with salt, pepper, and nutmeg. Pour over the cream and cover with pastry dough. Bake at 400° for 30 minutes or until browned.

36 • SOUTH AMERICA

2 pounds fish
3 onions, sliced
½ cup olive oil
3 tomatoes, chopped
½ cup water
2 teaspoons salt
pepper

½ teaspoon saffron (optional)
bay leaf
3 potatoes, boiled and cubed or in balls
2 green peppers, shredded
1 cup peas
strips of pimiento

(This can be made with cod.) Sauté the onions in oil; add the tomatoes, water, salt, pepper, saffron, and bay leaf; and simmer 10 minutes. Arrange the fish in a buttered casserole with the potatoes, green peppers, and peas around it. Pour over the sauce and garnish with pimiento strips. Cover and bake at 350° for 30 minutes.

37 • INDIA

2 cups salmon or haddock
2 onions, chopped
1 green pepper, chopped
butter
1 tablespoon curry powder

½ teaspoon salt
¼ teaspoon pepper
2 hard-boiled eggs
2 cups cooked rice

(This is a well-known dish called kedgeree, and I was brought up on it. My mother omitted the curry when we were children. It can be made with cooked and flaked or canned fish.) Sauté the onions and green pepper in butter until the onion is golden. Add the curry powder, salt, pepper, chopped egg whites, fish, and rice with 2 tablespoons butter. Mix well and heat through. Serve piled high with the egg yolks sieved on top.

Fish is excellent for certain kinds of luncheon, late-supper, and buffet dishes. The next four recipes—#38 through #41 —are such dishes.

6 fillets of sole
3 cups water
½ cup vinegar
salt
butter
1 cup shrimp, shelled and
    cleaned

2 teaspoons chopped parsley
¼ cup heavy cream
6 large potatoes, baked
¼ cup flour
1 cup milk
2 tablespoons red wine
pepper

Poach the sole in water with the vinegar and 1 teaspoon salt. Melt 1 tablespoon butter; add the shrimp, chopped parsley, and cream; and cook a few minutes. Slit the potatoes and remove a little of the pulp. Pour some of the shrimp mixture into each. Lay a folded fillet on top of each. Melt ¼ cup butter, stir in the flour, and gradually add milk, wine, salt, and pepper. Simmer until thickened. Pour over the stuffed potatoes. Reheat in the oven or under the broiler if necessary. Garnish with parsley.

2 pounds cod, cooked and
    flaked
¼ cup butter
¼ cup flour
2 cups milk or 1½ cups
    milk plus ½ cup white
    wine

6 potatoes, sliced and pan-
    fried
1 pound bacon, cooked
3 hard-boiled eggs, quar-
    tered
parsley

Melt the butter, stir in the flour, and gradually add the milk. Cook 10 minutes and season to taste. Combine with the fish and pour into the center of a hot platter. Surround with the fried potatoes and crisp bacon. Garnish with the eggs and parsley. (In Spain people make a dish similar to this. They sauté 4 sliced onions in butter with plenty of garlic along with the potatoes and add this mixture to the fish, using ½ cup white wine instead of the sauce.)

6 thick slices salmon
1 cup white wine
1 cup vinegar
1 teaspoon tarragon
dash Worcestershire sauce

salt
pepper
¼ cup tomato paste
grated Parmesan cheese

Marinate the fish 1 hour or more in a combination of the wine, vinegar, tarragon, Worcestershire sauce, salt, and pepper. Remove the fish from the marinade, spread it with tomato paste, and lay it in a buttered baking dish. Pour over the marinade and sprinkle with grated cheese. Bake at 350° for 30 minutes or until done. (This may be served with Hollandaise sauce.)

41 • SOUTH SEA ISLANDS

6 fish fillets, cooked and flaked	½ cup hot milk
1 can dry-pack sweet potatoes	1 egg, beaten
	flour
	fat for deep frying

Mash the sweet potatoes with the milk and season to taste. Add the egg and fish and shape into small balls. Dip in flour and fry in deep fat.

II • SHELLFISH

1 • SPAIN

6 lobsters, split	bay leaf
6 onions, chopped	½ teaspoon thyme
1 cup oil	1 teaspoon oregano
1 teaspoon chili powder	1 teaspoon chopped parsley
3 teaspoons salt	
1 cup brandy	1 square baking chocolate
¼ cup tomato paste	1 teaspoon saffron
3 cups chicken stock or bouillon	clove garlic, minced

Remove the lobster meat from the shells, reserving the liver and coral. Brown the onions in oil; put them in a baking dish with the lobster meat, chili powder, salt, and brandy. Set the brandy aflame. When the brandy stops burning, add the tomato paste, stock, bay leaf, thyme, oregano, and parsley. Bake at 350° for 30 minutes. Pound the liver, coral, chocolate, saffron, and garlic to a smooth paste. Mix with a little sauce from the lobster. Stir over low heat for a few minutes, add to the lobster mixture, and serve. (This is an ideal "company" dish because, although it takes time to prepare, it can be made, frozen in its serving dish, and reheated when ready to serve.)

6 lobsters, split
2 onions, chopped
¼ pound mushrooms,
    chopped
1 tablespoon flour
½ cup chicken stock or
    bouillon

1 teaspoon salt
cayenne pepper
½ cup bread crumbs
½ cup grated cheese
butter

Remove the lobster meat from the shells and save the shells. Cut the meat into small pieces. Sauté the onions and mushrooms in butter; stir in the flour; and gradually add the stock, lobster meat, salt, and pepper. Cook 10 minutes. Place the filling in the shells; sprinkle with bread crumbs and grated cheese and dot with butter. Bake or broil until browned.

3 • JAVA

4 lobster tails
1 cup diced celery
1 cup peas
1 cup diced carrots
1 cup shredded cabbage
4 green onions or scallions,
    sliced thin

¼ cup oil
1 teaspoon salt
1 teaspoon sugar
1 tablespoon soy sauce
1 cup chicken stock or
    bouillon

Boil lobster tails 10 minutes and rinse in cold water; remove the meat from the shells and cut it up. Fry the vegetables in oil 10 minutes. Add the lobster meat and remaining ingredients and simmer 5 minutes.

4 • ITALY

6 lobsters, split
butter
1½ dozen oysters
3 anchovies, chopped

1 cup bread crumbs
½ teaspoon dry mustard
pepper

Dot the lobsters with butter and broil until done. Place 3 oysters on each lobster half and sprinkle with a mixture of the anchovies, bread crumbs, mustard, and pepper. Dot with butter and broil 10 minutes.

3 lobsters, split
salt
pepper
butter
3 green onions or scallions,
    chopped
½ cup white wine

½ tablespoon minced onion
2 cups cream sauce
grated Parmesan cheese
2 teaspoons chopped parsley
1 teaspoon dry mustard
2 tablespoons whipped
    cream (optional)

Season the lobster with salt and pepper and dot with butter.
place on an oiled pan and bake at 400° for 20 minutes. Remove the meat and reserve the shells. Combine 2 tablespoons
butter, the green onions, and the wine and cook until the
liquid is reduced to one-fourth the original amount. Sauté
the minced onion in ½ tablespoon butter until golden and
add to the cream sauce with 1 tablespoon grated Parmesan
cheese. Add the cooked green onions, parsley, and mustard
and blend well. Mix three-fourths of this sauce with the
lobster meat and fill the shells. Mix the remaining sauce
with the whipped cream. Pour on top of the stuffed lobsters,
sprinkle with grated Parmesan cheese, and brown under the
broiler. (This can be prepared except for the last step—topping with sauce and grated cheese—and frozen. When ready
to serve, fix with toppings and reheat.)

6 • FRANCE

3 lobsters, split
butter
salt
pepper
2 tablespoons flour
2 cups chicken stock

½ cup sherry
1 tablespoon Worcestershire
    sauce
1 teaspoon paprika
pieces cheese

Brush the lobster with melted butter, sprinkle with salt and
pepper, and bake on an oiled pan at 400° for 20 minutes.
Remove the meat from the shells and reserve the shells. Melt
2 tablespoons butter, stir in the flour, gradually add the stock,
and cook until thickened. Add the sherry, Worcestershire
sauce, paprika, salt, pepper, and lobster meat. Pour into the
shells, top with pieces of cheese, and return to the oven until
bubbly and crisp.

169

7 • CHINA

6 lobsters, split
2 teaspoons salt
2 teaspoons Mei Yen,
   MSG, or Accent
clove garlic, minced
pepper

1 cup sherry
1 teaspoon powdered ginger
   or grated fresh
   ginger root
2 tablespoons soy sauce
1 cup peanut oil

Remove the lobster meat from the shells and place it in a baking dish. Mix all the ingredients except the oil and pour over the lobster. Cover and bake at 350° for 20 minutes or until cooked through. Heat the oil and pour over the lobster before serving.

8 • FRANCE

2 cups cooked lobster
   meat, cut up
¼ cup butter
¼ cup flour
2 cups milk
½ cup chopped almonds

2 egg yolks
2 tablespoons red wine
salt
pepper
6 slices toast, buttered
paprika

Melt the butter, stir in the flour, gradually add the milk, and simmer 10 minutes. Mix the lobster, almonds, egg yolks, and wine together and add to the sauce. Season with salt and pepper. Heat through. Serve on hot, buttered toast and sprinkle with paprika.

9 • JAPAN

2 pounds large shrimp
2 eggs, beaten
1 cup flour

½ teaspoon salt
1 cup milk
fat for deep frying

Clean and shell the shrimp, slit them down the back, and pound them open (this makes them "butterfly" shrimp.) Dip in a batter made of the eggs, flour, salt, and milk. Fry in deep fat until golden, about 3 or 4 minutes. (This dish may be served with the usual shrimp sauces or with chutney, lemon, or pineapple chunks.)

10 • CHINA

2 pounds large shrimp
soy sauce
2 eggs, beaten

flour
fat for deep frying

Shell and clean the shrimp. Dip them in soy sauce, in egg, in flour, and again in egg. Fry in deep fat until golden, about 3 or 4 minutes. (This dish may be served with shrimp sauce, chutney, lemon, or pineapple chunks.)

11 • FRANCE

2 pounds cooked shrimp
½ pound butter, melted
¼ teaspoon thyme
½ teaspoon tarragon
clove garlic, minced

½ cup red wine
1 cup fine bread crumbs
salt
chopped parsley

Combine all the ingredients except the shrimp and parsley. Butter 6 individual casseroles. Fill them with alternate layers of the bread crumb mixture and the shrimp, ending with the crumb mixture. Sprinkle the tops with parsley. Bake at 400° for 15 minutes or until brown.

12 • NORWAY

2 cups cooked shrimp
1 tablespoon butter
1 tablespoon rice or potato
   flour

1 cup milk
salt
pepper
croutons

Melt the butter, add the flour, and stir in the milk. Season with salt and pepper and simmer until thickened. Add the shrimp and heat through. Serve with croutons.

13 • ENGLAND

1½ cups flaked cooked
   crab meat
6 firm tomatoes
2 hard-boiled eggs
2 tablespoons butter
1 teaspoon salt

1 teaspoon prepared mustard
2 tablespoons lemon juice
2 eggs, beaten
¼ cup cream
grated Parmesan cheese

Hollow out the tomatoes and salt them. Mix the hard-boiled egg yolks with butter, salt, mustard, and lemon juice. Add the chopped egg whites and the beaten eggs mixed with cream. Mix in the crab meat. Stuff the tomatoes with this mixture and place them on a buttered pan. Bake at 400° for 10 minutes, sprinkle with cheese, and return to oven long enough to brown the top.

1½ pounds crab meat
3 tablespoons butter
3 tablespoons flour
2 cups milk

1 onion, minced
4 teaspoons chopped parsley
½ teaspoon thyme
toast fingers

Melt the butter, stir in the flour, and gradually add the milk. Season to taste. Add the crab meat, onion, parsley, and thyme and cook gently 15 minutes. Serve on toast fingers.

15 • HAWAII

2 pounds cleaned shrimp,
    lobster, or crab meat
2 cups shredded coconut
3¼ cups milk
½ cup butter
½ cup flour

1 tablespoon minced onion
2 tablespoons curry powder
1 teaspoon salt
1 teaspoon powdered ginger
2 tablespoons lemon juice

Soak the coconut in 2 cups milk for 1 hour. Simmer together 10 minutes; strain and reserve the coconut milk. Melt the butter and add the flour and onion, stirring until smooth. Gradually add 1¼ cups milk and the coconut milk and stir until thickened. Add the shellfish, curry powder, salt, ginger, and lemon juice and simmer 30 minutes.

16 • ENGLAND

2 pounds cleaned shrimp,
    lobster, or crab meat
¼ cup butter
¼ cup flour
2 cups milk

1 teaspoon salt
½ teaspoon pepper
2 tablespoons curry powder
2 egg yolks (optional)

Melt the butter, stir in the flour, and gradually add the milk and seasonings. Add the egg yolks if you like a richer sauce. Stir in the shellfish and cook in a double boiler over hot water until heated through.

17 • JAVA

2 pounds cleaned shrimp,
    lobster, or crab meat
½ cup shredded coconut
½ cup milk
½ onion, minced
butter
2 tablespoons curry powder

1 teaspoon chili powder
½ teaspoon powdered ginger
½ teaspoon salt
¼ teaspoon pepper
1 cup bouillon
1 tablespoon lemon juice

Soak the coconut in milk for 1 hour. Simmer 10 minutes; strain and reserve the coconut milk. Cook the onion in butter until golden; add the curry powder, chili powder, ginger, salt, pepper, shellfish, and bouillon. Simmer 20 minutes. Add the coconut milk and lemon juice and heat through.

18 • FRANCE

1 dozen oysters
2 tablespoons butter
2 teaspoons chopped parsley
½ teaspoon thyme

2 hard-boiled eggs, chopped
bread crumbs
lemon wedges

Remove the oysters from the shells, reserving the shells and liquid. Put the oysters in a pan with the liquid, butter, parsley, thyme, and chopped eggs and simmer 5 minutes. Return to the shells, sprinkle with crumbs, dot with butter, and bake at 375° until light brown. Serve with lemon wedges.

19 • FRANCE

2 pounds scallops, washed
    and drained
salt
pepper
1 cup mushrooms,
    chopped fine

½ cup chopped parsley
bread crumbs
butter
¼ cup white wine
lemon wedges

If the scallops are large, cut them up. Divide them into 6 baking shells and season with salt and pepper. Sprinkle each with mushrooms, parsley, and bread crumbs. Dot with butter and pour a little wine on each. Place the shells on a baking sheet and bake at 400° for 15 minutes or until browned. Serve with lemon wedges.

9

RICE
PILAFS AND RISOTTOS

Rice is used in many countries of the world and is a felicitous complement to both meat and fish. In cooking rice, I follow the practice of a French cook we once had. I cook the rice in stock—either consommé or chicken broth— the kind of stock being determined by whether the rice is to be served with meat or fowl. Stock adds richness to the rice. Sometimes I make fried rice, in butter or oil, with a little onion or whatever other additions I am inspired to try at the moment. I was brought up on the East Indian dish kedgeree, which is a tempting combination of salmon, rice, eggs, green peppers and curry. Rice probably reaches its apogee in the Javanese Rijsttaffel (which means, literally, "rice table"). It is served elaborately, with considerable ceremony. A rice dish is passed first, and then Javanese boys—from ten to twenty, depending on the number of side dishes—serve the exotic accouterments: highly seasoned meat, fish, fowl, vegetable and fruit delicacies.

174

1 • TURKEY

2 pounds boned lamb
¼ pound butter
sugar
1 cup uncooked rice

4 tomatoes, chopped
2 cups lamb broth or
    consommé
yogurt or cottage cheese

Cut the lamb into ½-inch cubes and brown in a little butter with a pinch of sugar. Remove from the pan. Add the remaining butter and rice and fry until brown. Return the meat to the pan, add the tomatoes and broth, season to taste, and simmer 20 minutes or until tender. Serve with yogurt or cheese on the side.

2 • ITALY

1 onion, chopped
clove garlic, minced
butter
1 pound Italian- or
    Polish-type sausage
¼ cup sliced mushrooms
4 tomatoes, peeled and

    chopped
1 can tomato paste
salt
pepper
4 cups cooked rice
grated Parmesan or
    Romano cheese

Sauté the onion and garlic in butter until golden. Dice the sausage, add it to the onion, and brown it. Add the mushrooms, tomatoes, tomato paste, salt, and pepper and cook 20 minutes, adding a little water if necessary. To serve, pour it over the hot rice and sprinkle with grated cheese.

3 • FRANCE

3 cups chicken broth
bay leaf
little minced garlic
    (optional)
salt
1 cup uncooked rice

2 tablespoons butter
1 tablespoon curry powder
    (optional)
2 or 3 egg yolks, beaten
    (optional)

Bring the broth to a boil with the bay leaf, garlic, and salt. Add the rice and cook about 20 minutes or until the broth is absorbed. Stir in the butter, curry powder, and egg yolks. Pack tightly into a well-buttered ring mold and turn out on a serving dish. (The center of the ring can be filled with creamed chicken, fish, or vegetable. The top of the dish can be sprinkled with grated Parmesan or Gruyère cheese and lightly browned under the broiler.)

4 • SPAIN

1 onion, chopped
clove garlic, minced
butter
2 frying chickens, cut up
bay leaf

6 tomatoes, quartered
1 green pepper, chopped
¼ teaspoon saffron
   (optional)
2 cups uncooked rice

Cook the onion and garlic in butter until golden; add the chicken and brown. Add the bay leaf and enough water to cover. Simmer 20 minutes. Combine the chicken pieces, 5 cups of the broth it was cooked in, tomatoes, green pepper, saffron, and rice and simmer 20 minutes or until the broth is absorbed. (For a buffet dish, garnish with hard-boiled eggs, fried parsley sprigs, pimiento strips, peas, and asparagus.)

5 • IRAQ

1 stewing chicken
1 cup uncooked rice
butter

1 cup slivered almonds
cinnamon or nutmeg
chopped fresh mint

Cut up the chicken, stew it, and reserve the broth. Cook the rice in 3 cups of the chicken broth, salted to taste, until the broth is absorbed (about 20 minutes). Lightly brown the pieces of chicken in butter; add the almonds and let them brown. Toss the rice and chicken together with 2 good dashes of cinnamon or nutmeg. Serve sprinkled with mint. (In Iraq practically everything is cooked in the grease of a fat-tailed sheep. You'll probably prefer butter.)

6 • ENGLAND

1 stewing chicken
4 strips bacon
1 onion, chopped
1 green pepper, chopped
1 cup uncooked rice
salt

pepper
2 cups drained canned or
   diced fresh tomatoes
1 tablespoon Worcestershire
   sauce
¼ cup red wine

Cut up the chicken, stew it, and reserve the broth. Cook the bacon and drain it. Cook the onion and green pepper in the bacon fat, add the rice and brown it lightly, and remove the excess fat. Add 3 cups of the broth from the chicken, salt, pepper, tomatoes, and Worcestershire sauce and cook 20 minutes or until broth is absorbed. Add the chicken pieces and crumbled bacon; heat through. Add the wine and serve.

176

7 • WEST INDIES

2 frying chickens
flour
olive oil
2 onions, chopped
2 cups drained canned or

diced fresh tomatoes
1 teaspoon thyme
2 teaspoons sugar
3 cups chicken broth
1 cup uncooked rice

Cut the chickens into pieces, season, dip in flour, and brown in oil. Remove the chicken and brown the onions. Add the tomatoes, thyme, sugar, chicken, and half the broth and simmer 30 minutes. Add the rice and the remaining broth and cook 20 minutes or until broth is absorbed. (This can be garnished with seedless raisins, olives, or chopped peanuts browned quickly in a little oil.)

8 • IRAN

1 stewing chicken
2 cups uncooked rice
peel of 2 oranges,
    cut in strips
¼ cup blanched almonds or

pistachio nuts
2 teaspoons sugar
¼ teaspoon saffron
    (optional)
½ cup melted butter

Cup up the chicken, cook it, and reserve the broth. Cook the rice in 6 cups of broth 20 minutes or until the broth is absorbed. Boil the orange peel and nuts in ¼ cup water with the sugar for 5 minutes; drain off the water and combine the peel mixture with the rice and saffron. Place half the rice on a serving dish and pour over half the butter. Place the chicken on the rice. Place the remaining rice on top, pour over the rest of the butter, and serve.

9 • FRANCE

2 lobsters
1 onion, chopped
little minced garlic
butter
2 cups uncooked rice

4 cups consommé
¼ teaspoon tarragon
3 tablespoons grated
    Parmesan cheese
chopped chives

Cook the lobsters and remove the meat from the shells. Sauté the onion and garlic in butter until golden. Add the rice and brown lightly. Add the consommé and tarragon and simmer 20 minutes or until liquid is absorbed. Stir in the cheese and a little butter. Toss lightly with the lobster meat. Season and sprinkle with chives.

2 lobsters
2 cups uncooked rice
5 cups chicken broth
½ onion, chopped
butter
½ cup white wine

1 tomato, peeled and
   chopped
1 tablespoon flour
2 tablespoons chopped
   parsley

Cook the lobsters and remove meat from shells. Cook the rice in 4 cups broth for 20 minutes or until broth is absorbed. Brown the onion lightly in butter; add the lobster, wine, and tomato; and bring to a boil. Melt 1 tablespoon butter, stir in the flour, gradually add 1 cup broth, and simmer 5 minutes. Combine the sauce with the lobster mixture and parsley, season to taste, and cook 5 more minutes. Pour over the rice. The lobster sauce can be kept hot in a double poiler if necessary. You can sprinkle with nutmeg or paprika.

11 • RUSSIA

1 cup whole mushrooms
2 cups cooked rice
1½ pounds shrimp
salt
pepper
paprika

grated cheese
4 tablespoons butter
4 tablespoons flour
1 tablespoon red wine
   (optional)

Cook the mushrooms in 2 cups boiling water until tender, drain, and reserve the liquid. Meanwhile, cook the shrimp. Combine the hot rice, shrimp, mushrooms, salt, pepper, and a dash of paprika. Put in a buttered baking dish, sprinkle with cheese, and bake at 400° until browned on top. Melt the butter, stir in the flour, gradually add the liquid from the mushrooms and the wine, and cook till thickened, seasoning to taste. Serve the sauce over the rice.

12 • WEST INDIES

2 cups shredded coconut
3 cups milk
1 onion, chopped
oil

salt
2 cups uncooked rice
1 teaspoon cinnamon

Soak the coconut in the milk 1 hour, simmer 10 minutes, and squeeze out the coconut, reserving the milk. Brown the onion lightly in oil. Add the coconut milk, salt, and rice and simmer 20 minutes or until the liquid is absorbed. Sprinkle with the cinnamon.

· 10 ·

SAUCES

Sauces have not been listed according to countries. Although many of them have recognizable origins, they have become so widely used in varied forms that it is difficult, and in some cases almost impossible, to trace them to their sources. Of course the French are pre-eminent in this field, having literally hundreds of white, brown, hot, cold, and *chaud-froid* sauces to their credit. Most other sauces probably were developed from one of these. Others, of course, show a different inspiration; those using soy sauce as an ingredient indicate an Eastern origin. There are many things we Americans can learn about sauces from the rest of the world; methods of preparation, variety and that *je ne sais quoi* that a good sauce can add to otherwise pedestrian dishes.

GENERAL RULES FOR CREAM OR WHITE SAUCE:

1. Thin cream sauce for soups:
   1 tablespoon butter, 1 tablespoon flour, 1 cup cream or milk

2. Medium cream sauce for sauces:
   2 tablespoons butter, 2 tablespoons flour, 1 cup cream or milk
3. Heavy cream sauce for croquettes:
   ¼ cup butter, ¼ cup flour, 1 cup cream or milk.

METHOD: Melt the butter, stir in the flour, and gradually add the cream or milk, stirring well. Simmer 10 minutes or cook in the top of a double boiler, but be sure to cook it thoroughly. (American cooking so often falls down on raw-flour cream sauce, too quickly turned out.) Season to taste with salt and pepper. If you like a richer sauce, add 1 or 2 egg yolks. Meat stock, broth, consommé, bouillon, or the water that vegetables were cooked in can be used as the liquid, instead of cream or milk, for a difference in flavor. When chicken or veal stock is used, the sauce is velouté sauce.

I • FOR VEGETABLES

1 • HOLLANDAISE

In the top of a double boiler melt ¼ pound butter with the juice of ½ lemon and 2 tablespoons water. This mixture can be set aside if you are not ready to finish the sauce. When you are ready to serve it, add 4 egg yolks, but be sure the top of the pot does not touch the hot water. Stir vigorously until well thickened and serve immediately. Do not allow to stand. If the sauce tends to curdle, remove it from the heat, add a dash of hot water, and stir vigorously and it will pull together again. For thinner sauce, use 2 or 3 egg yolks. This is the well-known favorite, Hollandaise sauce. It is falsely considered hard to make. It goes extremely well with asparagus, artichokes, broccoli, and fish. Made with tarragon vinegar instead of lemon juice, it is excellent on chicken or steak.

2 • TOMATO HOLLANDAISE

Mix 1 cup of Hollandaise sauce (Vegetable Sauce #1) with ¼ cup tomato paste and 2 teaspoons chopped parsley.

3 • ITALIAN CHEESE

Make medium cream sauce with 2 tablespoons butter, 2

tablespoons flour, and 1 cup cream or milk. Add 1 cup grated Parmesan or Parmesan and Romano cheese and stir over low flame until cheese is melted.

4 • SESAME

Toast ½ cup sesame seeds in a skillet, then crush them with a rolling pin. Mix with ¼ cup vinegar, ¼ cup soy sauce, and 2 tablespoons sugar. This is especially good with spinach or cabbage.

5 • VINAIGRETTE

Salad Dressing #2 (Vinaigrette), page 76.

II • FOR BEEF

1 • HORSERADISH

Add ¼ cup horseradish and salt to taste to 1 cup sour cream.

2 • MUSHROOM

Melt 2 tablespoons butter, stir in 2 tablespoons flour, and gradually add ⅔ cup consommé and then ½ cup cream or milk. Simmer 10 minutes. Add 3 chopped sour pickles or 1 chopped onion browned in butter with 1 pound of sliced mushrooms. Season to taste and add a little lemon juice if you wish.

3 • TARRAGON HOLLANDAISE

Combine 2 chopped green onions or scallions, 1 bay leaf, ⅛ teaspoon thyme, pepper, 4 teaspoons chopped parsley, and ¼ cup tarragon vinegar or cider vinegar with 2 teaspoons tarragon added. Simmer until reduced to 2 tablespoons. Strain and add to 1 cup Hollandaise sauce (Vegetable Sauce #1, page 180).

4 • ESPAGNOLE

Sauté 2 chopped onions and a clove of garlic minced in ¼ cup oil. Add 1 chopped carrot, 1 chopped green pepper, 2 teaspoons chopped parsley, 2 whole cloves (optional), 2 teaspoons salt, 1 teaspoon paprika, ¼ teaspoon chili powder, 1 bay leaf, 1 large can of tomatoes drained, and 2 slices of bacon cooked and crumbled. Simmer together 20 minutes.

5 • WINE

To the pan juices of fried steaks add ¼ cup red wine, stirring and scraping pan until the wine is almost evaporated. Add a little minced garlic, another ½ cup wine, 2 tablespoons tomato paste, ½ teaspoon salt, ¼ teaspoon pepper, and ½ teaspoon fennel seeds (optional). Simmer together a few minutes.

6 • HUNGARIAN SOUR CREAM

Sauté 1 tablespoon minced onion and ½ cup sliced mushrooms in butter a few minutes. Stir in 1 tablespoon flour, ¼ teaspoon paprika, and salt. Gradually add 1 cup sour cream. Heat but do not boil. You may add 2 tablespoons catsup if you wish.

7 • ITALIAN TOMATO

Combine 2 cups tomatoes, 3 cans tomato paste, 1 bay leaf, ½ teaspoon sweet basil, 4 tablespoons butter, ½ teaspoon salt, and ¼ teaspoon pepper. A little minced garlic and minced onion may be added. Simmer about 1 hour.

TIPS: The following sauces are particularly good for these uses:
For tenderloin, sirloin, T-bone steaks: 1, 3, 6.
For cube steaks, other small steaks, hamburgers: 2, 4, 5.
For hamburgers, meatballs: 6, 7.

III • FOR LAMB

These sauces are good for roast lamb, lamb chops, steaks, and leftover lamb. Cooked lamb can be sliced and heated quickly in sauce. However, simmer only a few minutes, until the meat is just heated through. Recooking toughens the meat.

1 • DILL

Use lamb juices from the roasting pan, skimming off the fat before measuring, or use canned meat broth. Melt 2 tablespoons butter, stir in 2 tablespoons flour, gradually add 1½ cups lamb juice, and simmer 10 minutes. Add 2 teaspoons sugar, 2 tablespoons vinegar, 2 tablespoons dill, and ½ teaspoon salt. Stir in 1 egg yolk.

2 • FRUIT

Combine ½ cup lemon juice, ½ cup orange juice, 2 teaspoons powdered sugar, 6 tablespoons chopped mint, a little salt, and a dash of nutmeg. Stir vigorously or put in a tightly covered jar and shake well.

3 • MINT

Dissolve 1 tablespoon sugar in ¼ cup boiling water; add to ½ cup vinegar, 3 teaspoons finely chopped mint, and a pinch of salt.

4 • CURRANT MINT

Melt ½ cup currant jelly with ½ cup mint jelly. Add ¼ cup lemon juice and ¼ cup orange juice.

5 • PICKLE

Use lamb juices from the roasting pan, skimming off the fat before measuring. Melt 2 tablespoons butter, stir in 2 tablespoons flour, gradually add ⅔ cup lamb juice, and simmer a few minutes. Add ½ cup cream or milk, 4 chopped sweet pickles, and 1 tablespoon chopped dill (optional).

6 • CURRANT

To 4 cups lamb gravy add ½ cup currant jelly and 1 teaspoon lemon juice.

7 • ENGLISH SHARP

Combine ½ cup vinegar, ¼ can tomato paste, ¼ cup water, 6 tablespoons Worcestershire sauce, 1 teaspoon dry mustard, minced onion, and 1 teaspoon salt. Bring to a boil and serve.

IV • FOR HAM AND CORNED BEEF

1 • CURRANT MUSTARD

Melt together equal parts of currant jelly, butter, and prepared mustard.

2 • MUSTARD

Mix 1 teaspoon prepared mustard, salt, pepper, and a little lemon juice. Fold into ½ cup whipped cream.

3 • RAISIN

Put 1 cup raisins and 4 whole cloves in a pan, just cover with water, and simmer 10 minutes. Mix 1 teaspoon cornstarch with ¾ cup brown sugar and add to the raisins, stirring until thickened. Add 1 tablespoon lemon juice, 1 teaspoon Worcestershire sauce, and ¼ teaspoon salt.

4 • HOT

Combine 2 tablespoons melted currant jelly with 1 tablespoon vinegar, 1 teaspoon horseradish, 1 tablespoon prepared mustard, juice and grated rind of 1 lemon, and juice and grated rind of 2 oranges.

5 • WINE

Combine and melt ¼ cup currant jelly, ¼ cup butter, and ¼ cup prepared mustard. Add juice of 1 lime and ½ cup red wine.

6 • ENGLISH Sweet-Sharp

Combine and melt ¼ cup currant jelly, ¼ cup butter, and ¼ cup prepared mustard. Add 1 finely chopped onion and ½ teaspoon thyme.

V • FOR COLD CUTS

1 • FRUIT

Combine ¼ cup applesauce, 2 tablespoons horseradish, and 1 cup of any fruit juice (orange is good).

2 • GINGER RAISIN

Combine 3 cups bouillon, ¼ cup chopped blanched almonds, 1 tablespoon vinegar, 1 tablespoon sugar, ¼ cup seedless raisins (optional), and 1 dozen ginger snaps broken up. Simmer until the mixture has thickened a little.

3 • MUSTARD

Sauce #2 for ham and corned beef, page 183.

VI • FOR CHICKEN AND PORK

1 • HUNGARIAN CREAM

Sauté 1 chopped onion in butter; stir in 2 tablespoons flour, 2 teaspoons Hungarian paprika, and ½ teaspoon salt; and gradually add 2 cups chicken broth. Simmer 10 minutes. Add 1 cup sour cream and 1 tablespoon dill or tarragon (optional). Heat but do not boil again.

2 • CHINESE BASIC

Heat 4 cups consommé. Mix 1 tablespoon cornstarch with ¾ cup water; 1 tablespoon soy sauce; 1 tablespoon Mei Yen, MSG, or Accent; and 1 teaspoon salt. Add to the consommé. Simmer until clear.

3 • HOLLANDAISE VARIATIONS

Sauce #1 and Sauce #2 for vegetables, page 180.
Sauce #3 for beef, page 181.

VII • FOR FISH

1 • TARRAGON

Combine 1 cup mayonnaise, 1 teaspoon tarragon or 2 tablespoons tarragon vinegar, 1 teaspoon chopped parsley, 1 teaspoon minced onion, 1 teaspoon chopped sour pickles, 1 teaspoon chopped chives, and ½ teaspoon capers (optional).

2 • FRENCH

Melt ¼ cup butter; add 1 teaspoon salt, pepper, 2 tablespoons lemon juice, 2 teaspoons chopped parsley, and a pinch of marjoram.

3 • AMANDINE

Melt butter in the pan in which the fish was cooked; heat until brown. Pour over the fish and sprinkle with slivered or chopped blanched almonds.

4 • WHIPPED CREAM

Mash the yolks of 2 hard-boiled eggs with 1 raw egg yolk, 1 teaspoon dry mustard, 1 tablespoon vinegar, ¼ teaspoon salt, ⅛ teaspoon pepper, and 1 tablespoon sugar. Fold into 1 cup whipped cream.

5 • GREEN

Cook a few spinach leaves and force through a sieve or put in the blender. Add 2 cups mayonnaise, 2 tablespoons chopped parsley, 1 tablespoon chopped chives, ¼ teaspoon chervil or tarragon, and salt and pepper to taste.

6 • ANCHOVY

Cream ¼ cup butter with 1 tablespoon anchovy paste and a few drops each of lemon juice and onion juice. Add pepper to taste.

7 • MUSTARD

Cream ¼ cup butter with 2 teaspoons dry mustard and a few drops of Worcestershire sauce.

8 • HOLLANDAISE

Sauce #1 (Hollandaise) for vegetables, page 180.

TIPS: The following sauces are particularly good used these ways:
For hot broiled or fresh fish: 1, 2, 3, 6, 7.
For cold fish: 4.
For hot or cold poached or baked fish; most often used with salmon: 5, 8.

• 11 •

GARNISHES
AND RELISHES

Any meal can be attractively served, and its piquancy judiciously emphasized, with the pleasing use of garnishes. Many cooks feel this kind of attention takes too much time, and so charm is sacrificed to what is thought of as efficiency. There is nothing so unappealing as an "efficient" meal. Food must not only be nutritious; it must charm the eye, the palate and the nostril. (What good is nutrition if the food is not appealing enough to eat? It is astonishing how often the so-called "difficult" eater succumbs to an attractively served meal.) The touch of foreignness can often add this attractiveness. The French put croutons in soups and salads; this has become accepted, and rightly so, as a simple, pleasing addition. Scandinavians favor brightening dishes with slices of beets and hard-boiled eggs. Polynesians place baked bananas on the platter with their meat. The Japanese have made a true art of serving food. Since food in Japan was not overly plentiful much of the time, and the variety rather

187

limited, the Japanese made every appeal to the eye and the sense of touch. Color, shape and combinations of texture became important. The Japanese can make a work of art of a radish. Only a nation with an appreciation of the spiritual importance of all these elements could make a religious ritual of tea drinking.

I • FOR SOUP AND SALADS

1 • France

Croutons: Dice white bread and deep fry or fry in butter in a skillet until golden. Or brush cubes of slightly stale bread with butter and put them in a 400° oven until golden. A pinch of garlic powder, onion powder, or herbs can be added to the butter. Grated Parmesan cheese can be sprinkled on the hot croutons.

2 • Italy

Toss together ½ cup grated Parmesan cheese, 2 tablespoons chopped parsley, 1 teaspoon thyme or marjoram, and 4 cups dry bread crumbs. Sprinkle on soup or salad.

3 • Germany

Cream ½ pound Roquefort cheese with ¼ pound butter. Add a little grated dark rye bread or pumpernickel. Form into balls and chill. Serve with or in tossed green salad.

4 • Switzerland

Melt ½ pound Swiss cheese in a double boiler with 2 tablespoons butter; add salt and 3 tablespoons flour. Cool and stir in 4 egg yolks. Spread on both sides of bread slices with the crust removed. Dip bread into beaten egg whites and fry in deep fat. Cut each slice into three strips and serve hot.

5 • Italy

Dip slices of hard cheese in slightly beaten egg and then in bread crumbs and brown on both sides quickly in hot fat.

6 • England

Work together ½ pound grated cheddar cheese, ½ cup butter, 1 cup flour, and 1 teaspoon salt. Roll into balls the size of marbles. Place on a buttered baking sheet and bake at 350° for 10 minutes.

7 • ENGLAND

Dip Saltine crackers in cold water and place in 400° oven. They will puff up and brown.

8 • FRANCE

Heat ¾ cup milk or consommé with a slice of onion. Strain and pour gradually over 1 slightly beaten egg, adding salt, pepper, and nutmeg (optional). Pour into a shallow buttered pan and bake at 350° for 10 minutes or until set. Cool and cut into cubes with a wet knife. Delicious in consommé.

9 • ITALY

Beat 2 tablespoons flour into 2 beaten egg whites. Add 2 tablespoons grated Parmesan cheese, salt, pepper, a dash of Worcestershire sauce, and chopped chives. Drop by teaspoonful into boiling soup or stew. Cover and simmer 5 minutes.

10 • ITALY

Remove the centers of cucumbers with an apple corer. Blend cream cheese, a little milk, chopped chives, salt, and a dash of paprika. Stuff mixture into cucumbers. Chill until firm and slice.

11 • ENGLAND

To Lake Cornet cream puff batter—recipe #4, Cookies and Small Confections, page 210—add a combination of ½ cup grated cheese and ½ cup flour. Drop ½ teaspoon at a time into hot butter and fry until golden.

12 • HUNGARY

Sprinkle soups or salads with caraway or poppy seeds or with a combination of chopped hard-boiled egg yolks and chopped parsley.

13 • CHINA

Beat 2 eggs with ¼ teaspoon salt; pour into an oiled skillet, tilting pan to spread thin. Cook until firm, turn out, and cut into strips. Serve in clear soups and salads and on meat-and-rice dishes.

14 • FRANCE

Put 1½ cups flour into a bowl with 1½ teaspoons salt. Make a well in the center. Drop in 2 egg yolks and 1 tablespoon melted butter. Stir well and fold in the beaten whites of 2 eggs. Add either a pinch of curry powder or a pinch of saffron or a pinch each of parsley and marjoram. Drop by teaspoonful onto boiling soup or stew. Cover and simmer 10 minutes or until dumplings float to the top.

15 • AUSTRIA

Roll out pastry dough and sprinkle well with grated cheese. Fold over and roll out again. Sprinkle with cheese and cut into shapes. Bake at 450° until slightly browned.

16 • RUSSIA

Float a dollop of whipped cream on creamed soups. For special occasions, add a dab of caviar in the center.

17 • HOLLAND

Blend together 6 tablespoons butter, 2 hard-boiled egg yolks, salt, pepper, and nutmeg. Form into balls. Chill and drop into creamed soups.

18 • HUNGARY

Combine 1 cup mashed potatoes, 1 egg, ½ cup butter, and 1 cup flour. Mix well and roll out. Cut into strips, brush with egg yolk, and sprinkle with caraway seeds. Bake on a buttered sheet at 375° until lightly browned.

19 • MEXICO

Fry tortillas in hot deep fat. Drain.

20 • SPAIN

Cut bread slices into rounds. Fold ⅔ cup grated cheese into 1 beaten egg white with a dash of paprika. Spread on the bread rounds about ¼ inch thick. Brown in 400° oven.

II • FOR MAIN COURSES

1 • FRANCE

Slit the shells of 1 pound chestnuts; boil the nuts in water to cover for 30 minutes; remove hulls and skins. Simmer with celery stalks (optional) in enough consommé to cover until tender. Mash with hot milk, butter, salt, and pepper. Serve in mounds with paprika sprinkled on top. (Chestnuts can also be chopped and sprinkled on vegetables or salad.)

2 • ITALY

Cook squash or pumpkin and mash with hot milk, butter, salt, and pepper. Add a little flour, shape into balls, dust with flour, and fry in deep fat until golden. Sprinkle with brown sugar, plain or melted. (Serve with pork or ham.)

3 • MALAYA

Boil 6 eggs and cut them in half. Melt 4 tablespoons butter, stir in 4 tablespoons flour, and gradually add 2 cups milk, ½ teaspoon salt, ¼ teaspoon pepper, and 1 tablespoon curry powder. Simmer 5 minutes. Warm the eggs in this sauce. Instead of curry powder, you can use 1 onion sliced and browned in butter and ¼ teaspoon nutmeg.

4 • AUSTRIA

Garnish halved hard-boiled eggs with a pinch of horseradish, paprika, and a little French dressing.

5 • ENGLAND

In a skillet brown pecans or almonds in fat with a pinch of garlic or curry powder. Drain the nuts on paper and salt them.

6 • WEST INDIES

Cook cornmeal or grits and chill until firm. Cut into small strips; dip in bread crumbs, in beaten egg, and again in bread crumbs; and fry in butter or deep fat until golden.

7 • HUNGARY

Cook fine noodles, rinse with cold water, and drain. Fry in deep fat until golden.

8 • FRANCE

Simmer stalks of celery in consommé until tender. Drain and chill in French dressing. Top with anchovy fillets if you wish.

9 • SWEDEN

Stuff one cooked and pitted prune into another. Wrap with a strip of bacon and secure with a toothpick. Fry in deep fat. (Superb with game.)

10 • FRANCE

Simmer whole mushroom caps in French dressing until tender.

11 • FRANCE

Wash and drain sprigs of parsley. Drop them into hot deep fat and cook until they float. Drain and salt.

12 • ITALY

Scoop out firm tomatoes and fill with croutons. Sprinkle with a little olive oil and sweet basil and broil until slightly shriveled.

13 • SPAIN

Cut tomatoes in half. Sprinkle the cut sides with olive oil, salt, pepper, and oregano and broil.

14 • ENGLAND

Cut tomatoes in half and sprinkle with salt, pepper, bread crumbs, grated cheese, and dots of butter. Broil. Can be served plain or topped with the following: In the top of a double boiler cook 2 tablespoons vinegar, ¼ cup butter, 1 teaspoon prepared mustard, 1 tablespoon Worcestershire sauce, salt, pepper, and 1 slightly beaten egg; stir until thickened.

15 • SAMOA

Peel and bake bananas whole or split lengthwise. Or cook in a little butter in a skillet.

16 • HAWAII

Peel bananas and split lengthwise. Spread with a mixture of 1 tablespoon butter, 2 tablespoons flour, salt, pepper, and cinnamon and/or nutmeg. Either broil or place in a pan with a little white wine and simmer until done.

17 • HAWAII

Peel and split 3 bananas lengthwise; place split side down in a baking dish. Spread with a mixture of ½ cup strawberry or other jelly and 1 tablespoon lemon juice. Bake at 350°, basting regularly, for about 20 minutes or until done.

18 • ITALY

Simmer small whole mushrooms in butter until lightly browned. Place in a buttered baking dish; sprinkle with bread crumbs, marjoram, and grated Parmesan cheese; and dot with butter. Broil.

19 • HUNGARY

Place small whole mushrooms in a buttered baking dish. Cover with sour cream; sprinkle with salt, pepper, chopped parsley, minced onion, and a little lemon juice. Bake at 350° for 20 minutes or until done. Paprika may also be used.

20 • ITALY

Put 1 pound small whole mushrooms in a skillet with olive oil, a little minced garlic, 2 chopped anchovy fillets, 2 peeled and chopped tomatoes, and ½ teaspoon chopped mint or ¼ teaspoon mint flakes. Cook 10 minutes, stirring frequently. This can be served on or with meat or as a luncheon dish on toast.

21 • FRANCE

Lightly sauté 2 cups small whole mushrooms in butter with a little minced garlic and 2 tablespoons minced onion. Add 2 tablespoons red wine and 1 tablespoon chopped dill. (Especially good with chicken.)

22 • MALAYA

Melt 4 tablespoons butter in a skillet; add 2 tablespoons curry powder and ½ teaspoon salt. Add 1 can pineapple chunks with the juice and simmer 12 to 15 minutes.

23 • GERMANY

Slice and core unpeeled apples and fry them in butter.

12

PANCAKES

Here is my downfall! As I read diaries kept during my various trips I am almost embarrassed to note that in every country I seemed deliberately to have set out to eat pancakes—and then eulogized them! As I think of each country I become absolutely nostalgic over its pancakes and of each one I think, "Now this *is* the best." So, of all my favorites, I have chosen a number for this section (thinking that no one but myself would want a whole book of them) and some suggestions for fillings. The innumerable ways of serving these little delicacies of eggs, milk and flour are as varied as the countries from which they come: the French *crêpes de volaille* filled with minced chicken, the silver-dollar-sized pancakes served with lingonberries in Sweden, the huge German *Apfel Pfannkuchen*. All these have a fond place in my memory, and I hope they will in yours.

I • PANCAKE BATTERS

METHOD: Mix all ingredients till smooth. (You may use the blender if you wish.) Grease a skillet with butter, oil, or margarine. Pour a little batter into the hot skillet, tilting the pan so that the batter spreads evenly. When the pancake is set and lightly golden on one side, turn it and cook it until it is golden on the other side. These pancakes may be cooked in large skillets—German or Dutch style—and eaten flat or rolled up with honey, jam, hot applesauce seasoned with nutmeg, or other fillings. They may also be made very small in the special Swedish skillets or in a 6-inch skillet for individual servings. Note the omission of baking powder and shortening in foreign pancakes.

1 • HUNGARY (12 medium pancakes)

1 cup flour, 2 eggs, 1½ cups milk, ½ teaspoon salt.

2 • GERMANY (1 large pancake)

¼ cup flour, 2 eggs, 6 tablespoons milk, ¼ teaspoon salt. (This is made in an 8-inch skillet. Thinly sliced onions may be spread on top before the pancake sets and shortly before it is turned. This pancake may be baked in the oven at 350° for 20 minutes.)

3 • SWEDEN (24 small pancakes)

1 cup flour, 3 eggs, 2 cups milk, ¼ teaspoon salt, 2 tablespoons sugar.
(Serve with lingonberries if they are available or with any other berries. Swedish cooks let this batter stand 2 hours before using, so mix it ahead of time if you wish.)

4 • RUSSIA (12 medium pancakes)

¼ cup flour, 4 eggs, 1 cup sour cream, ¼ teaspoon salt.
(Serve with melted butter, sour cream, and caviar or thinly sliced smoked salmon. The Russians use buckwheat flour for this.)

5 • FRANCE (10 medium pancakes)

¾ cup flour, 3 eggs, 1½ cups milk, ¼ teaspoon salt.
(Serve with jam or jelly and sprinkle with powdered sugar.)

6 • MEXICO (12 medium pancakes)

¼ cup flour, 6 eggs, ¼ cup water, 2 tablespoons cornmeal, ¼ teaspoon salt.

7 • POLAND (10 medium pancakes)

¼ cup flour, 3 eggs, ½ cup milk, ¼ teaspoon salt.
(This pancake is not turned in cooking. When it is set, spread with jam, sprinkle with powdered sugar, and serve.)

8 • HOLLAND (10 medium pancakes)

1¼ cups flour, 2 eggs, 1 cup milk, ¼ teaspoon salt (½ pound crumbled cooked bacon may be added to the batter).

9 • AUSTRIA (12 medium pancakes)

1½ cups flour, 2 egg yolks, 2 cups milk, ¼ teaspoon salt, ¼ cup sugar.
(Try this served with brown sugar, as people do in Vienna.)

II • PANCAKES FILLINGS

Americans are apt to overlook the possibilities of the European pancake, remembering only their own thicker breakfast griddle cake. However there are not only as many pancakes as there are countries but also countless varieties within each country. To avoid overlapping, I have used recipes that are representative of only a few countries. These varied and adaptable pancakes will add immeasurably to your lunches and late suppers. They may be stacked flat, one on top of the other, and kept warm in a low oven; the filling may be spread between the layers; and the pancakes may be cut into pie-shaped wedges for serving. The pancakes may also be filled individually, rolled up, and kept warm in the oven by laying one pancake flat over all the others. The Hungarians tuck in the ends of these filled, rolled pancakes; dip them in egg: roll them in crumbs; and fry them in deep fat. Any of these preparations may be done days in advance, and the pancakes may be frozen and reheated when you are ready to use them.

1 • MEAT FILLINGS

Any meat mixture under meatballs and hash, pages 128-132.

2 • POLAND

1 cup chopped boiled ham with ½ cup sour cream (or 1 cup deviled ham).

196

3 • HUNGARY

1 cup cooked lobster or crab meat, ½ cup sour cream, 1 slice bread soaked in milk, ½ tablespoon parsley, salt, pepper.

4 • FRANCE

1 cup velouté sauce, 2 cups cooked minced chicken, turkey or tuna fish. (For velouté sauce, see general rules for cream or white sauce, page 179.)

5 • HUNGARY

1 cup sautéed sliced mushrooms, ¼ cup sour cream, 1 egg, salt, pepper.

6 • AUSTRIA

1 cup finely chopped cabbage cooked in butter, salt, pepper.

7 • GERMANY

When pancake has set, place 1 chopped and browned apple or thin slices of onion on top. Pour a little extra batter over this. Allow to set slightly. Turn and brown the second side.

8 • SWEDEN

Fill pancakes with jam, jelly, and lingonberries (and whipped cream if you wish) and dust with powdered sugar.

13

BREADS AND BISCUITS

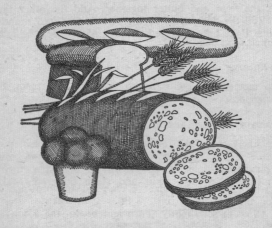

I have seen bread being made in ways that would make an American not only view it with interest but sometimes almost with alarm. In Iran, chunks of dough are thrown against the side of the house and left to bake in the sun. When they are baked through and dry, they drop to the ground. In many other parts of the world the bread is quite different from ours. It is often made under what we would consider unsanitary conditions, fried in strange fats, and made from grains that are not palatable to us. But some of the unusual breads are quite delightful. China has a bread called "doilies," which is served with the famous Peking Duck. It is very simple: ½ yeast cake, ½ cup water, ½ teaspoon salt, 2 cups flour; knead for 10 minutes; let rise 4 hours; divide into 15 to 20 pieces, roll into thin strips, and steam. But I have found that wherever corn is grown, the bread of that area is a kind we tend to like. Russian breads and other European breads have a familiar aspect. The recipes in this section are culled mainly from European sources. I have also included some quick breads and our family favorite, the *croissant* of France, which, with *café au lait,* is the eye-opener for many Frenchmen.

1 • ENGLAND (SCONES)

2 cups flour
4 tablespoons butter
2 tablespoons sugar
2 teaspoons cream of tartar

1 teaspoon soda
½ teaspoon salt
¾ cup milk

Work the flour and butter together. Add the other ingredients. Roll the dough out ½ inch thick. Cut into rounds like biscuits. Bake on a buttered sheet at 450° for 12 minutes or until lightly browned.

2 • SCOTLAND (SCONES)

1¼ cups flour
½ teaspoon soda
1 teaspoon cream of tartar
1 teaspoon sugar

pinch salt
1 egg
½ cup milk

Combine all the ingredients and drop by spoonful onto a hot, greased griddle. When brown on one side, turn and brown the other side. Split and serve buttered. Makes 6 scones.

3 • RUMANIA (CORNMEAL FINGERS)

1 cup yellow cornmeal
1½ tablespoons salt
4 cups water
¼ cup softened butter

¼ cup grated Parmesan,
   Gruyère, or Swiss
   cheese

Add cornmeal gradually to boiling, salted water, stirring constantly. Cook 20 minutes. Turn into a buttered 8-inch square pan and chill until firm. Cut into strips 1 inch by 2 inches, split each strip in half, spread with butter, and sprinkle with cheese. Put the halves together again and spread the tops with butter and sprinkle with cheese. Place on a buttered sheet and bake at 400° for 15 minutes or until lightly browned.

There are many things you can do with baked hard rolls and French, Vienna, and small loaves of rye bread. The following six recipes—#4 through #9—are simple ways of adding variety to meals. You can also try these fillings for baked potatoes: slash the potatoes with a cross and squeeze the sides gently to force the potatoes open; fill with any of the fillings in the following six recipes.

4 • ESTONIA

6 hard rolls (baked or half
    baked)
1 cup cottage cheese
1 egg
4 tablespoons butter

salt
2 teaspoons caraway seeds
½ cup sour cream
1 tablespoon sugar

Split the rolls in half lengthwise. Combine all the other ingredients and spread on the cut sides of the rolls. Bake or
broil until brown. Serve at once.

5 • AUSTRIA

rolls or French, Vienna, or
    rye bread
⅓ pound bleu cheese
¼ cup minced ripe olives

½ cup butter
2 tablespoons lemon juice
3 slices bacon, cooked and
    crumbled

Split the rolls or bread lengthwise. You may toast them if
you wish. Spread them with a combination of the remaining
ingredients. Bake or broil till bubbly.

6 • AUSTRIA

rolls or French, Vienna, or
    rye bread
½ pound butter
2 cloves garlic, crushed, or
    1 teaspoon garlic

powder
½ cup chopped parsley
1 tablespoon chopped chives
curry powder or anchovy
    paste (optional)

Split the rolls or bread and spread with a mixture of the
remaining ingredients. Bake or broil till bubbly.

7 • ENGLAND

rolls or French bread
½ pound butter
½ pound grated cheddar

cheese
2 tablespoons chopped
    chives

Split the rolls or bread. Combine all the other ingredients
and spread on the cut sides. Bake or broil until brown.

8 • FRANCE

French bread or rolls
½ pound butter
2 cloves garlic, crushed or

1 teaspoon garlic
powder
sesame seeds

Split the bread or rolls lengthwise. Cream the butter and garlic together and spread on the bread. Toast the sesame seeds in a skillet until browned. Sprinkle on top of the bread. Bake or broil.

9 • FRANCE

rolls or French bread   *2 or 3 herbs (basil, thyme,*
½ cup chopped onion   *oregano)*

Split the bread. Spread with butter and sprinkle with chopped onion and 2 or 3 herbs. Bake or brown under broiler.

10 • RUSSIA (CHEESE PASTRY)

½ pound butter   *2 tablespoons melted butter*
2 cups flour   *¼ teaspoon salt*
1 cup sour cream   *1 teaspoon sugar*
2 eggs   *1 pound cream cheese*

Cut the butter into the flour, add 2 tablespoons sour cream, and work together. Roll into a ball, wrap in wax paper, and chill until firm. Roll out ⅛ inch thick on a floured board; cut into 1½-inch circles. Pinch into cup shapes. Combine all the ingredients. Fill each pastry cup with 2 teaspoons of the mixture. Bake at 375° for 20 minutes or until very light brown.

11 • HUNGARY (HAM PUFF)

¼ cup bread crumbs   *½ cup grated cheese*
3 tablespoons butter   *1 cup minced or deviled*
4 eggs, separated   *ham*
¾ cup sour cream

Combine the bread crumbs, butter, egg yolks, sour cream, cheese, and ham. Beat the egg whites stiff and gently fold the ham mixture into them. Drop by spoonful onto a buttered baking sheet. Bake at 350° for 15 minutes or until lightly browned.

12 • FRANCE (CRESCENT ROLLS OR CROISSANTS)

1 package yeast   *¼ teaspoon salt*
2 cups flour   *1 pound butter, softened*
¾ cup milk

Dissolve the yeast in a little warm water, mix with ½ cup

flour, cover, and let rise. Mix the remaining flour, milk, and salt, making a smooth dough, and combine with the yeast sponge. Cover and let rise 20 minutes. Roll out in a rectangle ½ inch thick and spread with the butter. Fold the outside thirds over the middle section, fold in half in opposite direction and roll out. (This is called a turn.) Repeat this folding process. Chill well. Repeat this folding process two more times. Chill again. Divide the dough into two parts. Roll out very thin into 10-inch circles. Cut each like a pie into 8 wedges. Roll up from the wider edge to the narrower and place in crescent shapes on a baking sheet. Cover and let rise until doubled in bulk. Brush with milk and bake at 350° for 10 minutes or more until lightly browned.

13 • AUSTRALIA (CURRY BISCUITS)

¾ cup flour	¼ cup grated cheese
½ teaspoon baking powder	1 egg yolk
	2 tablespoons milk
2 teaspoons curry powder	⅛ teaspoon salt
¼ cup butter	⅛ teaspoon dry mustard

Mix the flour, baking powder, and curry powder; cut in the butter and add the cheese. Mix the egg yolk, milk, salt, and mustard and work in. Roll out ¼ inch thick and cut into rounds. Bake on a buttered sheet at 400° for 12 minutes. (You can also add curry powder and cheese to your own or a prepared biscuit mix. And there are other simple tricks, such as (1) adding a little crumbled cooked bacon or chopped ham or caraway seeds to the dough; (2) substituting sour cream or tomato juice for the milk; (3) topping the biscuits, before baking, with either 1 cup bleu cheese with a little milk or 1 cup blueberries with a little milk or 1 cup raspberries with a little sugar; and (4) topping each unbaked biscuit with a slice of Edam or other cheese.)

14 • GERMANY (BLITZ KUCHEN)

2 cups flour	1 cup sour cream
½ cup shortening	1 teaspoon soda
2 cups brown sugar	1 egg
1 teaspoon baking powder	1 teaspoon vanilla
½ teaspoon salt	½ cup ground nuts

Work together the flour, shortening, sugar, baking powder, and salt as for pastry dough. Mix 2 cups of this mixture with the sour cream, soda, egg, and vanilla. Pour into a buttered square pan. Combine the remaining mixture with the ground nuts and sprinkle on top. Bake at 350° for 35 minutes. Serve hot.

15 • AUSTRIA (PLUM BUNS)

1 package yeast	2 tablespoons softened butter
2½ cups flour	¼ cup sugar
½ cup milk	2 tablespoons melted butter
¼ teaspoon salt	½ cup plum jam
1 egg	

Dissolve the yeast in a little warm water with a pinch of sugar. Add 3 tablespoons flour, cover, and let rise until doubled in bulk. Combine the remaining flour, milk, salt, egg, softened butter, and sugar. Beat in the yeast sponge. Let rise until doubled in bulk. Roll out ¼ inch thick. Cut into strips 2 inches by 3 inches. Place a dab of jam at one end of each strip and roll up. Place strips close together in a buttered pan. Brush with melted butter and let rise until doubled. Bake at 350° for 20 minutes or until lightly browned. Serve hot.

16 • HUNGARY (POPPY-SEED BALLS)

½ package yeast	4 tablespoons softened
2¼ cups flour	butter
¾ cup milk	sugar
¼ teaspoon salt	crushed poppy seeds
5 egg yolks	

Dissolve the yeast in a little warm water. Add 1 cup flour, milk, salt, egg yolks, butter, and 4 tablespoons sugar, beating until smooth. Cover and let rise 30 minutes. Add another cup of flour and stir until springy. Add the remaining flour and shape into balls the size of marbles. Place on a buttered baking sheet and let rise until doubled in bulk. Bake at 300° until very lightly browned. Crush the poppy seeds with a rolling pin and combine with an equal amount of sugar. Dip the balls in melted butter and roll them in the poppy-seed mixture.

17 • FRANCE (BRIOCHE)

1 package yeast	12 tablespoons butter,
½ cup water	softened
4 cups flour	1 egg yolk
1 teaspoon salt	little milk
4 eggs	

Dissolve the yeast in ¼ cup warm water, add 1 cup flour, and let rise. Put the remaining flour and the salt into a bowl and work in the eggs, butter, and, gradually, the remaining ¼ cup water, working the dough until it is springy. Add the yeast mixture, cover, and let rise until doubled in bulk. Punch down. Shape the dough into balls and place in buttered brioche or muffin tins or on a buttered sheet. Make a cross-shaped incision in the top of each and insert a smaller ball of dough. Let rise until half again as large. Beat the egg yolk and milk together lightly and brush over the tops. Bake at 400° about 20 minutes or until golden brown.

18 • ENGLAND (CRUMPETS)

1 package yeast	1½ cups lukewarm milk
½ cup lukewarm water	2 tablespoons melted butter
2 eggs	½ teaspoon salt
3 cups flour	1 teaspoon sugar

Dissolve the yeast in the water. Beat the eggs. Beat in the remaining ingredients. Add the yeast. Cover and let stand 15 minutes. Fill buttered muffin tins two-thirds full. Bake at 450° for 10 minutes or until lightly browned. Serve hot.

19 • HUNGARY (BACON BALLS)

1 package yeast	4 eggs
4 cups flour	1 pound bacon, cooked
1 cup sour cream	and crumbled
1 teaspoon salt	1 egg yolk, slightly beaten
½ teaspoon pepper	

Dissolve the yeast in a little warm water. Add the flour, sour cream, salt, pepper, eggs, and bacon and knead well. Roll out ½ inch thick and cut into 1-inch rounds. Brush with the beaten egg yolk. Place on a greased baking sheet and let rise 30 minutes. Bake at 375° for 15 minutes.

20 • HOLLAND (MUFFINS)

1 package yeast	1 teaspoon sugar
2 cups flour	¼ teaspoon salt
⅔ cup milk	

Dissolve the yeast in a little warm water. Add the flour, milk, sugar, and salt. Pour into hot, buttered muffin tins; fill two-thirds full. Bake at 450° for 10 minutes or until brown. This dough is not left to rise at any time.

14

DESSERTS

I have come to the conclusion that the whole world likes sweets. I don't know of any place that I have been that they were not served. The array of foreign desserts is vast, and I have singled out some of my favorites as a closing for this book. They are mainly European in origin. Although the rest of the world—Asia, Africa, the islands of the Pacific—offer some pleasing desserts, these are often not practical to make, since certain of their ingredients are unobtainable here. Australia and New Zealand tend to have English desserts. South America is often influenced by Spain; South Americans are fond of using honey, chocolate, almonds, fruit and native liqueurs. I have included a recipe for Fruit Flambé which is characteristic of French desserts and simple even for the neophyte cook. Another that I have included I use frequently for entertaining because, although it is a soufflé, it holds well. In France it is called *Fils d'Or,* or Golden Thread, because of the trickles of apricot jam running through the egg whites.

I • FRUIT DESSERTS

1 • ENGLAND (CUSTARD APPLES)

6 baking apples
2 cups milk
2 eggs, slightly beaten

¼ cup sugar
⅛ teaspoon salt
½ teaspoon vanilla

Bake the apples. Combine the milk, eggs, sugar, and salt and cook in a double boiler over hot water until the mixture thickens. Add the vanilla. To serve, pour the mixture over the baked apples.

2 • HUNGARY (BAKED APPLES)

6 baking apples
3 tablespoons sugar
2 egg yolks, beaten

1 tablespoon lemon juice
½ cup white wine

Bake the apples. Beat the sugar into the egg yolks; add to the lemon juice and wine. Cook in the top of a double boiler over hot water until thickened. Pour the mixture over the hot baked apples.

3 • FRANCE

small melons   *Port or sweet dessert wine*

Make a small hole in each melon and pour in the wine. Chill. Cut in half, remove the seeds, and serve.

4 • CHINA

honeydew melon   *powdered ginger*

Cut the melon into slices and sprinkle with ginger.

5 • SWITZERLAND

blueberries   *cream*
cinnamon

Sprinkle blueberries with cinnamon and serve with cream.

6 • FRANCE (FRUIT FLAMBÉ)

6 peaches or pears
4 tablespoons melted butter
4 tablespoons lemon juice

1 cup sugar
liqueur
slivered almonds

Slice the peaches or pears and put them in a shallow baking dish or chafing dish. Cover the fruit with a combination of the butter, lemon juice, sugar, and ½ cup of your favorite liqueur. Bake in a 400° oven for 20 minutes or cook in a chafing dish. When sugar is dissolved and fruit is cooked, pour in extra liqueur and set aflame. When flame has burned out, sprinkle with almonds and serve.

II • PUDDINGS AND SOUFFLÉS

1 • LATVIA (MOLDED NUTS)

1 tablespoon gelatin	2 tablespoons rum or liqueur
1 cup sugar	½ pint cream, whipped
1 pound nuts, ground	

Soak the gelatin in ¼ cup cold water. Add 1 cup boiling water and combine with the sugar, nuts, and rum or liqueur. Let cool slightly. Fold in the whipped cream. Pour into a buttered mold and chill until firm, about 2 hours. Unmold and serve.

2 • SWITZERLAND (CHOCOLATE RUM MOLD)

½ pound baking chocolate	ladyfingers
½ pound butter	rum
1 cup powdered sugar	

Melt the chocolate over hot water. Cream the butter and sugar together and add the chocolate. Dip the ladyfingers in rum and line the bottom and sides of a mold. Pour in half the chocolate mixture. Place a layer of ladyfingers on top. Pour in the remaining chocolate. Top with ladyfingers. Chill until firm. Unmold on a serving plate.

3 • FRANCE (CUSTARD)

6 egg yolks, beaten	1 cup brown sugar
2 cups cream	fresh strawberries or
2 tablespoons sugar	raspberries (optional)

Cook the egg yolk, cream, and sugar in the top of a double boiler over hot water for about 3 minutes. Pour into a baking dish and cool. Sprinkle completely with brown sugar and put under the broiler flame until caramelized. Watch carefully, as sugar can burn. Serve with berries if desired.

4 • POLAND (PUDDING)

8 slices bread
little milk
3 eggs, separated
4 tablespoons butter
½ cup sugar

¼ teaspoon cinnamon
1 pound sour cherries,
  pitted
¼ cup chopped almonds

Break up the bread and soften it in a little milk. Beat the egg whites until stiff. Combine the bread, butter, sugar, cinnamon, egg yolks, cherries, and almonds. Fold in the egg whites. Pour into a buttered baking dish and bake at 400° for 15 minutes or until set.

5 • FRANCE (DESSERT OMELET)

6 eggs
6 tablespoons sugar
1 tablespoon butter

powdered sugar
rum

Beat the eggs slightly with the sugar. Melt the butter in a skillet or chafing dish. Pour in the eggs. Cook the omelet, loosening the sides and tilting the pan to spread the liquid. When the omelet is set, fold it over and sprinkle it with powdered sugar. Warm the rum slightly, pour it over the omelet, and ignite it.

6 • SOUTH AMERICA

6 eggs, separated
salt
2 tablespoons sugar

1 teaspoon vanilla
4 ripe bananas, chopped fine

Beat the egg yolks, salt, sugar, and vanilla together. Add the bananas. Beat the egg whites stiff and fold into the banana mixture. Bake in a buttered dish at 350° for 20 minutes or until set or divide in two and cook in a skillet.

7 • FRANCE (MOUSSE)

3 ounces sweet chocolate
4 eggs, separated

1 cup sugar
1½ cups heavy cream

Melt the chocolate over hot water and cool slightly. Beat the egg yolks, add the sugar, and beat until light. Beat in the chocolate. Beat the egg whites stiff and fold in the chocolate mixture. Whip the cream and fold into the mixture. Pour into a 2-quart mold and freeze until firm. This makes a very rich and creamy mousse. (If you like a mocha flavor, add 2 tablespoons of very strong coffee with the chocolate.) Serve with plain or whipped cream.

8 • FRANCE (SOUFFLÉ)

4 egg whites
¼ cup sugar
3 tablespoons apricot jam

fresh or frozen fruit
¼ cup rum or liqueur

Beat the egg whites until stiff. Beat in the sugar and fold in the jam. Butter the top of a double boiler, pour in the mixture, and cook over boiling water 1 hour. This will keep for a while over hot water. Be sure to keep it covered all the time it is cooking. Turn out on a serving dish. Surround with a colorful variety of fresh or frozen fruits. Warm the rum or liqueur, pour over the soufflé, and ignite.

9 • FRANCE (SOUFFLÉ)

3 tablespoons butter
2 tablespoons flour
2 cups milk
2 tablespoons sugar

6 eggs, separated
1 teaspoon strawberry jam
little grated lemon rind
(optional)

Melt the butter, stir in the flour, and gradually add the milk, sugar, egg yolks, jam, and lemon rind. Beat the egg whites stiff. Fold in the hot mixture. Pour into a buttered baking dish. Set in a pan of hot water and bake at 350° for 40 minutes or until puffed and set.

III • COOKIES AND SMALL CONFECTIONS

1 • ENGLAND (COOKIES)

¾ cup butter
¾ cup sugar
1 egg, separated
1¾ cups flour

½ teaspoon salt
1 teaspoon vanilla
½ cup ground nuts

Cream the butter and sugar together; add the beaten egg yolk, flour, salt, and vanilla. Spread thin on a baking sheet, cover with beaten egg white, and sprinkle with nuts. Bake at 325° for 30 minutes or until baked through. Cut while warm into desired shapes.

2 • ITALY (CREAM PUFFS)

1 cup boiling water
½ cup butter
½ teaspoon salt
1 tablespoon sugar
1 cup flour
4 eggs
1 tablespoon each grated

orange and lemon
  rind
vanilla or chocolate pudding
2 tablespoons rum or
  liqueur (optional)
chopped candied peel
  (optional)

When water is boiling, add butter, salt, and sugar, stirring until butter is melted. Add the flour all at once and stir vigorously over heat until the mixture leaves the side of the pan completely. Remove from heat and, with a wooden spoon, beat in one egg at a time. Add the orange and lemon rind. Drop by tablespoonful onto a greased cookie sheet, allowing room for expansion. Bake at 425° for 15 minutes, reduce heat to 375°, and bake until lightly browned. Fill with pudding, adding rum or liqueur to it if you wish. The puffs can be garnished with candied peel.

3 • SWEDEN (COOKIES)

2¼ cups flour
1 cup sugar
1 cup butter
½ teaspoon cream of

tartar
½ teaspoon salt
½ teaspoon soda
1 teaspoon vanilla

Work all the ingredients together with a pastry blender. Roll into balls the size of marbles. Bake on a greased sheet at 350° for 12 minutes or until lightly browned.

4 • FRANCE (CAKE CORNETS)

2 egg whites
½ cup sugar
½ cup flour
¼ teaspoon salt

3 tablespoons butter
1 teaspoon vanilla
¼ teaspoon cinnamon
  (optional)

Beat the egg whites stiff and fold in the sugar; add the flour, salt, butter (which has been melted and cooled slightly), vanilla, and cinnamon. Drop by tablespoonful onto a hot pan and quickly spread thin. Bake at 450° until golden. While warm, roll quickly around a pencil or into cone shapes. Serve plain or with sweetened whipped cream. (In Sweden people serve these cornets filled with whipped cream mixed with strawberry or raspberry jam.)

5 • HUNGARY

¾ cup flour
¼ cup milk
½ cup wine
¼ cup sugar

3 eggs, beaten
fat for deep frying
fresh sweet Bing cherries
powdered sugar

Make a batter of the flour, milk, wine, sugar, and eggs. Dip cherries in the batter and fry in deep fat until brown. Drain and dip in powdered sugar.

6 • FRANCE (PANCAKES)

pancake recipe #5,
    page 195

fillings:
1 cup bleu cheese, milk,

1 box or can of
    blueberries
jam or jelly
hot applesauce, dash of
    nutmeg

Make the pancakes in a small skillet. Blend the cheese with enough milk to soften; mix in the berries. If you use canned berries, drain before using. Spread the filling on the pancakes, roll up, and keep warm in a very low oven, with one pancake laid over the top. Sprinkle with powdered sugar before serving. (These pancakes can be frozen and reheated when ready to serve. They can also be rolled without a filling and frozen. To serve, thaw and warm in a chafing dish with a little butter and with ½ cup orange juice and a little lemon juice too, if you wish. Baste with flaming rum or liqueur.)

IV • PIES AND TARTS

1 • NEW ZEALAND (APRICOT NUT PIE)

⅔ cup shortening
1¼ cups flour
½ teaspoon salt
3 eggs
½ cup butter
¼ cup sugar

1 cup apricot preserves
¼ cup ground nuts or
    shaved almonds or ½
    cup vanilla cookie
    crumbs

Make the pastry by cutting the shortening into the flour and salt and then working in 1 egg. Chill well. Roll out and line a pie pan. For the filling, combine 2 eggs, butter, sugar, and apricot preserves and beat together thoroughly. Pour into the pie shell. Sprinkle the nuts or crumbs on top. Bake at 375° for 30 minutes or until browned.

2 • GERMANY (TART)

1 cup butter
2 cups flour
sugar
⅛ teaspoon salt
1 egg

1 tablespoon ice water
cream or milk
sliced peaches
¾ cup ground nuts

Make the pastry by cutting the butter into the flour, sugar, and salt and then working in the egg and ice water. Wrap in wax paper and chill until firm. Divide in half and line two pie or tart pans. Brush with cream or milk. Arrange rows of sliced peaches on the pastry. Sprinkle with nuts and sugar and bake at 375° for 30 minutes.

3 • ITALY (COCOA TART)

¾ cup sugar
¼ teaspoon salt
⅓ cup cocoa
1 cup ground nuts

4 eggs, separated
1 teaspoon vanilla
cake or cookie crumbs

Mix sugar, salt, cocoa, and nuts. Beat the egg yolks; then beat them with the cocoa mixture and vanilla. Beat the egg whites stiff and fold in the cocoa mixture. Butter a 9-inch square baking pan and sprinkle with crumbs. Pour in the mixture. Bake at 350° for 30 minutes or until set. Serve hot.

4 • RUSSIA (CHEESE PASTRY)

Recipe #10, Bread and Biscuits, page 201.

V • CAKES

1 • FRANCE (BAKED ALASKA)

angel food or sponge cake
    or baked pastry shell
1 quart very firm ice cream
4 egg whites

¼ cup light corn syrup
1 teaspoon cream of tartar
powdered sugar

Place a 1-inch-thick layer of cake on a baking sheet. (Have the cake 2 inches larger than the ice cream.) Place the ice cream in the center of the cake or pie shell. Cover with meringue made by beating the egg whites stiff and then beating in the corn syrup and cream of tartar. Sprinkle the top with powdered sugar and bake in a 500° oven until lightly browned. Place on a serving dish and serve immediately. Try this with peppermint ice cream on a hot summer day.

2 • AUSTRIA (CHOCOLATE BUTTERMILK CAKE)

1½ cups sugar
2¼ cups sifted flour
1½ teaspoons soda
½ teaspoon salt
¼ pound butter
¾ cup buttermilk
3 large eggs
1 teaspoon vanilla
2 ounces sweet chocolate

apricot jam

frosting:
5 ounces baking chocolate
¼ pound butter
2 tablespoons hot water
2 eggs
2 cups powdered sugar

Mix and sift the dry ingredients together. Make a well in the center. Place the butter, buttermilk, eggs, and vanilla in the well. Beat at medium speed for 2 minutes. Melt the chocolate with ¾ cup boiling water in a double boiler. Add to the first mixture and beat one minute. Pour into an 8-inch-by-12-inch buttered baking dish. Bake at 375° for 40 minutes or until done. Cool. Spread a layer of jam over the cake. Melt the chocolate and butter over hot water and beat them together with the remaining ingredients. Spread on top of the apricot jam.

3 • HUNGARY (PANCAKE CAKE)

⅓ cup butter
⅓ cup sugar
⅔ cup flour
2 cups milk
8 eggs, separated
1 teaspoon vanilla

grated sweet chocolate

meringue:
3 egg whites
3 tablespoons sugar
½ teaspoon vanilla

Melt the butter and gradually add the sugar, flour, and milk, stirring until thickened. Cool and add the egg yolks and vanilla. Beat the egg whites stiff and fold into the mixture. Make the pancakes in a buttered 12-inch skillet. As they are done, pile them like layers of a cake, sprinkling each with grated chocolate. While you are doing this, keep them warm in a very low oven. To make the meringue, beat the egg whites stiff and then beat in the sugar and vanilla. Spread on top of the pile of pancakes. Bake at 325° until lightly browned. Serve immediately. Cut in wedges like a cake. If you prefer, you may omit the meringue and just sprinkle grated chocolate on top. (This cake can be wrapped in aluminum foil, frozen, and reheated when ready to serve.)

INDEX OF RECIPES

*Parenthetical references indicate the regional character
of dish and the recipe number within the special group.*

Acorn squash (W. Indies 6), 67
amandine sauce (3), 185
anchovy-eggplant salad (Italy 3), 71
anchovy-olive stuffing (Italy 5), 62
anchovy omelet (Sweden 3), 35
anchovy-Parmesan omelet filling
    (Italy 9), 38
anchovy salad dressing (25), 79
anchovy sauce (6), 186
appetizers, *see* HORS D'OEUVRES
apples, baked (Hungary 2), 206
apples, fried (Germany 23), 193
apricot nut pie (N.Z. 1), 211
artichoke hearts, baked (Italy 2), 40
artichoke hearts, fried (Italy 1), 40
artichokes stuffed w. chicken (Fr.
    20), 140
Asparagus
    crumbed (Poland 1), 40
    w. egg, parsley (Belgium 2), 40-41
    -beet-apple salad (Balkans 2), 71
    w. cheese (Poland 4), 41
    w. creamy dressing (Fr. 6), 41
    Hollandaise (Fr. 3), 41
    pie (Switz. 8), 42
    on toast (Fr. 7), 41
    -romaine salad (Germany 14), 72-
        73
    vinaigrette (Fr. 5), 41
Avocado
    -chili salad (Mex. 4), 75
    -cucumber salad (Mex. 1), 71
    -egg dip (S. America 30), 16
    -romaine salad (Fr. 2), 75
    salad, molded (Guatemala 1), 74-
        75
    -shrimp salad (Polynesia 6), 74
    -sour cream soup (Mex. 2), 18
    -spinach salad (Fr. 3), 75
    -tomato dip (Mex. 31), 16

Bacon balls (Hungary 19), 204
bacon-cheese omelet filling (Eng. 5),
    37
Baked Alaska (Fr. 1), 212
baked eggs, 34-35; *see also under*
    EGGS
baked fish, *see under* FISH
banana pudding (S. Africa 6), 208
Bananas
    baked (Samoa 15), 192
    broiled (Hawaii 16), 192
    w. chicken (W. Indies 43), 147
    w. jelly (Hawaii 17), 193
    -tangerine salad (Philippines 6), 75
basic salad dressing (15), 78
bean sprout-bamboo-watercress salad
    (Far East 5), 71
BEEF, 81-96

Casseroles
    adapting stew recipes for, 91
    w. bacon, beer (Germany 33), 91
    dried beef, noodles (Germany
        36), 92
    w. mushrooms, wine, herbs (Fr.
        35), 92
    w. sour cream (Russia 34), 92
    w. sour cream, paprika (Hungary
        37), 93
chili-tomato meatballs (Mex. 7),
    129
cooked, in meatballs (Fr. 17), 132
-curry soup (S. Africa 12), 20
ground, in French bread shell
    (Mex. 48), 96
Hash, 93-95
    w. apple (Denmark 42), 94
    w. fried eggs (Austria 40), 94
    w. potatoes, parsley (Eng. 43), 94
    w. raisins, almonds (Cuba 39), 93
    w. onions, potatoes (Fr. 38), 93
    w. rice, sour cream (Hungary
        44), 95
    95
meatballs, browned in butter (Nor-
    way 11), 130
w. mushrooms and bamboo shoots
    (Japan 47), 96
Parmesan-flavored meatballs (Italy
    8), 129
rice-tomato meatballs (Russia 10),
    130
Round Steak, 81-83
    w. bacon (Austria 7), 83
    baked (Russia 3), 81
    baked (Switz. 4), 82
    marinated, baked (W. Indies 5),
        82
    w. onions (Holland 2), 81
    w. sherry (Holland 8), 83
    w. sour cream (Hungary 1), 81
    in wine (Denmark 6), 82
    in wine-lemon sauce (Yugosl. 9),
        83
sauce for spaghetti (Italy 45), 95
soy-ginger meatballs (China 6),
    128-29
Stews, 86-91
    w. beer, herbs (Belgium 26), 89
    w. beer, spices (Germany 25),
        89
    w. caraway (Austria 31), 90-91
    w. chili (Mex. 23), 88
    w. chili, ginger (Burma 29), 90
    w. gingersnaps (Russia 22), 88
    w. olives (Chile 28), 90
    w. paprika, parsley (Yugosl. 27),
        89

w. paprika, sour cream (Hungary 20), 87
w. peanut butter (Ecuador 19), 87
w. red wine, herbs (Fr. 30), 90
w. rice (Chile 32), 91
suggestions for cooking, 86-87
w. wine, herbs (Italy 21), 87-88
w. wine, mustard (Denmark 24), 88-89
Swedish meatballs (Sweden 5), 128
sweet and pungent (Malaya 46), 95-96
Tenderloin, 83-86
breaded (Italy 15), 85-86
w. butter sauce (Fr. 16), 86
in cream (Czech. 10), 84
herbed (Fr. 14), 85
roast (Fr. 18), 86
sautéed (Fr. 17), 86
w. sour cream (Hungary 13), 85
in white wine (S. America 12), 84-85
in wine (Italy 11), 84
Tongue, 96-98
w. almonds (S. America 1), 97
in aspic (Fr. 2), 97
in batter (Hungary 6), 98
w. raisins and almonds (Poland 5), 98
w. soy sauce (China 4), 97-98
in spicy sauce (Italy 3), 97
see also MEATBALLS AND MEAT LOAVES
beef-cheese soup (Eng. 3), 18
beef-soup, see under SOUPS, Beef Stock Base
beet-orange salad (Scand. 5), 75
Beets
in sour cream (Poland 1), 45
w. tarragon (Russia 2), 45
in wine-consommé (Austria 3), 45-46
beet salad dressing (24), 79
blitz kuchen (Germany 14), 202-03
blueberries (Switz. 5), 206
BREADS AND BISCUITS, 198-204
bacon balls (Hungary 19), 204
blitz kuchen (Germany 14), 202-03
brioche (Fr. 17), 203-04
cheese-bacon rolls (Austria 5), 200
cheese-filled rolls (Estonia 4), 200
cheese pastry (Russia 10), 201
cornmeal fingers (Rumania 3), 199
croissants (Fr. 12), 201-02
crumpets (Eng. 18), 204
curry biscuits (Australia 13), 202
"doilies" (China), 198
garlic bread or rolls (Austria 6), 200
garlic sesame bread (Fr. 8), 200-01
ham puffs (Hungary 11), 201
muffins (Holland 20), 204
onion-herb rolls (Fr. 9), 201
plum buns (Austria 15), 203
poppy-seed balls (Hungary 16), 203
rolls w. cheddar cheese (Eng. 7), 200
scones (Eng. 1), 199
scones (Scotland 2), 199
bread-cherry pudding (Poland 4), 208
brioches (Fr. 17), 203-04
Broccoli
w. almonds (Fr. 5), 46-47
w. bacon (Germany 1), 46
w. chives (Eng. 2), 46

Hollandaise (Fr. 4), 46
sautéed (Italy 6), 47
w. wine (Italy 3), 46
Buffet Dishes
fish, 165-67
see also CASSEROLES; STEWS; MEAT-BALLS; CHICKEN

Cabbage
w. bacon (Germany 12), 51
buttered (Holland 10), 50
w. butter, jelly (Eng. 13), 51
methods of cooking, 47
red (Austria 14), 51
-rice soup (Italy 8), 19
w. sour cream, caraway (Austria 11), 50
Stuffed
w. beef (Fr. 3), 48
w. beef (Poland 4), 48
w. beef, pork (Holland 6), 49
w. beef, pork (Rumania 8), 49-50
w. beef, rice (Russia 7), 49
w. cooked meat (Austria 5), 48-49
w. lamb (Austria 1), 47-48
w. pork, rice (Hungary 9), 50
cake cornets, Fr. 4), 210
Cakes, 212-13
Baked Alaska (Fr. 1), 212
chocolate buttermilk cake (Austria 2), 213
pancake cake (Hungary 3), 213
calf's liver w. eggs (Italy 1), 32
cantaloupe-mixed vegetable salad (Balkans 10), 72
caraway garnish (Hungary 12), 189
carp poached in beer (Germany 17), 158
see also FISH, Poached
Carrots
buttered (Eng. 3), 52
in butter-wine sauce (Fr. 1), 51-52
w. soy sauce (Philippines 2), 52
CASSEROLES, 91-93
adapting stew recipes for, 91
Beef
bacon, beer (Germany 33), 91
sour cream (Russia 34), 92
sour cream, paprika (Hungary 37), 93
wine, herbs (Fr. 35), 92
Chicken, 145-48
w. asparagus, almonds (Fr. 46), 148
w. bananas (W. Indies 43), 147
w. cream, mushrooms (Eng. 15), 138
w. cream, wine (Fr. 16), 138
in cream sauce (Hungary 37), 145-46
crumbed, in sour cream (Ukraine 44), 148
w. macaroni (Italy 36), 145
w. Parmesan (Eng. 15), 138
w. pearl onions (Fr. 45), 148
w. pineapple juice (China 42), 147
w. potatoes (Scotland 38), 146
w. spices (India 40), 146-47
w. tomatoes (S. America 41), 147
w. wine, prunes, raisins (Belgium 39), 146
diced sausage casserole (Austria 3), 127

dried beef, noodles (Germany 36), 92

Fish, 203-207; see recipes under FISH, Casseroles

freezing, 149

ground cooked meat-rice (Yugosl. 2), 127

ground meat combination (S. America 1), 126-27

Lamb
(India 26), 111
(Russia 22), 110

veal with pastry cover (Eng. 15), 102-03

see also individual meats; Rice; STEWS

Cauliflower
baked (Poland 1), 52
butter-crumbed (Sweden 3), 53
w. chicken breasts (China 21), 140
-olive-anchovy salad (Italy 13), 72
sautéed (Italy 2), 53

caviar-oyster hors d'oeuvres (Russia 21), 14

celery-anchovy garnish (Fr. 8), 191

Cheese
cheddar cheese balls (Eng. 24), 14-15
cheddar cheese balls (Fr. 25), 15
cheddar cheese rolls (Eng. 7), 200
balls (Fr. 23), 14
balls for salads (Fr. 16), 73
-egg toast (Switz. 2), 38
pastry (Russia 10), 201
-rice balls (India 22), 14
sauce (3), 180-81
-sherry dip (Eng. 32), 16
soufflé (Fr. 1), 38
soup (Eng. 3), 18

cherries in batter (Hungary 5), 211

chestnut garnish (Fr. 1), 190-91

chestnuts w. chicken (Bulgaria 27), 142

CHICKEN, 134-51
-almond-grape salad (Fr. 2), 73
w. artichokes (Fr. 20), 140
breasts, w. cauliflower (China 21), 140
breasts, deep-fried (Russia 18), 139
Casseroles, 145-48; see recipes under CASSEROLES, Chicken
with cherries (Russia 22), 140-41
w. cherries, pistachios (Arabia 8), 136
w. Chinese vegetables (China 3), 134-35
-chutney salad (India 4), 74
w. coconut (Hawaii 13), 137
in cream-wine sauce (Fr. 16), 138
crumbed, baked in cream (Poland 12), 137
Curries, 149-51
basic (Java 47), 149
w. buttermilk (India 50), 150
w. coconut (India 48), 149-50
w. soy sauce, sherry (China 49), 150
w. wine (Eng. 51), 150-51
w. dried peas and wine (S. America 6), 135
w. grape jam (Spain 4), 135
-herb-curry hors d'oeuvres (India 26), 15
hors d'oeuvres (Scand. 19), 139-40
w. lemon, tomato, oregano (Greece 9), 136

-lobster loaf (Scand. 19), 139-40
marinated, deep-fried (China 17), 139
marinated, fried (Italy 10), 136-37
marinated, simmered (Santo Domingo 11), 137
w. paprika, sour cream (Austria 7), 136
w. paprika, sour cream (Hungary 5), 135
w. peas, almonds (Africa 14), 137-38
w. rice, nuts, orange peel (Iran 8), 177
w. rice, tomatoes (Eng. 6), 176
w. rice, tomatoes (Spain 4), 176
w. rice, tomatoes (W. Indies 7), 177
salad (Eng. 3), 74
sauces for, 184-85
soy-flavored (China 2), 134
Stews, 141-45
with cabbage (Hungary 29), 142-43
w. chestnuts (Bulgaria 27), 142
w. ham, wine (Italy 28), 142
w. herbs, vegetables (Fr. 32), 144
w. nuts, spices (India 35), 145
w. olives, prawns (Central America 25), 141-42
w. pineapple (Hawaii 33), 144
w. raisins, olives (Mex. 31), 143
w. soy sauce (Indonesia 24), 141
w. spices, nuts (India 35), 145
w. spinach (Africa 30), 143
w. tomatoes (Italy 34), 144-45
suggestions for stewing, 141
in wine sauce (Russia 1), 134

chicken liver filling (Germany 4), 37

chicken liver-mushroom hors d'-oeuvres (Russia 17), 13-14

chicken livers in onions (Italy 23), 141

chicken livers and water chestnuts (China 1), 11-12

chicken soup, see under SOUPS, Chicken

chicory, cooked (Belgium 1), 53

chili-horseradish dip (Eng. 36), 16

Chinese sauce, basic (China 2), 185

Chinese vegetable combination (China 4), 69

Chinese vegetables w. chicken (China 3), 134-35

chocolate buttermilk cake (Austria 2), 213

chocolate rum mold (Switz. 2), 207

chopped ham or bacon hors d'oeuvres (Eng. 4), 12

Chopped Meat Dishes
beef-pork-lamb combinations (S. America 1), 126-27
w. cooked meat, rice (Yugosl. 2), 127
see also BEEF; MEATBALLS AND MEAT LOAVES

chutney-butter hors d'oeuvres (Eng. 16), 13

chutney salad dressing (21), 78

cocktail dips, 15-16; see under HORS D'OEUVRES

cocoa tart (Italy 3), 212

Coconut
in baked fish (South Sea Isl. 23), 160
w. chicken (Hawaii 13), 137

216

w. rice (W. Indies 12), 178
w. spinach (Hawaii 4), 66
cod in cream sauce (Eng. 39), 166
Consommé
  w. egg (Fr. 5), 18
  w. oats (Austria 9), 19-20
  w. poached egg (Italy 6), 18-19
  see also Soups
cookies, see under Desserts
corn w. lima beans (Fr. 2), 44-45
cornmeal fingers (Rumania 3), 199
cottage cheese omelet filling (Hungary 6), 37
cottage cheese salad dressing (22), 78-79
Crab Meat
  -curry hors d'oeuvres (Eng. 6), 12
  on toast (Fr. 14), 172
  in whole tomatoes (Eng. 13), 171
cranberry salad (Eng. 7), 75
cream dressing (17), 78
cream-potato soup (Austria 15), 21
cream puffs (Italy 2), 210
cream sauce, basic, 179-80
cream sauce, Hungarian (1), 184-85
croissants (Fr. 12), 201-02
croutons (Fr. 1), 188
crumpets (Eng. 18), 204
Cucumbers, 53-56
  -avocado salad (Mex. 1), 71
  in butter-cream sauce (Austria 7), 55
  garnish (Italy 10), 189
  methods for stuffing, 53-54
  sautéed (Fr. 8), 55-56
  Stuffed
    w. bacon, onion, tomato (Fr. 2), 54
    w. beef, ham (Italy 5), 55
    w. meat, rice (Austria 3), 54
    w. mushrooms (Fr. 4), 54-55
    w. sausage (Holland 1), 54
    w. tuna fish (Italy 6), 55
currant jelly dip (Eng. 34), 16
curried pineapple (Malaya 22), 193
curried pork (Philippines 34), 124-25
curried potatoes (India 5), 64
Curries
  Chicken, 149-51
    basic (Java 47), 149
    w. coconut (India 48), 149-50
    w. soy sauce, sherry (China 49), 150
  kedgeree (India 37), 165
  Lamb, 113-14; see also Lamb
curry-beef soup (S. Africa 12), 20
curry biscuits (Australia 13), 202
curry-cream-chicken soup (India 8), 23-24
curry-flavored dip (India 28), 15
curry-flavored poached fish (India 15), 158
curry salad dressing (6), 77
custard (Fr. 3), 207
custard apples (Eng. 1), 206

Desserts, 205-13
  Cakes, 269-270
    Baked Alaska (Fr. 1), 212
    chocolate buttermilk cake (Austria 2), 213
    pancake cake (Hungary 3), 213
  Cookies and Small Confections, 209-11
    cake cornets (Fr. 4), 210

cherries in batter (Hungary 5), 211
cookies (Eng. 1), 209
cookies (Sweden 3), 210
cream puffs (Italy 2), 210
dessert pancakes (Fr. 6), 211
Fruit desserts, 206-07
  baked apples (Hungary 2), 206
  blueberries (Switz. 5), 206
  custard apples (Eng. 1), 206
  fruit flambé (Fr. 6), 206-07
  honeydew w. ginger (China 4), 206
  melon w. wine (Fr. 3), 206
Pies and Tarts, 211-12
  apricot nut pie (N.Z. 1), 211
  cheese pastry (Russia 10), 201
  cocoa tart (Italy 3), 212
  peach tart (Germany 2), 212
Puddings and Soufflés, 207-09
  banana pudding (S. America 6), 208
  bread-cherry pudding (Poland 4), 208
  chocolate rum mold (Switz. 2), 207
  custard (Fr. 3), 207
  dessert omelet (Fr. 5), 208
  egg soufflé (Fr. 9), 209
  molded nuts (Latvia 1), 207
  mousse (Fr. 7), 208-09
  soufflé w. liqueur (Fr. 8), 209
deviled ham in pancakes (Hungary 36), 125
dill dressing (12), 77
dill sauce (1), 182
"doilies" for Peking Duck (China), 198
dressings, salad, see Salad Dressings
Duck
  honey-brown sugar (China 1), 151
  -orange salad (Fr. 1), 73
  w. tomatoes (Spain 3), 151-52
  w. white wine (Italy 2), 151
dumplings (Fr. 14), 190

Egg-curry garnish (Malaya 3), 191
egg dressing (7), 77
Egg Foo Yung (China 2), 35
egg garnish (China 13), 189
Eggplant, 56-57
  -anchovy salad (Italy 3), 71
  baked (Italy 2), 56
  baked, w. tomatoes, green pepper (Italy 4), 56-57
  Hollandaise (Fr. 3), 56
  hors d'oeuvres (Syria 5), 12
  w. olives (Algeria 1), 56
  salad (Italy 17), 73
  -tomato dip (Fr. 35), 16
  w. tomatoes and cottage cheese (Algeria 5), 57
Eggs, 31-38
  Baked, 34-35
    w. ham or bacon (Eng. 2), 34
    w. potatoes (Fr. 4), 34-35
    in sour cream (Austria 1), 34
    in whole tomato (Italy 3), 34
  egg-cheese toast (Switz. 3), 38
  Fried, 32-33
    in browned bread (Poland 2), 32-33
    w. calf's liver and sweetbreads (Italy 1), 32
    w. mushrooms (Austria 4), 33

217

w. potatoes and frankfurters
(Germany 3), 33
Omelets, 35-38
w. anchovies (Sweden 3), 35
basic recipe, 36-37
Egg Foo Yung (China 2), 35
filled, 36-38
w. fish fillets (Philippines 7), 36
w. mashed potatoes (Fr. 4), 35-36
onion-parsley (Portugal 5), 36
spinach-cheese (Austria 6), 36
Poached, 33-34
w. consommé (Italy 6), 18-19
w. ham (Fr. 1), 33
method, 33
w. spinach (Italy 2), 33
w. tomatoes (Mex. 3), 34
in wine sauce (Fr. 4), 34
Scrambled, 31-32
w. cheese (Austria 4), 32
method, 31-32
w. mushrooms (Poland 6), 32
w. mushrooms bamboo shoots
(China 2), 32
w. orange juice (Mex. 7), 32
w. smoked salmon (Russia 5), 32
w. soy sauce, sugar (Japan 1), 32
w. tomatoes (Spain 3), 32
soufflé (Fr. 1), 38
Espagnole sauce (4), 181

Filled omelets, 36-38; see also Omelet
Fillings
fillet of sole, see FISH
fillet of veal, see VEAL
fillings for baked potatoes, 199-201
fillings for pancakes, see PANCAKES
FISH, 154-67
Baked, 159-62
w. cream, coconut (South Sea
Isl. 23), 160
fillets, stuffed (S. America 24),
161
fillets w. wine (Fr. 21), 160
w. ginger, coconut (India 25), 161
in milk (Austria 28), 162
salmon, marinated (Fr. 40), 166-67
salmon, stuffed (Alaska 22), 160
salmon, whole (Fr. 20), 159-60
whole, stuffed (Poland 36), 161
w. wine, chocolate (Spain 27), 162
balls (South Sea Isl. 41), 167
Casseroles, 162-65
w. herbs, wine, tomatoes (Fr.
32), 163-64
w. ginger, peppers, scallions
(Philippines 31), 163
w. pastry cover (Russia 35),
164-65
w. potatoes, onions, tomatoes
(Chile 29), 162
w. rice, tomatoes, wine (Spain
34), 164
w. sauerkraut, mushrooms (Poland 30), 163
w. sour cream, mushrooms
(Hungary 33), 164
w. tomatoes, potatoes (S. America 36), 165
cod in cream sauce (Eng. 39), 166
fillet of sole in lime juice (Polynesia 5), 74

Fillets, Sautéed, 154-56
w. almonds (Fr. 8), 156
w. buttermilk, lemon (India 1),
154
w. ginger, soy sauce (Japan 6),
155
w. onion, tomato (Austria 2), 154
w. raisins, nuts (Italy 7), 155
w. sherry, soy sauce (China 3),
154-55
w. soy sauce, sesame seeds
(Korea 4), 155
w. tomatoes (Fr. 9), 156
w. vinegar, brown sugar (Philippines 5), 155
fillets w. shrimp (Fr. 38), 166
filling for omelet (Japan 2), 37
kedgeree (India 37), 165
omelet (Philippines 7), 36
Poached, 156-59
w. cabbage, potatoes, caraway
(Germany 16), 158
carp w. beer (Germany 17), 158
w. cauliflower, peas (Japan 18),
159
curry-flavored (India 15), 158
w. onions, tomatoes, olives (Russia 11), 157
pike in milk (Hungary 12), 157
w. spices (W. Indies 14), 157
trout in wine vinegar (Hungary
13), 157
in wine (Fr. 19), 159
sardines, broiled (Eng. 8), 12-13
sauces for, 185-86
smoked salmon filling for omelet
(Russia 7), 37
smoked salmon hors d'oeuvres
(Sweden 14), 13
smoked salmon w. scrambled eggs
(Russia 5), 32
suggestions for frying, 154
suggestions for poaching, 156
see also SHELLFISH
frankfurters w. lentil soup (Germany
2), 25
frankfurters w. split pea soup (Czech.
3), 26
French bread stuffed w. beef (Mex.
48), 96
French dressing, basic (5), 76
French sauce (2), 185
fried eggs, see under EGGS
fruit flambé (Fr. 6), 206-07
fruits, see under DESSERTS; SALADS;
individual fruits
fruit salad w. cheese balls (Fr. 8), 75
fruit sauce (2), 182-83
fruit shop (Norway 1), 27-28

Garlic-sesame bread (Fr. 8), 200-01
GARNISHES, 187-93
apple, fried (Germany 23), 193
banana (Hawaii 17), 193
banana (Samoa 15), 192
banana-jelly (Hawaii 17), 193
beaten egg (Fr. 8), 189
caraway (Hungary 12), 189
celery-anchovy (Fr. 8), 191
cheddar (Eng. 6), 188-89
cheese-batter (Eng. 11), 189
cheese-parsley (Italy 2), 188
cheese rounds (Spain 20), 190
chestnut (Fr. 1), 190-91
cornmeal strips (W. Indies 6), 191
croutons (Fr. 1), 188

deep-fried parsley (Fr. 11), 192
dumplings (Fr. 14), 190
egg (China 13), 189
egg-butter balls (Holland 17), 190
egg-curry (Malaya 3), 191
egg-horseradish (Austria 4), 191
fried noodles (Hungary 7), 191
hard cheese (Italy 5), 188
for main courses, 190-93
mushroom (Fr. 10), 192
mushroom (Italy 18), 193
mushroom-anchovy-tomato (Italy
    20), 193
mushrooms, baked (Hungary 19),
    193
mushrooms in wine (Fr. 21), 193
nut (Eng. 5), 191
Parmesan (Italy 9), 189
pastry-cheese (Austria 15), 190
pineapple-curry (Malaya 22), 193
poppy-seed (Hungary 12), 189
for pork, 116-17
potato-egg strips (Hungary 18), 190
prune-bacon (Sweden 9), 192
Roquefort (Germany 3), 188
saltine (Eng. 7), 189
for soups, salads, 31, 188-90
squash balls (Italy 2), 191
stuffed cucumber (Italy 10), 189
Swiss cheese (Switz. 4), 188
tomato-cheese (Eng. 14), 192
tomato-crouton (Italy 12), 192
tomato-oregano (Spain 13), 192
tortillas, fried, (Mex. 19), 190
tor veal, 100
whipped cream (Russia 16), 190
ginger-raisin sauce (2), 184
Green Beans
baked (Italy 2), 42-43
deep-fried (Italy 5), 43
sautéed (Fr. 3), 43
tips for cooking, 44
w. bacon (Hungary 1), 42
w. herbs (Russia 8), 44
w. onions (Italy 7), 44
in sour cream (Austria 6), 43-44
w. soy sauce (China 4), 43
Green Peppers, Stuffed, 61-63
w. anchovies, olives (Italy 5), 62
w. beef and almonds (Mexico 1),
    61
w. chicken (Fr. 6), 62
methods of preparing, 61
w. pork and rice (Hungary 2), 61
w. sausages and sour cream (Aus-
    tria 3), 61-62
w. seafood (China 4), 62
green sauce (5), 185-86
ground beef-vegetable soup (Philip-
    pines 11), 20

Haddock, *see* Fish
halibut, *see* Fish
Ham
in pancakes (Hungary 36), 125
chopped, hors d'oeuvres (Eng. 4),
    12
-chutney-chili hors d'oeuvres (N. Z.
    2), 12
ground, w. eggs (Eng. 2), 34
and melon hors d'oeuvres (Italy
    15), 13
-onion soup (Spain 10), 19-20
puffs (Hungary 11), 201
slices, rolled (S. America 35), 125

Hash
Beef, 93-95
w. beaten egg (Germany 41), 94
beef-apple (Denmark 42), 94
beef-onion-potato (Fr. 38), 93
beef-potatoes-parsley (Eng. 43),
    94
beef-raisin-almond (Cuba 39), 93
beef-rice-sour cream (Hungary
    44), 95
w. fried eggs (Austria 40), 94
Lamb, 111-13
baked (Italy 28), 112
suggestions for preparing, 111
w. mushrooms (Fr. 27), 112
w. rice and chili (Indonesia 29),
    112
w. rice and eggs (W. Indies 30),
    113
Pork, *see recipes above under*
    Hash, Lamb
hearts of palm Hollandaise (Fr. 1),
    59
herb dressing (11), 77
herbed green beans (Russia 8), 44
herb omelet filling (Fr. 3), 37
herb omelet filling (Switz. 10), 38
Hollandaise sauce (1), 180
tarragon Hollandaise (3), 181
tomato Hollandaise (2), 180
horseradish sauce (1), 181
Hungarian cream sauce (1), 184-85
Hungarian sour cream sauce (6), 182
honeydew melon w. ginger (China 4),
    206
Hors d'Oeuvres, 11-16
avocado-egg dip (S. America 30),
    16
avocado-tomato dip (Mex. 31), 16
caviar-oyster (Russia 21), 14
cheddar cheese balls (Eng. 24), 14-
    15
cheddar cheese balls (Fr. 25), 15
cheese balls (Fr. 23), 14
cheese pastry (Russia 10), 201
cheese-shrimp dip (Eng. 32), 16
chicken-herb-curry balls (India 26),
    15
chicken-lobster spread (Scand. 19),
    139-40
chicken livers and mushrooms
    (Russia 17), 13-14
chili-horseradish dip (Eng. 36), 16
chopped ham or bacon (Eng. 4), 12
chutney-butter (Eng. 16), 13
cocktail dips, 15-16
crab meat-curry (Eng. 6), 12
cream cheese-caraway dip
    (Hungary 33), 16
cream cheese-caraway dip (Latvia,
    27), 15
currant jelly dip (Eng. 34), 16
curry-flavored dip (India 28), 15
eggplant (Syria 5), 12
eggplant-tomato dip (Fr. 35), 16
ham-chutney-chili (N. Z. 2), 12
ham and melon (Italy 15), 13
lobster-almond (Fr. 9), 13
lobster-artichoke (Fr. 7), 12
mushrooms stuffed w. fish (Fr. 3),
    12
oysters w. bacon (Eng. 10), 13
oysters on toast rounds (Fr. 20), 14
pancakes, filled (Eng. 18), 14
rice-cheese balls (India 22), 14
sardines, broiled (Eng. 8), 12-13

scallops and mushrooms (Fr. 13), 13

shrimp in marinade (Sweden 11), 13

shrimp-soy sauce (China 12), 13

smoked salmon-cream cheese (Sweden 14), 13

sour cream-fennel dip (Hungary 29), 16

water chestnuts and chicken livers (China 1), 11-12

Italian cheese sauce (3), 180-81
Italian tomato sauce (7), 182

Jelly salad dressing (23), 79

Kedgeree (India 37), 165

LAMB
  casserole w. eggplant (Russia 22), 110
  onion-tomato (India 26), 111
    see also CASSEROLES, LAMB
  Chops, 105-08
    baked w. tomatoes (Iraq 16), 107-08
    breaded (Hungary 10), 106
    broiled w. anchovies (Italy 14), 107
    broiled, curried (Australia 15), 107
    broiled w. mint (Morocco 12), 106
    broiled w. mushrooms (Fr. 17), 108
    marinated (S. Africa 9), 106
    marinated, broiled (Turkey 13), 107
    in piecrust (Australia 11), 106
    cooking time, 103
  Curries, 113-14
    browned in butter, sugar (India 31), 113
    w. coconut (Hawaii 34), 114
    w. eggplant, garlic (India 33), 114
    w. tomatoes, consomme (Eng. 32), 113
  Hash, 111-13
    baked (Italy 28), 112
    w. eggs and rice (W. Indies 30), 113
    w. mushrooms (Fr. 27), 112
    w. rice and chili (Indonesia 29), 112
    suggestions for preparing, 111
  Leg
    roast (Arabia 2), 103-04
    roast, with coffee (Sweden 5), 104
    roast, w. herbs (Fr. 7), 105
    roast, w. mint (Eng. 3), 104
    roast, w. mushrooms (Austria 8), 105
    roast, w. vinegar (Poland 6), 105
    w. wine (Italy 4), 104
    w. rice (Turkey 1), 175
  Stews, 108-11
    w. corn, lima beans (S. America 21), 109-10
    w. garden vegetables (Fr. 20), 109
    w. onions, potatoes (Ireland 25), 111
    w. sour cream (Hungary 23), 110

w. spices (Indonesia 19), 109
  suggestions for preparing, 108
  w. wine (Fr. 24), 110-11
lamb-lemon soup (Turkey 3), 28
leftover pork (Poland 32), 124
lemon-chicken-rice soup (Greece 10), 24
lentil-curry soup (India 1), 25
lentil-frankfurter soup (Germany 2), 25
lettuce, baked (Spain 2), 57-58
lettuce cooked in cream (Fr. 1), 57
lettuce salad w. croutons (Fr. 12), 72
lima beans w. corn (Fr. 2), 44-45
lima beans w. cream (Germany 3), 45
lima beans w. onion (Italy 1), 44
Lobster, 167-70
  -almond hors d'oeuvres (Fr. 9), 13
  -artichoke hors d'oeuvres (Fr. 7), 12
  baked, w. cheese (Fr. 6), 169
  w. oysters (Italy 4), 168
  -chicken loaf (Scand. 19), 139-40
  w. creamy stuffing (Eng. 5), 169
  filling for omelets (Japan 2), 37
  flamed w. brandy (Spain 1), 167
  w. rice (Sweden 10), 178
  w. sherry, ginger (China 7), 170
  stuffed, broiled (W. Indies 2), 168
  on toast (Fr. 8), 170
lobster tails with vegetables (Java 3), 168

Macaroni w. chicken (Italy 36), 145
meat, see under individual meats;
  CASSEROLES; STEWS; HASH
MEATBALLS AND MEAT LOAVES, 127-32
  w. bacon (W. Indies 14), 131
  beef-pork in sour cream (Austria 13), 131
  beef-pork in sour cream (Austria 15), 131-32
  beef-pork in wine sauce (Denmark 16), 132
  browned in butter (Norway 11), 130
  chili-tomato (Mex. 7), 129
  w. cooked beef (Fr. 17), 132
  w. Parmesan cheese (Italy 8), 129
  w. rice (Russia 10), 130
  in sour cream (Poland 12), 130-31
  soy-ginger (China 6), 128-29
  w. soy sauce (Japan 9), 130
  suggestions for serving, 127
  Swedish (Sweden 5), 128
  veal-beef-sausage combination (Cuba 4), 128
    see also BEEF; CHOPPED MEATS;
    CASSEROLES
meatball soup (Spain 13), 20
meat salads, 73-74
meat sauce for spaghetti (Italy 45), 95
melon-ham hors d'oeuvres (Italy 15), 13
melon in wine (Fr. 3), 206
melon salad (Fr. 9), 75
melon soup (China 8), 30
mint-lemon consommé (Guatemala 1), 18
mixed greens w. cheese balls (Fr. 16), 73
mixed vegetable salad (Indonesia 7), 71
mixed vegetable salad w. croutons (Fr. 8), 72

molasses salad dressing (14), 78
molded nut dessert (Latvia 1), 207
mousse (Fr. 7), 208-09
muffins (Holland 20), 204
Mushrooms
  w. anchovies and tomatoes (It. 20), 193
  baked (Hungary 19), 193
  baked (Italy 2), 58
  broiled (Italy 18), 193
  in butter (Spain 1), 58
  -chicken liver hors d'oeuvres (Russia 17), 13-14
  w. fried eggs (Austria 4), 33
  omelet filling (Poland 1), 37
  sauce (2), 181
  -scallop hors d'oeuvres (Fr. 13), 13
  w. scrambled eggs (Poland 6), 32
  stuffed w. fish (Fr. 3), 12
  stuffing for cucumbers (Fr. 4), 54-55
  in wine (Fr. 21), 193
mustard greens (China 1), 58-59
mustard salad dressing (26), 79
mustard sauce (3), 185
mustard sauce (7), 186

Noodles, fried (Hungary 7), 191
noodles w. dried beef (Germany 36), 92
nut cookies (Eng. 1), 209
nut garnish (Eng. 5), 191

Oatmeal soup (Austria 9), 19
Omelet Fillings, 37-38
  anchovy-Parmesan (Italy 9), 38
  chicken liver (Germany 4), 37
  cottage cheese-sour cream (Hungary 6), 37
  fish or lobster (Japan 2), 37
  ham-Swiss cheese (Eng. 5), 37
  herb (Fr. 3), 37
  mint-basil (Switz. 10) 38
  mushroom (Poland 1), 37
  smoked salmon, anchovies, caviar (Russia 7), 37
  tomato-pepper (Spain 8), 37
  variations, 38
Omelets, 35-38
  basic recipe, 36-37
  dessert (Fr. 5), 208
  filled, 37-38
  see also under EGGS
Onion
  -bean sprout soup (E. Indies 11), 24
  -cheese soup (Fr. 4), 18
  -ham soup (Spain 10), 19-20
  -parsley omelet (Portugal 5), 36
  -wine soup (Austria 7), 19
  salad dressing (18), 78
onions, baked (Bermuda 1), 59
onions stuffed w. chicken livers (Italy 23), 141
orange-beet salad (Scand. 5), 75
orange-duck salad (Fr. 1), 73
oyster-bacon hors d'oeuvres (Eng. 10), 13
oysters, baked (Fr. 18), 173

Pancakes, 194-97
  batters, 194-96
  dessert pancakes (Fr. 6), 211
  w. deviled ham (Hungary 36), 125
  filled (Fr. 18), 14

Fillings, 196-97
  apple (Germany 7), 197
  cabbage (Austria 6), 197
  ham-sour cream (Poland 2), 196
  lingonberries and jam (Sweden 8), 197
  meat (1), 196
  methods, 196
  mushroom-sour cream (Hungary 5), 197
  seafood (Hungary 3), 197
  velouté sauce, meat or fish (Fr. 4), 197
  pancake cake (Hungary 3), 213
pastry-cheese garnish (Austria 15), 190
peach tart (Germany 2), 212
peanut butter-chicken soup (Africa 9), 24
peanut butter-chicken soup (W. Africa 1), 21
Peas, 59-60
  w. pearl onions (Fr. 2), 60
  puréed, baked (Fr. 4), 60
  w. rice (Austria 1), 59-60
  w. soy sauce (China 3), 60
  tips on cooking, 59
peppers, green, see GREEN PEPPERS
Pheasant
  in red wine (Fr. 3), 152
  w. sauerkraut, white wine (Germany 1), 152
  w. sour cream (Austria 2), 152
pike, poached (Hungary 12), 157; see also FISH, Poached
pickle salad dressing (19), 78
pickle soup (Poland 3), 30
pies, see under DESSERTS
pineapple, curried (Malaya 22), 193
pineapple w. chicken (Hawaii 33), 144
plum buns (Austria 15), 203
poached eggs, 33; see also under EGGS
poppy-seed balls (Hungary 16), 203
poppy-seed garnish (Hungary 12), 189
PORK, 114-25
  Chops, 114-118
    baked w. cheese (Philippines 2), 115
    baked w. potatoes (Sweden 8), 116
    w. figs, rice (Philippines 13), 118
    w. honey-Worcester marinade (Germany 17), 119
    marinated (Mex. 1), 114
    marinated (S. America 12), 117-18
    w. mozzarella, prosciutto (Italy 10), 117
    w. pineapple (Hawaii 3), 115
    w. rice, tomato (Near East 14), 118
    sherry-lemon (Holland 16), 118-19
    w. sour cream (Hungary 4), 115
    w. sour cream, caraway (Austria 6), 116
    in soy sauce (Indonesia 11), 117
    stuffed (Austria 15), 118
    w. white wine (Fr. 7), 116
    w. wine fennel (Italy 5), 115-16
    in wine-tomato sauce (Italy 9), 117
  curry-rice (Philippines 34), 124-25
  diced roast (E. Indies 20), 120

garnishes for, 116-17
Hash
    baked (Italy 28), 112
    w. eggs, rice (W. Indies 30), 113
    w. mushrooms (Fr. 27), 112
    w. rice, chili (Indonesia 29), 112
leftover (Poland 32), 124
Roast
    w. caraway (Austria 23), 121
    w. orange juice (W. Indies 18),
        119
    w. prunes (Sweden 21), 120
    w. sausage (Mexico 22), 121
    w. spices (Central America 19),
        120
sauces for, 184-85
Spareribs
    baked (China 25), 121
    w. caraway (Austria 26), 122
    crumbed, fried (S. America 24),
        121
Stews
    w. caraway, horseradish (Austria
        27), 122
    w. herbs, white wine (Italy 30),
        123
    w. pearl onions (Russia 31), 123
    w. pimiento and tomato (Spain
        28), 122
    w. sauerkraut, sour cream
        (Hungary 29), 123
stir-fried (China 33), 124
suggestions for cooking, 119
see also MEATBALLS AND MEAT
    LOAVES
pork ball-vegetable soup (China 14),
    21
pork-watercress soup (China 7), 27
Potato
    -bacon salad (Germany 4), 71
    -cream soup (Austria 15), 21
    -sardine salad (Scand. 11), 72
    -turnip soup (Spain 10), 30
    -veal salad (Latvia 16), 103
    -watercress soup (Portugal 8), 27
    -wine salad (Fr. 15), 73
Potatoes, 63-64
    baked w. eggs (Fr. 4), 34-35
    curried (India 5), 64
    w. fried eggs (Germany 3), 33
    mashed, in omelet (Fr. 4), 35-36
    w. onions, cheese (Fr. 1), 63
    w. sour cream (Poland 2), 63-64
    stuffed (Hungary 3), 64
    stuffed (Italy 4), 64
    stuffed w. fish, shrimp (Fr. 38) 166
poultry, see under CHICKEN; DUCK;
    PHEASANT
prune-bacon garnish (Sweden 9), 192
puddings, see under DESSERTS
purée of spinach (Fr. 5), 66

Red cabbage w. wine (Austria 14), 51
relishes, see GARNISHES
Rice, 174-78
    w. almonds (Iraq 5), 176
    -cheese balls (India 22), 14
    w. chicken, nuts, orange peel (Iran
        8), 177
    w. chicken, tomatoes (Eng. 6), 176
    w. chicken, tomatoes (Spain 4), 176
    w. chicken, tomatoes (W. Indies
        7), 177
    w. coconut (W. Indies 12), 178
    w. lamb (Turkey 1), 175
    w. lobster (Sweden 10), 178

    w. mushrooms (Russia 11), 178
rijsttafel, 149
    in ring mold (Fr. 3), 175
    w. sausage (Italy 2), 175
    suggestions for preparing, 174
rijsttafel, 149
Roquefort garnish (Germany 3), 188
round steak, 81-83; see also under
    BEEF
Russian dressing (9), 77

SALAD DRESSINGS, 76-79
    anchovy (25), 79
    basic (15), 78
    beet (24), 79
    chutney (21), 78
    cooked (4), 76
    cottage cheese (22), 78-79
    cream (17), 78
    curry (6), 77
    dill (12), 77
    egg (7), 77
    French, basic (5), 76
    herb (11), 77
    jelly (23), 79
    molasses (14), 78
    mustard (26), 79
    onion (18), 78
    pickle (19), 78
    Russian (9), 77
    sesame seed (20), 78
    sour cream (1), 76
    soy (8), 77
    suggestions for using, 79
    sweet (13), 77
    tarragon (16), 78
    tomato (10), 77
    Thousand Islands (3), 76
    vinaigrette (2), 76
SALADS, 70-75
    asparagus, beets, apples (Balkans
        2), 71
    asparagus-romaine (Germany 14),
        72-73
    Avocado
        -chili (Mex. 4), 75
        molded (Guatemala 1), 74-75
        -romaine (Fr. 2), 75
        -shrimp (Polynesia 4), 74
        -spinach (Fr. 3), 75
    banana-tangerine (Philippines 6),
        75
    bean sprout-bamboo shoot (Far
        East 5), 71
    cauliflower-olive-anchovy (Italy
        13), 72
    cheese balls for (Fr. 16), 73
    chicken (Eng. 3), 74
    chicken-almond-grape (Fr. 2), 73
    chicken-chutney (India 4), 74
    cooked mixed vegetables vinaigrette
        (Fr. 9), 72
    cranberry (Eng. 7), 75
    cucumber-avocado (Mex. 1), 71
    duck-orange (Fr. 1), 73
    eggplant (Italy 17), 73
    eggplant-anchovy (Italy 3), 71
    fillet of sole-lime juice (Polynesia
        5), 74
    fruit, 74-75
    fruit with cheese balls (Fr. 8), 75
    garnishes for, 188-89
    ingredients for, 70
    lettuce w. croutons (Fr. 12), 72
    meat, 73-74
    melon (Fr. 9), 75

222

mixed greens-cheese balls (Fr. 16), 73
mixed greens-sesame (Far East 6), 71
mixed vegetable (Indonesia 7), 71
mixed vegetables-cantaloupe (Balkans 10), 72
mixed vegetables w. croutons (Fr. 8), 72
orange-beet (Scand. 5), 75
potato-bacon, hot (Germany 4), 71
potato-sardine (Scand. 11), 72
potato-wine (Fr. 15), 73
shrimp-sprout (Far East 7), 74
veal-potato (Latvia 16), 103
vegetable, 70-73
Salmon
baked stuffed (Alaska 22), 160
baked whole (Fr. 19), 159
marinated, baked (Fr. 40), 166-67
see also Smoked Salmon; FISH
sardine-potato salad (Scand. 11), 72
sardines, broiled (Eng. 8), 12-13
SAUCES; 179-86
amandine (3), 185
anchovy (4), 186
basic cream, 179-80
basic white, 179-80
for beef, 181-82
for chicken, 184-85
Chinese, basic (2), 185
dill (1), 182
for fish, 185-86
Espagnole (4), 181
French (2), 185
fruit (2), 182-83
ginger raisin (2), 184
green (5), 185-86
Hollandaise (1), 180
  tarragon (3), 181
  tomato (2), 180
horseradish (1), 181
Hungarian cream (1), 184-85
Hungarian sour cream (6), 182
Italian cheese (3), 180-81
Italian tomato (7), 182
for lamb, 182-83
mushroom (2), 181
mustard (3), 184
mustard (7), 186
for pork, 184-85
sesame (4), 181
sour cream (6), 182
tarragon (1), 185
tips, 182, 186
tomato Hollandaise (2), 180
for vegetables, 180-81
vinaigrette (2), 76
whipped cream (4), 185
wine (5), 182
sausage casserole (Austria 3), 127
sausage w. rice (Italy 2), 175
scallop-mushroom hors d'oeuvres (Fr. 13), 13
scallops, baked (Fr. 19), 173
scones (Eng. 1), 199
scones (Scotland 2), 199
scrambled eggs, 31-32; see also under EGGS
seafood, see SHELLFISH; FISH
sesame sauce (4), 181
sesame seeds w. mixed greens (Far East 6), 71
sesame seed salad dressing (20), 78
SHELLFISH, 167-73
  w. coconut (Hawaii 15), 172

Crab Meat, 171-72
-curry hors d'oeuvres (Eng. 6), 12
on toast (Fr. 14), 172
in whole tomatoes (Eng. 13), 171
curried (Eng. 16), 172
Lobster, 167-70
-almond hors d'oeuvres (Fr. 9), 13
-artichoke hors d'oeuvres (Fr. 7), 12
baked, w. cheese (Fr. 6), 169
broiled, w. oysters (Italy 4), 168
-chicken loaf (Scand. 19), 139-40
w. creamy stuffing (Eng. 5), 169
w. flaming brandy (Spain 1), 167
w. rice (Fr. 9), 177
w. rice (Sweden 10), 178
w. sherry, ginger (China 7), 170
stuffed, broiled (W. Indies 2), 168
on toast (Fr. 8), 170
lobster tails (Java 3), 168
marinated shellfish w. spices, coconut (Java 17), 172-73
oyster-bacon hors d'oeuvres (Eng. 10), 13
oyster hors d'oeuvres (Fr. 20), 14
oysters, baked (Fr. 18), 173
scallop-mushroom hors d'oeuvres (Fr. 13), 13
scallops, baked (Fr. 19), 173
Shrimp, 170-71
-avocado salad (Polynesia 6), 74
-bean sprout salad (Far East 7), 74
butterfly (Japan 9), 170
in cream sauce (Norway 12), 171
deep-fried (China 10), 170-71
w. fish fillets (Fr. 38), 166
hors d'oeuvres (Sweden 11), 13
in individual casseroles (Fr. 11), 171
in marinade (Sweden 11), 13
marinated, deep-fried (China 17), 139
-soy sauce hors d'oeuvres (China 12), 13
shrimp, see above under SHELLFISH
smoked salmon hors d'oeuvres (Sweden 14), 13
smoked salmon w. scrambled eggs (Russia 5), 32
sole, see FISH
Soufflés
egg-cheese (Fr. 1), 38
see also under DESSERTS
SOUPS, 17-30
Beef Stock Base
  beef-cheese (Eng. 3), 18
  beef-curry (S. Africa 12), 20
  browned meatball (Spain 13), 20
  cabbage-rice (Italy 8), 19
  cheese-onion (Fr. 4), 18
  consommé w. egg (Fr. 5), 18
  consommé w. oats (Austria 9), 19
  consommé w. poached egg (Italy 6), 18-19
  ground beef and vegetable (Philippines 11), 20
  ham-onion (Spain 10), 19-20
  mint-lemon (Guatemala 1), 18
  onion-wine (Austria 7), 19
  pork ball-vegetable (China 14), 21
  potato-cream (Austria 15), 21

sour cream-avocado, chilled
(Mex. 2), 18
Chicken base
cream-curry (India 8), 23-24
cream-herb, chilled (Fr. 6), 23
fruit-ginger (Hawaii 3), 22
leek-wine (Belgium 4), 22
onion-bean sprout (E. Indies 11),
24
peanut butter (Africa 9), 24
peanut butter (W. Africa 1), 21
rice-lemon (Greece 10), 24
-vegetable (Chile 2), 21-22
walnut-sour cream (Fr. 12), 24
water chestnut-egg (China 5), 22-
23
yam (W. Indies 7), 23
fruit (Norway 1), 27-28
garnishes for, 20, 25, 188-90
lamb-lemon (Turkey 3), 28
melon (China 8), 30
pickle (Poland 9), 30
potato-turnip (Spain 10), 30
suggested variations, 25
tapioca-cream (Norway 4), 28-29
tomato-wine (Hungary 2), 28
Vegetable
lentil-curry (India 1), 25
lentil-frankfurter (Germany 2),
25
potato-watercress (Portugal 8), 27
spinach (Italy 5), 26
spinach w. pork (China 6), 27
split pea-frankfurter (Czech. 3),
26
Soups, Vegetable (continued)
split pea-ham-frankfurter (Poland
4), 26
watercress-pork (China 7), 27
sour cream-avocado, chilled soup
(Mex. 2), 18
sour cream w. baked eggs (Austria
1), 34
sour cream-fennel dip (Hungary 29),
16
sour cream salad dressing (1), 76
soy dressing (8), 77
spaghetti w. meat sauce (Italy 45),
95
Spareribs
baked (China 25), 121
w. caraway (Austria 26), 122
crumbed, fried (S. America 24),
121
Spinach
w. bacon (Holland 2), 65
w. bacon (Italy 3), 66
-cheese omelet (Austria 6), 36
w. chicken (Africa 30), 143
w. coconut (Hawaii 4), 66
w. peanuts (China 1), 65
w. poached eggs (Italy 2), 33
puréed, baked (Fr. 5), 66
spinach soup (Italy 5), 26
spinach soup w. pork (China 6), 27
split pea-frankfurter soup (Czech. 3),
26
split pea-ham-frankfurter soup
(Poland 4), 26
Squash, 66-68
acorn, baked (W. Indies 6), 67-68
baked (Italy 3), 67
fried (Italy 2), 67
in piquant sauce (Hungary 5), 67
sautéed (Greece 4), 67
garnish (Italy 2), 191

Stews
beef stews, see under Beef
chicken stews, see under Chicken
lamb stews, see under Lamb
veal stews, see under Veal
Pork
caraway-horseradish (Austria
27), 122
w. herbs, white wine (Italy 30),
123
w. pearl onions (Russia 31), 123
w. pimiento, tomato (Spain 28),
122
w. sauerkraut, sour cream
(Hungary 29), 123
see also Casseroles
stuffed cabbage, see Cabbage, Stuffed
Stuffings
beef (Fr. 3), 48
for Cabbage
beef (Poland 4), 48
beef-pork (Holland 6), 49
beef-pork (Rumania 8), 49-50
beef-rice (Russia 7), 49
cooked meat (Austria 5), 48-49
for Cucumber or Zucchini
bacon-onion-tomato (Fr. 2), 54
beef-ham (Italy 5), 55
meat-rice (Austria 3), 54
mushroom (Fr. 4), 54-55
sausage (Holland 1), 54
tuna fish (Italy 6), 55
for Green Peppers
anchovy-olive (Italy 5), 62
beef-almond (Mex. 1), 61
chicken (Fr. 6), 62
pork-rice (Hungary 2), 61
sausage-sour cream (Austria 3),
61-62
seafood (China 4), 62
lamb (Middle East 2), 48
sausage (Austria 1), 47-48
sweetbreads w. eggs (Italy 1), 32
sweet potatoes, w. mint (Fr. 3), 65
sweet potatoes, w. oranges (W. Indies
2), 65
sweet and pungent beef (Malaya 46),
95-96
sweet salad dressing (13), 77
Swiss chard w. chicken (Africa 30),
143

Tapioca-cream soup (Norway 4), 28-
29
tarragon dressing (16), 78
tarragon sauce (1), 185
tarts, see under Desserts
tenderloin, see under Beef
Thousand Islands dressing (3), 76
tomato dressing (10), 77
tomato Hollandaise sauce (2), 180
tomato-pepper omelet filling (Spain
8), 37
tomato sauce, Italian (7), 182
tomato-wine soup (Hungary 2), 28
Tomatoes
baked w. eggs (Italy 3), 34-35
broiled (Eng. 14), 192
w. crab stuffing (Eng. 13), 171
w. poached eggs (Mex. 3), 34
stewed w. spices (Philippines 1), 68
Tongue, 96-98
w. almonds (S. America 1), 97
in aspic (Fr. 2), 97
in batter (Hungary 6), 98

224

w. raisins and almonds (Poland 5), 98
w. soy sauce (China 4), 97-98
in spicy sauce (Italy 3), 97
trout, poached (Hungary 13), 157; *see also* FISH

VEAL
casserole w. pastry cover (Eng. 15), 102-03
cold, in salad (Latvia 16), 103
chops, *see* Cutlets, below
Cutlets, 98-100
  baked, w. mushrooms (Poland 8), 100
  in batter (Germany 4), 99
  in beer-onion sauce (Germany 5), 99
  breaded (Italy 2), 98-99
  in butter, wine (Italy 1), 98
  w. caviar (Russia 6), 99
  w. onions, carrots (Fr. 7), 99-100
  w. sour cream (Austria 3), 99
Fillets, 100-02
  w. cashews (W. Indies 12), 101
  w. cheese (Italy 9), 100
  w. chicken livers (Italy 10), 100
  w. mushrooms (Hungary 11), 101
  w. prunes (Sweden 13), 101
  stuffed, rolled (Fr. 14), 102
garnishes for, 100
veal-potato salad (Latvia 16), 103
round, tips on preparing, 81
Stews
  caraway, horseradish (Austria 27), 122
  w. herbs, white wine (Italy 30), 123
  w. pearl onions (Russia 31), 123
  w. pimiento, tomato (Spain 28), 122
  w. sauerkraut, sour cream (Hungary 29), 129
see also MEATBALLS AND MEAT LOAVES
vegetable-chicken soup (Chile 2), 21-22
vegetable-ground beef soup (Philippines 11), 20

VEGETABLES, 39-69
Asparagus, 40-42
  butter-crumbed (Poland 1), 40
  w. cheese (Poland 4), 41
  w. creamy dressing (Fr. 6), 41
  w. egg, parsley (Belgium 2), 40-41
  Hollandaise (Fr. 3), 41
  pie (Switz. 8), 42
  on toast (Fr. 7), 41
  vinaigrette (Fr. 5), 41
artichoke hearts, baked (Italy 2), 40
artichoke hearts, fried (Italy 1), 40
artichokes w. chicken (Fr. 20), 140
Beets, 45-46
  in sour cream (Poland 1), 45
  w. tarragon (Russia 2), 45
  in wine and consommé (Austria 3), 45-46
Broccoli, 46-47
  w. almonds (Fr. 5), 46-47
  w. bacon (Germany 1), 46
  w. chives (Eng. 2), 46
  Hollandaise (Fr. 4), 46
  sautéed (Italy 6), 47
  w. wine (Italy 3), 46
cabbage, 47-51

w. bacon (Germany 12), 51
w. butter-currant jelly (Eng. 13), 51
buttered (Holland 10), 50
methods of cooking, 47
red, w. wine (Austria 14), 51
sour cream-caraway (Austria 11), 50
stuffed, 47-50; *see recipes under* Cabbage, Stuffed
Carrots
  buttered (Eng. 3), 52
  in butter-wine sauce (Fr. 1), 51-52
  w. soy sauce (Philippines 2), 52
Cauliflower
  baked (Poland 1), 52
  butter-crumbed (Sweden 3), 53
  w. chicken (China 21), 140
  sautéed (Italy 2), 53
chicory, cooked (Belgium 1), 53
cooking tips, 39-40
corn w. lima beans (Fr. 2), 44-45
Cucumbers, 53-56
  in butter-cream sauce (Austria 7), 55
  sautéed (Fr. 8), 55-56
  stuffed, 54-55; *see recipes under* Cucumbers, Stuffed
Eggplant, 56-57
  baked (Italy 2), 56
  baked, w. tomatoes (Italy 4), 56-57
  Hollandaise (Fr. 3), 56
  w. olives (Algeria 1), 56
  hors d'oeuvres (Syria 5), 12
  w. tomatoes, cottage cheese (Algeria 5), 57
  -tomato dip (Fr. 35), 16
Green Beans
  w. bacon (Hungary 1), 42
  baked (Italy 2), 42-43
  deep-fried (Italy 5), 43
  w. herbs (Russia 8), 44
  w. onions (Italy 7), 44
  sautéed (Fr. 3), 43
  in sour cream (Austria 6), 43-44
  w. soy sauce (China 4), 43
Green Peppers, Stuffed, 61-63
hearts of palm Hollandaise (Fr. 1), 59
lettuce, baked (Spain 2), 57-58
lettuce cooked in cream (Fr. 1), 57
Lima Beans
  w. cream (Germany 3), 45
  w. corn (Fr. 2), 44-45
  w. onion (Italy 1), 44
Mixed
  Chinese vegetables in oil (China 4), 69
  in olive oil (W. Indies 2), 69
  in sour cream (Austria 3), 69
  in tomato juice (Germany 1), 68
Mushrooms
  baked (Italy 2), 58
  in butter (Spain 1), 58
mustard greens (China 1), 58-59
onions, baked (Bermuda 1), 59
onions stuffed w. chicken livers (Italy 23), 141
Peas, 59-60
  w. pearl onions (Fr. 2), 60
  puréed, baked (Fr. 4), 60
  w. rice (Austria 1), 59-60
  w. soy sauce (China 3), 60
  tips on cooking, 59

Potatoes, 63-64
  baked w. eggs (Fr. 4), 34-35
  curried (India 5), 64
  w. fried eggs (Germany 3), 33
  in omelet (Fr. 4), 35-36
  w. onions, cheese (Fr. 1), 63
  w. sour cream (Poland 2), 63
  stuffed (Hungary 3), 63-64
  stuffed (Italy 4), 64
Spinach, 65-66
  w. bacon (Holland 2), 65
  w. cheese (Italy 3), 66
  w. chicken (Africa 30), 143
  w. coconut (Hawaii 4), 66
  w. peanuts (China 1), 65
  w. poached eggs (Italy 2), 33
  puréed, baked (Fr. 5), 66
Squash, 66-68
  acorn squash, baked (W. Indies
    6), 67-68
  baked (Italy 3), 67
  fried (Italy 2), 67
  sautéed (Greece 4), 67
  see also Zucchini
Sweet Potatoes
  w. bananas and almonds (Hawaii
    1), 64
  mashed, w. mint (Fr. 3), 65
  w. oranges (W. Indies 2), 65
Swiss chard w. chicken (Africa
    30), 143
Tomatoes
  baked w. eggs (Italy 3), 34
  w. poached eggs (Mex. 3), 34
  stewed, w. onion (Portugal 2),
    68

  stewed, w. spices (Philippines 1),
    68
  stuffed w. crabmeat (Eng. 13),
    171
Zucchini, 53-55
  fried (Italy 1), 66
  methods for stuffing, 53-54
  see also Cucumbers; Squash
see also under individual vegetables
vegetable salads, 70-73
vegetable salad vinaigrette (Fr. 9), 72
Venison
  in wine sauce (Austria 1), 126
  w. sour cream (Norway 2), 126
vinaigrette sauce (2), 76

Walnut soup (Fr. 12), 24
water chestnuts and chicken livers
    (China 1), 11-12
watercress-potato soup (Portugal 8),
    27
watercress-pork soup (China 7), 27
whipped cream sauce (4), 185
whitefish, see FISH
white sauce, basic, 179-80
wine sauce (5), 182
wine-tomato soup (Hungary 2), 28

Yam-chicken soup (W. Indies 7), 23

Zucchini, 53-55
  fried (Italy 1), 66
  methods for stuffing, 53-54
  see also Cucumbers; Squash